ON
PURPOSE

ON PURPOSE

HOW WE CREATE THE MEANING OF LIFE

PAUL FROESE

OXFORD
UNIVERSITY PRESS

OXFORD
UNIVERSITY PRESS

Oxford University Press is a department of the University of
Oxford. It furthers the University's objective of excellence in research,
scholarship, and education by publishing worldwide.

Oxford   New York
Auckland   Cape Town   Dar es Salaam   Hong Kong   Karachi
Kuala Lumpur   Madrid   Melbourne   Mexico City   Nairobi
New Delhi   Shanghai   Taipei   Toronto

With offices in
Argentina   Austria   Brazil   Chile   Czech Republic   France   Greece
Guatemala   Hungary   Italy   Japan   Poland   Portugal   Singapore
South Korea   Switzerland   Thailand   Turkey   Ukraine   Vietnam

Oxford is a registered trademark of Oxford University Press
in the UK and certain other countries.

Published in the United States of America by
Oxford University Press
198 Madison Avenue, New York, NY 10016

Cataloging-in-Publication Data on file with the Library of Congress.
ISBN 978–0–19–994890–1

9 8 7 6 5 4 3 2 1
Printed in the United States of America
on acid-free paper

For Jana, Milo, and Sasha

The ultimate possible attitudes to life are

irreconcilable, and hence their struggle can

never be brought to a final conclusion.

Max Weber

contents

ON
PURPOSE

1

purpose

> Life is said to be intolerable unless some
> reason for existing is involved, some purpose
> justifying life's trials.
>
> *Emile Durkheim*[1]

What is your purpose in life?

It's not an easy question to answer. And I won't attempt to answer it for you. The purpose of this book is to investigate how other people create the meaning of their lives.

In his bestselling *The Purpose Driven Life*, Rick Warren promises to take you on a *"40-day spiritual journey* that will enable you to discover the answer to life's most important question: What on earth am I here for?" This is certainly an important question. Leo Tolstoy said it was the *only* important question and spent his lifetime trying to answer it. Desperate to realize his true calling at age 82, Tolstoy fled his family to live as a wandering pilgrim but died soon afterward. Warren comforts us by asserting that we, unlike Tolstoy, can find our true purpose in a mere 40 days.

Nearly 3 out of 5 Americans say they are currently trying to "find themselves."[2] In fact, purpose is so valued that it has a multifaceted industry dedicated to providing it. From Oprah Winfrey to late-night infomercials, purpose fascinates and engages a broad range of television viewers. And the publishing industry has made a fortune off the American quest for purpose, from Warren's evangelical self-help book to Stephen Covey's *The 7 Habits of Highly Effective People*; Arianna Huffington's *Thrive: The*

Third Metric to Redefining Success and Creating a Life of Well-Being, Wisdom, and Wonder; and Eckhart Tolle's *A New Earth: Awakening to Your Life's Purpose*, a Western introduction to Eastern enlightenment.

Why are Americans so passionate about purpose? The first and most simple answer is that the quest for life's meaning is as old as the first philosophy. But it turns out that we have other, more practical reasons to be interested in purpose: a sense of purpose provides direction, moral assurance, self-confidence, and better health and well-being. So it's no wonder that people search for purpose, nor that there are a multitude of people willing to sell you a life purpose at the right price. Warren says you can have a purpose-driven life in just 40 days for the low price of $14.99 (in paperback). Who would turn down such a deal? Could it possibly be that easy?

what is purpose?

"The experience of boredom is prone to the presence of routinized activities lacking intrinsic meaning." You can say that again. This finding comes from a medical study of 646 Flemish mental health patients. Ghent University researchers found that "emphasis on task completion functions as a mechanism to create meaning."[3] In other words, boredom, apathy, and lack of enthusiasm are the results of purposeless routine.

But why would someone get bored in the first place? We are always inundated with new sensory and cognitive stimuli. As William Barrett noted, "A universe . . . where no moment is ever the stale replica of another would be a supremely interesting universe."[4] In our universe, no moment is ever the same, so life *should* be supremely interesting.

Consider a Georgia O'Keeffe painting of a flower. It shows how a single blossom can reveal the intricate marvels of the universe. O'Keeffe wrote, "Nobody sees a flower, really—it is so small—we haven't the time, and to see takes time."[5] You are supposed to stop and smell the roses for good reason. If you look and touch and smell the flowers, you will notice a symphony of colors and patterns, not to mention a rich palette of aromas and textures. Flowers can be endlessly fascinating.

But they aren't, usually. Why? Because our experience of a single flower has little to no purpose. O'Keeffe looked at flowers with a larger purpose: artistic, aesthetic, and spiritual. She took the time to see, because she found it meaningful. Her artistry captures our attention and can inspire us to look for and see what is fascinating about flowers. The act of looking becomes interesting only when it is purposeful; we must have a reason to look, and O'Keefe's art provides an enthralling one.

Purpose is the personal meaning we give to any experience.

The meaning of many experiences is simple and direct. We watch television to relax; we play basketball because it is fun. Enjoyable experiences are meaningful because they fulfill an obvious desire to feel immediate pleasure and achievement. It is no mystery why we seek out these experiences again and again. What is mysterious is why we willingly subject ourselves repeatedly to experiences that are *not* fun but arduous, exhausting, and bothersome. Kids find this tendency in adults quite strange; they ask why we have to go to work and why they have to go to school. Adults have answers to these questions—we *must* do these things because they serve a long-term or higher purpose. From this adult perspective, an arduous or unappealing task is transformed into a purposeful step toward moral goodness and future well-being.

Education specialist William Damon says that children must feel there is a purpose to their schoolwork in order to flourish in class and beyond.[6] He finds that "where no larger purpose exists, short-term goals and motives usually lead nowhere and soon extinguish themselves in directionless activity."[7] Consequently, a crucial aspect of our early development is the sense that schoolwork, housework, politeness, and hygiene are meaningful, for both moral and self-interested reasons.

Our ability to find things like schoolwork meaningful is highly beneficial not only to ourselves but also to others. Many of our day-to-day trials are justified because they eventually yield positive individual and collective outcomes. Psychologist Martin Seligman asserts that our physical and psychological well-being is dependent upon having a "Meaningful Life," which "consists in belonging to and serving something that you believe is bigger than the self, and humanity creates all the positive institutions to allow this: religion, political party, being green, the Boy Scouts, or the family."[8] Seligman stresses that a healthy life's purpose must extend beyond pure self-interest to focus on something that is *bigger than the self.*

Social life provides a host of objects that are bigger than the self: family, friends, profession, community, politics, art, nation, and God. We attach our lives to one or more of these objects and their accompanying narratives to create a purpose-driven life. If we have the freedom and the resources, the number of possible purposes is nearly infinite. As philosopher Charles Taylor notes, we now have the freedom to believe in one, none, or many philosophies of life.[9] The question becomes: which one will you choose?

some choices

Around 70 percent of Americans indicate that they "know" their "purpose in life," which suggests that they could articulate the meaning of their life if asked.[10] While this statistic does not reveal what each respondent means by a "purpose in life," it is good place to begin. In the United States, people tend to want to assert that they are leading purposeful lives; in fact, the concept of purpose is something of an American cultural meme. Countless books, self-help strategies, management and coaching approaches, infomercials, talk shows, psychological assessments, and nuggets of spiritual guidance emphasize the need for a purpose. There is a strong sense that we should get busy and find our purpose quickly—it seems downright un-American to be directionless.

Still, over half of Americans are actively trying to "discover" themselves, and around 40 percent say that they are still searching for "purpose in life."[11] Clearly, the meaning of life is confusing, because people will simultaneously say that they know their purpose in life and that they are still searching for it. This reflects the popular notion that finding a purpose in life is an ongoing process, a belief that helps keep the self-help industry vibrant and lucrative.

The kinds of people who are more likely to *know* their purpose in life is telling. Religious people are the most likely to say they have a clear purpose in life and that this calling is "part of a larger plan" (see Figure 1.1).[12] This is also true of people who say that they are "spiritual."

It makes sense that religious and spiritual people are confident about their life's purpose. Religions provide clear and all-encompassing systems of meaning. Religions also speak directly to the hardest questions in life. Confucius, the Buddha, Moses, Jesus, and Muhammad were no strangers to the extremes of human suffering. As Victor Frankl noted of his time

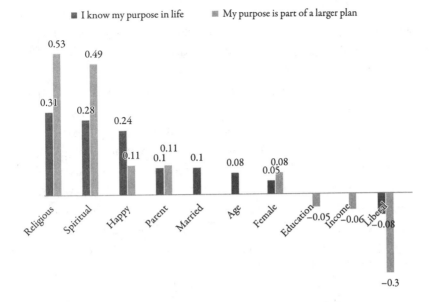

■ I know my purpose in life   ■ My purpose is part of a larger plan

0.53 0.49 0.31 0.28 0.24 0.11 0.11 0.1 0.1 0.08 0.08 0.05 −0.05 −0.06 −0.08 −0.3

Religious Spiritual Happy Parent Married Age Female Education Income Liberal

Figure 1.1 | Who knows their purpose in life?

Data: Numbers indicate correlation coefficients. Positive numbers show the likelihood that the 2 responses are related; for instance, religious people are *more* likely to say their purpose is part of a larger plan. Negative numbers indicate the inverse; for instance, liberal people are *less* likely to know their purpose in life.

Source: Baylor Religion Survey, Wave 4. N = 1572

in Auschwitz, our need for higher meaning is greatest when life is most harsh.[13] Indeed, the world's grand religious traditions were all born out of deep turmoil. Religions thus offer meaning to both the breadth and the depth of human experience.

Consider the tradition of Islam. It begins with a grand narrative told through some of the world's greatest poetry; it prescribes a daily routine of worship and contemplation; and it provides a detailed picture of the moral universe to guide believers through life's tough decisions. But that is not the entirety of Islam. There is also the art, symbolism, and sensuality of the tradition. Alain de Botton explains that "Muslim artisans covered walls of houses and mosques with repeating sequences of delicate and complicated geometries, through which the infinite wisdom of God might be intimated."[14] In this way, even Islamic architecture contributes to a believer's sense of purpose because the meaning of life is communicated everywhere, in walls and designs as well as rituals and doctrine. Religions are amazing attempts to satisfy our deep need for a meaningful existence. They blend stories, values, art, ceremony, and community to render a holistic sense of purpose. That's why science and technology do not undermine religious meaning in general as much as challenge specific religious doctrines. Science leaves the sensual, existential, communal, and imaginative elements of spirituality untouched.[15]

For instance, the United States is the most technologically and economically advanced country in the world, yet religious confidence remains high. Approximately 60 million Americans believe the Bible "should be taken literally, word-for-word, on all subjects."[16] An additional 100 million Americans believe that while the Bible must be interpreted, it is "perfectly true" if interpreted properly. In other words, most Americans are pretty certain about the meaning of life—it has been written down and if you want to know it, you can just pick up a Bible.

But if biblical literalism is not your bag, countless other spiritual options are available. There are Islam, Judaism, Buddhism, Hinduism, Taoism, folk, and New Age religions—you get the picture. In turn, we subdivide these traditions by schools of thought or denominations. In the Christian world, there are Catholicism and Protestantism, which can be further broken down into Methodists, Presbyterians, Episcopalians, Baptists, Congregationalists, Lutherans, Anglicans, Anabaptists, Pentecostals, Charismatics, and so on.

But even with all these holistic systems of meaning on offer, not everyone finds their purpose in faith. Indeed, secular philosophies and values are gaining popularity. For instance, Americans with higher incomes and more education are *as* likely to find life meaningful but are much *less* likely to think of their life as part of some larger plan (see Figure 1.1). Perhaps access to more resources and a broader knowledge of diverse systems of meaning make us less inclined to see our life as part of some universal design for humanity. This more secular and multicultural perspective reflects a move away from conservative, traditional religion but a continued embrace of meaningful personal philosophies.[17]

As a whole, secular purposes are pretty upbeat. They tend not to get weighed down by discussions of evil or damnation but rather posit a world composed of clear values, achievable goals, and astonishing progress. While religions tie the purpose of life back to God or some other supernatural force, secular purposes tend to explain the moral significance of specific pursuits on their own terms. Activities like business, art, science, and sports take on meanings bigger than the self.

Take football, for instance. *Friday Night Lights* was a television series about Texas high-school football. Before each game, players on the fictional Dillon Panthers team would, to great effect, chant, "Clear eyes, full hearts, can't lose." This simple six-word mantra nicely sums up thousands of hours of self-help recordings. The Dillon Panthers' chant communicates the basic elements of a clearly articulated purpose to living. It tells the players how to behave—directly and honesty ("clear eyes"). It tells them how to feel—enthusiastic and passionate ("full hearts"). And it tells them what to strive for and expect—victory ("can't lose"). While there is no reference to God or the supernatural, this simple dictum forms the basis of a life philosophy bigger than football.

Is it true that the Dillon Panthers can't lose? We certainly expect players who share a common goal to be more closely tied to one another, to work harder, and to cooperate more. Winning coaches know this and do much more than teach athletic skills or strategize plays; they have the ability to instill in their players a sense of meaning and morality that extends beyond the field. Basketball legend Phil Jackson explains that his personal faith, which ranges from "Christian mysticism to Zen Buddhism to Native American ritual," is the creative source of his coaching philosophy.[18] For Jackson and many others, sport can embody a life's purpose.

Business is another activity in which many people find meaning. Roy M. Spence, author of *It's Not What You Sell, It's What You Stand For*, argues that corporate America needs more than just the profit motive. It needs meaning: "An effective purpose reflects the importance people attach to the company's work—it taps their idealistic motivations—and gets at the deeper reason for an organization's existence beyond just making money."[19]

The creative life is another popular articulation of secular purpose. Artists, musicians, writers, and thinkers dedicate their lives to the creative process, which for many defies any formulaic or commercial goal. It is what psychologist Otto Rank called the "creative urge," and it leads individuals to pursue artistic beauty and inspiration as their highest goals. In fact, the inspiration felt by highly creative people is often described as emerging from some higher reality. They are in touch with something transcendent that they often don't understand, cannot verbalize, and cannot control.

Saxophonist great John Coltrane felt this way, explaining, "My music is the spiritual expression of what I am—my faith, my knowledge, my being." Through music alone, Coltrane sought to speak directly to the "souls" of his listeners. Many listened and some were transformed. The Saint John Coltrane African Orthodox Church of San Francisco was established in 1971 and exists to this day, testifying to the fact that artists can inspire new ways to create a purpose-driven life.

The scientific project also offers an imaginative and selfless meaning to life—one guided by a devotion to knowledge. Albert Einstein described the wonders of such a life:

> Only those who realize the immense efforts and, above all, the devotion without which pioneering work in theoretical science cannot be achieved are able to grasp the strength of the emotion out of which alone such work, remote as it is from the immediate realities of life, can issue . . . The scientist's religious feeling takes the form of a rapturous amazement at the harmony of natural law.[20]

The scientist is similar to the creative artist and business entrepreneur; each seeks to build something for humanity—something bigger than the self. While these meanings are essentially secular, they can, and often do, overlap easily with religious concepts.

Social change is another popular life purpose. Activists find meaning working for social movements and political causes that will benefit generations to come. American Revolutionary Nathan Hale reportedly proclaimed, "I only regret that I have but one life to give for my country," before he was executed by British soldiers for spying. While gallantly theatrical and probably fictional, Hale's sentiment is demonstrably shared by protesters and soldiers around the globe who are willing to die for a political or national cause.

Interestingly, political liberals in the United States are *less* likely than conservatives to know their life's purpose (see Figure 1.1). Differences between American conservatives and liberals go far beyond policy preferences. These ostensibly political identities now define a whole host of cultural and lifestyle preferences, including stark differences in how a person imagines the purpose of life. In general, conservatives are much more secure in their sense of purpose and are more likely to believe in a singular and ultimate Truth.

The modern world gives us a multitude of purposes from which to choose. For many, traditional religions and political Truths become deeply embedded in how they experience life. Some doggedly follow professional pursuits, which provide a moral narrative of service and devotion. Still others feel that nothing strikes a chord; they remain skeptical of the suggested metaphors, narratives, or ideologies that guide other lives. In all cases, social context determines which path is ultimately chosen.

If there's anything that unites all these purposes, it's other people. Love and friendship are at the very center of each life purpose, because the kinds of love and friends we have establish not only the kinds of goals we pursue but also the reasons to pursue them. In this way, our most intimate relations are critical in determining whether we will be captivated by an O'Keeffe flower, will tenaciously serve Allah, will be quietly spiritual, will feel politically inspired, or will be cynical about everything.

Being less sure of life's meaning or the existence of a larger plan doesn't necessarily mean a person doesn't find life meaningful.[21] We cannot simply separate people into two camps, those with purpose and those without. Rather, it makes more sense to think about why certain people accept core assumptions about life and express popular articulations of its purpose while others do not.

some assumptions

Popular discourse about purpose tends to be vague and overgeneralized, perhaps out of necessity. Individual lives are too idiosyncratic for any one-size-fits-all meaning of life to satisfy everyone. Still, publishers offer a bounty of books that claim to give us the tools to find our own purpose. These purveyors of purpose offer us a guiding narrative. In fact, the "success story" is the primary mode by which the purpose of life is articulated. Oprah Winfrey is beloved by millions for her spiritual lessons about the meaning of life; she regularly shares stories about herself and others who have overcome tragedy to find a higher purpose.[22] Like

Oprah, many famous and influential Americans share their personal narratives to motivate the masses so that we too can find success, happiness, and inner peace.

Exemplars of "successful" living are assumed to be of help to the rest of us. These popular stories share a common motif—namely, that life is given great and joyous meaning by committing to a passion, a love, or a faith. "Faith" tends to refer to some ambiguous religious or spiritual belief system, the specifics of which are to be worked out by one's denomination of choice. "Love" tends to refer to romantic partnering, the specifics of which are to be worked out by one's matching-making site of choice. Finally, "passion" tends to refer to career, the specifics of which are to be worked out by one's interest of choice.

Instead of specifics, popular purpose discourse is built on three basic assumptions:

Assumption 1. Life's purpose is within you.

In *The Purpose Driven Life*, Rick Warren promises that by the end of his book "you will know God's purpose for your life and will understand the big picture—how all the pieces of your life fit together."[23] This is quite a bold promise, but Warren's idea that self-reflection yields purpose is commonly accepted. While they differ on specifics, Christian, New Age, and self-help books point to a similar source of your *True* purpose—the self. We are asked to *look inward*, over and over again. The assumption is that our inner vision will render a better understanding of ultimate reality and our place within it.

Warren encourages readers, "Don't just *read* this book. *Interact with it.* Underline it. Write your own thoughts in the margins. Make it *your* book. Personalize it!"[24] Warren is part of a popular evangelical movement that has swept the United States in the last few decades and is characterized by the message that we can all have a deeply *personal* relationship with God.[25] Following this ethic, Warren stresses the role of the self in the cosmic order, making him sound more like a self-help guru than an old-timey fire and brimstone preacher. The message is that God isn't in some cold distant realm, he resides *within* us.

Tony Robbins has become a leader in the self-help industry by promising that "simple secrets" can "turn your dreams into reality."[26]

Robbins, like Warren, stresses a deeper self, writing that "we're all here to contribute something unique, that deep within each of us lies a special gift . . . Each of us has a talent, a gift, our own bit of genius waiting to be tapped."[27] Whether helping us to see a universal Truth or realize a source of personal power, Robbins emphasizes the need to do it in your own special way. He maintains that the secret to releasing your potential is not a doctrine, but rather a Power that is already *within* you.

Assumption 2. Life's purpose is transformative.

Warren, Robbins, and countless other purpose luminaries assert that their techniques will enable us to focus on new goals, establish new habits, become better people, and completely change our lives. Religious proselytizers work under the belief that if someone is willing to learn sacred Truths, she can expect to experience spiritual rebirth. Dedicated meditators describe a process of enlightenment where being in the moment expands into a blissful eternity. Life coaches offer tips on how to tap into our hidden and limitless powers. All of these strategies suggest that your ultimate purpose in life will transform you—if you work at it.

A good example of this assumption can be found in, of all places, Woody Allen's *Hannah and Her Sisters*. Allen's character thinks he has a terminal disease and sets out to find the meaning of life by experimenting with a host of philosophies, from Catholicism to Krishna consciousness. His search eventually leads to a form of Marxism (Groucho, not Karl); his is a spiritual quest that perfectly aligns with a popular conception of how we discover our purpose—we begin with a dire need to find the meaning of life and, after testing various doctrines and faiths, we experience a life-altering epiphany.

In *The 7 Habits of Highly Effective People*, Stephen R. Covey turns this narrative into a plan of action. He lays outs a series of life lessons that will transform the reader from depressed slug to satisfied success, provided the reader has the proper doggedness. Covey warns that "'lift off' takes a tremendous effort, but once we break out of the gravity pull [of old habits], our freedom takes on a whole new dimension."[28]

The religious convert, the failure turned success, and the wallflower turned beauty queen all illustrate the ability of individuals to transform themselves. They find a new calling, a new self, and a new meaning to life. Books and movies are filled with such stories. Our heroine is depressed, aimless, and morally lost. She looks within. She discovers her life's meaning and becomes balanced, goal-oriented, and virtuous. She finds her purpose and it transforms her.

Assumption 3. Life's purpose feels good.

Psychological research confirms that individuals who express a strong sense of purpose are better able to cope with life's difficulties and more likely to be happy, self-confident, optimistic, and healthy (both mentally and physically).[29] In turn, a lack of purpose is correlated with self-destructive behaviors.[30] Being without purpose is often an indicator of clinical depression and even reduces a person's ability to stave off disease.[31] Simply put, having a purpose in life feels great. It can help us physically, psychologically, and spiritually. It also makes us feel good about what we have and what we are doing.

For instance, a CEO is driven by making money, but is this how she would describe the purpose of her life? Probably not. She would likely expound on her grander significance as a creator of jobs or products that enrich the lives of others. Similarly, a rising pop star will set his sights on greater fame, but is this how he will describe his goals? He will likely express a deeper wish to bring joy to his throngs of fans. In this way, pragmatic pursuits of wealth and status are often reframed as callings. A moral purpose helps us to feel good about our experience of life—whatever that may be.

Purveyors of purpose promise to make us feel *good* about life. They assert that our purpose is the means to that end. It is not just about self-improvement, it is about improving one's sense of self. And the best way to feel good about yourself is to feel *moral*. For that reason, purveyors of purpose deal, more than anything else, in virtue. They assert that we can find our personal significance and it will be morally satisfying.

Are these core assumptions warranted? Perhaps, but they are most definitely incomplete. You *might* have a morally satisfying and transformative purpose deep within you, but you might not. It all depends on your environment.

communities of purpose

We cannot simply ask whether a self-help guru, like Tony Robbins, or a religious proselytizer, like Rick Warren, or a spiritual celebrity, like Oprah Winfrey, is correct. Their wisdom and strategies *will* make sense to certain individuals—their popularity proves it. Still, how helpful they are depends entirely on the extent to which people around them share their systems of meaning. Outside these systems, their advice is meaningless.

For instance, biblical literalism is *felt* within certain communities. Few, if any, literalists would argue that the Bible will help you if you don't believe in it. We cannot simply read the words to feel their effect; we have to *believe* in them. The feeling requires something other than the text—it requires a community in which the Bible is understood to be True. Faiths are not things we can turn on by reading a passage, they become instilled in us through our history, our culture, our community—everything that forms our identity. These factors determine which articulations of a purpose-driven life make sense and what Truths will be found within ourselves.

This is the core finding of this book. The way we imagine and talk about life's purpose depends on social situations, locations, and eras.

This book also questions some popular assumptions about the meaning of life.

Question 1: Life's purpose is discovered within you, but how did it get there?

Steven Pavlina, a successful self-help author and popular blogger on personal development, provides his readers with simple strategies to improve their lives by finding their "true purpose." Here is one of Pavlina's exercises:

1. Take out a blank sheet of paper or open up a word processor where you can type (I prefer the latter because it's faster).
2. Write at the top, "What is my true purpose in life?"
3. Write an answer (any answer) that pops into your head. It doesn't have to be a complete sentence. A short phrase is fine.
4. Repeat step 3 until you write the answer that makes you cry. This is your purpose.[32]

I had 25 people of different backgrounds take this "test."[33] Full disclosure: no one actually cried. Still, the findings are instructive and reflect some larger trends. As one might expect, many (11) wrote unambiguously religious answers. For instance:

> My purpose today and every day is to glorify God in all that I do and to live like Christ.

> My purpose is to love. God created me in His image, out of love, in order to love Him. That is my first, and should be, foremost purpose in life.

> My purpose is to strive for complete happiness, which can only be achieved by following Jesus and attempting to be more Christ-like.

All of these respondents felt their purposes deeply. Still, what is felt within must be conceptualized in order to be communicated. People who think God is within them first need to understand the concept of God. Georg Simmel states it simply: "We believe in God because we feel Him, although we really cannot feel Him until we have accepted His existence."[34]

There is a lot happening within us—churning emotions, competing concepts, confusing signals, and deep anxieties. What does it all mean? Religious traditions provide the language to make sense of it all. They give words to these feelings. Thus, Hindus *feel* that they have been reincarnated. Devout Catholics *feel* the holiness of the pope. And Muslims *feel* the presence of Allah. All of these feelings are real and profound, yet descriptions of these feelings follow predictable cultural and community patterns. Meaning is socially ordered.

Some of my respondents (10) described a desire to help others, not out of some religious ethic but through a professional calling. For instance, one woman wrote:

> I aspire to be a family and marriage therapist. I see the brokenness around me and the challenges that come from divorce and unstable homes. I want to be part of the restoration process.

A few (3) focused on the importance of nurturing their relationships. Another woman indicated:

> I strive to keep my marriage strong, and raise my kids to be the best people I could hope for. I also try hard to help care for my parents.

These values are agnostic, spanning both religious and secular perspectives. Like explicitly religious purposes, they draw on culturally popular articulations about what a true purpose entails—the value of serving one's family and community.

Purveyors of modern purposes rely heavily on these core cultural values. They don't provide revelations of meaning so much as articulate basic beliefs that many communities already embrace. Dedicated viewers of Winfrey or the followers of Robbins are not so much converts as people who happen upon a spokesperson saying the things they already wanted to hear.

Similarly, Rick Warren's *Purpose Driven Life* undeniably inspires millions. But people who find Warren's book motivational are most likely embedded in a community, church, or family that already seeks such advice.[35] Christ must *feel* real to a person for Warren's sentiments to have meaning. For those who don't already feel Christ, Warren's text will remain mere sounds and inscriptions.

Novelist David Mitchell has written, "Who and what run deeper than why." This perfectly encapsulates how life's meaning is at once within us but also socially determined.[36] We ask ourselves about life's meaning with questions of *why*—"why am I here?"; "why did God do that?"; "why is there suffering?"; "why should I care?" In the end, our answers, which appear to come from deep within us, are largely a reflection of *who* we trust and *what* they tell us. Our family, friends, authority figures, culture, and history are the *whos* and *whats* that determine which answers feel true. So, life's purpose is discovered within you, BUT it was planted there by society.

And finally, if you were doing the math, you will have noted that I have forgotten one of my respondents. His true purpose was not religious or humanitarian or filial. Contemplating Pavlina's question, he simply wrote "I don't know" over and over again.

Does this gentleman lack a culture or community to provide him with the concepts that will give his inner feelings direction and significance? Can he not express *why* he is significant because there is no *who* or *what* to guide him? No, he—like everyone else—is guided by a vocabulary that is part of his culture. In fact, his response is an especially interesting one because it, more than the others, is distinctly modern. Feeling a lack of purpose is a growing trend in human history. The man who doesn't know his purpose may be the most modern. He has internalized the concept of purposelessness to the point that when he looks *within* he *expects* to find nothing.

Throughout the book I investigate how modernity has changed the way we think about the problem of life's meaning. Most importantly, modernity has made the idea of purpose a *choice*. Only then could meaninglessness become a possibility.

Question 2: Life's purpose is transformative, but how?

More than anything else, popular discussions assert that purpose is physically, emotionally, and spiritually transformative. It all comes down to your commitment to a suggested practice or strategy.

But studies of conversions and dramatic life changes tell a slightly different story. John Lofland and Rodney Stark studied how the Unification Church (more popularly known as the Moonies) gained members.[37] Converts to the Church undeniably discovered a higher purpose; they become convinced that Reverend Sun Myung Moon was a divine prophet and committed their lives to the service of his vision. Did these converts pore over Moon's writings and ideas and look deeply inward to finally discover their true purpose? Not really, most joined the group without knowing what the Moonies were about.

Lofland and Stark found that conversion has little to do with people seeking a life's purpose and a lot to do with people finding themselves in a new social situation. Their landmark study demonstrated that individuals only embraced the doctrines of Reverend Sun Myung Moon *after* they had already joined his group. This, at first glance, appears counterintuitive. Why would someone join a religious cult if he didn't believe in their teachings? Lofland and Stark's argument is that faith requires social support; therefore, changes in faith require dramatic changes in social circumstances to occur *first*.

Most of the Moonie converts went looking for friends and companionship and ultimately found faith. They were not full-time spiritual seekers but rather lonely individuals who happened upon a group of welcoming companions who turned out to be members of a cult. Once inside the cult, the newcomers learned the group's systems of meaning and then became devotees of Reverend Moon.

This model of conversion reverses the popular narrative—people don't search for answers and find a new purpose; they tend to find themselves in a network of people who envelop them in a new system of meaning. Over time and with a little TLC, the newbie internalizes the reality of the group. Simply put, meaning follows practice, not the other way around.

Lofland and Stark's study reveals the extent to which our immediate social circle defines how we understand our *self*. In fact, they found that most converts narrate a story of their own conversion that doesn't match the facts. They speak about singular epiphanies—those moments when Truth is felt deeply within—even though the actual conversion process was gradual. It was only when a person felt himself to be a valued member of the group that he internalized its purpose.

The self-help industry promises epiphanies. Purveyors of purpose assert that we can uncover a lifelong positive self-image. But the strategies they prescribe to elicit your *enchanted self* are dependent on social context. The best strategies in the world can't help us if we have no social support. Purpose is certainly transformative, but finding one's enchanted self is mainly a result of luck. You have to be in the right networks at the right time.

Question 3: Life's purpose feels good, but is it good?

Amanda Lindhout is a social activist and author from Canada who was kidnapped by Somali Islamists and held for 15 months during which she was constantly subjected to torture and rape. She describes her horrific ordeal in the book *A House in the Sky*. What makes her story so incredible and inspiring is that she developed a profound empathy for her abusers and now testifies to the healing power of forgiveness.

To survive the physical and psychological torture of her captivity, Lindhout writes:

> In my mind, I built stairways. At the end of stairways, I imagined rooms. These were high, airy places with big windows and a cool breeze moving through. I imagined one room opening brightly onto another room until I'd built a house . . . I built many houses, one after another, and those gave rise to a city—a calm, sparkling city near the ocean, a place like Vancouver. I put myself there, and that's where I lived, in the wide-open sky of my mind.[38]

Lindhout looked deep within herself and found an expansive vision of beauty and serenity. This imaginative world gave her a reason to keep living through unspeakable horrors. But most amazing of all, it gave her a means by which to see her assailants in a different light; from inside her "house in the sky" she was able to humanize them.

Amanda Lindhout shows us what is good about having a higher purpose. It can save us from hopeless despair and redeem humanity even when it is at its worst. Looking inward, Lindhout found her true purpose—her ability to forgive.

By humanizing her abusers, Lindhout recognized that their fears and pains resembled hers. We should also note that they, like Lindhout, were driven by a clear purpose. As Islamist rebels they believed themselves to be serving Allah and working toward a grander vision of the "good society." They envisioned their own house in the sky—a nation guided by Shariah law and deep piety. But the rest of us, including most Muslims throughout the world, see their purpose as evil.

A life's purpose can be evil. Certain purposes are unhealthy and intentionally destructive. Still, individuals who have what most of us might deem nefarious purposes are fully convinced of their goodness. These individuals live within tight-knit communities that establish Truth. Faith in a higher purpose can lead to self-sacrifice, but it can also justify great atrocities.

Religious and ideological enclaves instill strong beliefs about what is True purpose. Belief in Truth can inspire the most vicious intolerance as well as the most altruistic love. Either way, the social mechanisms are the same. The morality of life's purpose is socially determined.

Still, most purveyors of purpose ignore the idea of evil purposes and describe deviant pursuits as *lacking* in purpose. They assume that life's meaning is necessarily positive. Business ethicists often stress this point. Nikos Mourkogiannis, a corporate strategist and author of *Purpose: The Starting Point of Great Companies*, explains Enron's collapse as the result of an absence of purpose. He writes, "Enron had strategy—indeed, it had many strategies. But strategies are about means; they cannot be an end in themselves. An end is a reason. Enron lacked a reason—it lacked Purpose."[39]

For Mourkogiannis, purpose is "part of your moral DNA." It is within you. And business ventures that lack it, he argues, will fail. For him, Enron didn't implode because it had the wrong ethic; it failed because it didn't have *any* ethic. But even though Enron might have lacked an ethic, it did not lack a purpose, as Mourkogiannis states. Rather, Enron embodied the purpose of profit—at any cost. It was a nefarious purpose.

Mourkogiannis's advice is most meaningful to an American audience, which values entrepreneurship and capitalism.[40] America's moral culture celebrates fierce competition and swift achievement. Filled with Mourkogiannis's ethic of fair play, the "good" businessman is also one step ahead of his competitor, cutting the deal, creating the product, and pleasing the consumer in record time. This creates a frenetic tempo and renders the workforce perpetually afraid of falling behind. Keeping pace becomes the modern professional's primary purpose in life. This state of affairs unintentionally infuses a purpose-driven life with a feeling of being constantly overwhelmed.

For career-driven professionals, urgency is felt everywhere—the morning alarm, the calendar marking hourly commitments, the rapid rhythms of weekly interactions, and the overall tempo of society. Modern life produces workaholics, some of whom have the resources to never work again yet still work themselves to death. They are victims of the rapid tempo of our capitalist culture. Other cultural tempos create perpetual boredom, and individuals never realize a purpose in life. How we experience time dominates our consciousness and in turn determines whether life feels frantic, worthless, or satisfying.

How we understand moral Truth and experience time vary across communities and cultures. Purveyors of purpose understand their own purpose to be *good*, but only within particular perceptions of Truth and time. They preach to a choir within their own system of meaning. So, life's purpose feels good to them, but whether it is good for us depends on our circumstances.

my purpose

Throughout this book, I argue that history, norms of self, communities of Truth, cultural tempos, and power dynamics determine how each of us understands the meaning of life. I paint a picture of society that may sometimes seem like a totalitarian force that determines everything, even our most intimate thoughts. Indeed, I initially thought I would find that people had little say in defining their own purposes.

But while social forces do have tremendous power to guide our understanding of life, I actually found that people have the agency to bend the meaning of their lives in highly imaginative ways. Imagination enables all of us to create purposes that society never taught us. Imagination allows us to choose from competing options, empathize with others, weave stories, and fantasize entire worlds. Imagination is what makes each individual purpose unique. It creates ideals that make collective action possible but can also subvert shared values and make conflict inevitable.

This book is intended to engage the imagination of readers. I weave data and ideas from national and international surveys, interviews, observations, literature, and previous research to discuss the social sources of life's meaning. But unlike the offerings from other books on purpose, I have no clever life strategies, grand revelations, or divine inspiration to recommend. As Max Weber deftly put it, "the ultimate possible attitudes to life are irreconcilable."[41] I cannot pretend to have found the universal key to living a satisfying life or achieving some long-desired goal. Rather, I hope to demonstrate that how we create life's meaning shifts with changing times and locations.

The following is an attempt to think more deeply about how we collectively create different purposes.

2

the good within

I do not know why we are here, but I am
pretty sure it is not in order to enjoy ourselves.

Ludwig Wittgenstein

What is your purpose in life? Does it make you happy?

If there is one obvious finding in the vast literature about human purpose it is this:

People who believe their life has a purpose are happier.[1]

People who cannot articulate a purpose tend to be, at the very least, mildly pessimistic about life, and the saddest people are those urgently searching for a purpose.[2]

But most people don't search for a purpose *in order* to be happy. Happiness is mainly luck. While purpose and happiness are strongly related, they remain distinct. As psychologist Daniel Gilbert puts it, we might "stumble on happiness," but it is unlikely to be the result of careful planning.[3]

In fact, the idea that personal happiness *should* be your purpose is very unpopular—brute egoism is often thought to be crass and obnoxious. Toddlers everywhere are routinely taught that it is *better* to share and show concern for others than behave selfishly. Ralph Waldo Emerson uttered this still common sentiment: "The purpose of life is not to be happy, it is to be useful, to be honorable, to be compassionate, to have it make some difference that you have lived and lived well."[4]

In sum, life is supposed to be about *more* than happiness. We are supposed to do something important, adhere to some ethic, and serve a greater good. We live for a goal, a principle, or a destiny—not just for pleasure. Wittgenstein was correct; we are not here in order to enjoy ourselves. We are here for some other purpose—a higher purpose.

Yet sometimes fate smiles upon us. Having purpose gives us a sense of moral significance, which turns out to feel really good.

Happiness is the lucky by-product of *moral egoism*—our universal urge to be good people.

moral egoism

Having witnessed the brutalities of nineteenth-century Russian life, Fyodor Dostoevsky noted a sad truth, "People speak sometimes about the bestial cruelty of man, but that is terribly unjust and offensive to beasts, no animal could ever be so cruel as a man, so artfully, so artistically cruel."[5]

It may be bleak, but Dostoevsky's insight is not all that shocking. We are inundated by stories of evil men. Television appears to depend on them for its livelihood—between the vivid and candid coverage of school shootings and terrorist attacks, networks stage graphic tales of killers in cop show after cop show. In fact, the entertainment industry labors tirelessly to up the ante of artistic cruelty—who will produce the new *Saw* movie or the next Dexter-type villain?

And these tales of artful evil depict their anti-heroes as purpose driven. It is not a haphazard madness that drives the archetypal serial killer, but cunning sadism with creative flair. Consequently, we are not at all surprised that humans are artistically cruel. In fact, we have become captivated by the idea. Maybe we always have been.

But we are also enthralled by heroes. They are the flip side of Dostoevsky's assertion. They illustrate what is exceptionally good about the human; namely, no animal could ever be as courageous, or so gallantly altruistic, as a human.

This is consistent with two basic assumptions social scientists hold about the moral nature of humans. The first is both obvious and mildly unflattering. It is the assumption of *rational egoism*—we are all, at heart, shrewdly self-interested. Economists routinely use this micro-foundation (the assumption of Rational Choice) to model human behavior. A commercial from Capital One states it simply, "According to research, everybody likes more cash . . . well, almost everybody," and cuts to a supremely uninterested infant. The dissenting baby is cute because he doesn't understand what is obvious to everyone.

The rational egoist is mainly driven by money, which he can exchange for status, excitement, and even sexual allure. He will be cruel or kind depending on what is in it for him. With enough money on offer, you can get him to do almost anything. Does he sound familiar?

A second basic assumption about the nature of humans is that we are, at heart, guided by higher values. Sociologist Christian Smith pleasingly and concisely defines the human as a "moral believing animal."[6] Our *moral instinct* explains our ability to adhere to values even when they do not serve our self-interest. We sacrifice our time, pleasures, and fantasies in deference to social values. We turn the other cheek not because we are too cowardly or too weak to strike back but because we feel that it is righteous. The human is genetically programmed to perceive the world through a moral lens; we are taught morality but also experience it instinctively.

Often, these two core assumptions (that we are rational egoists or that we are moral believing animals) are placed in opposition. But both assumptions are valid; humans are driven by values *and* self-interest.[7]

At root, we are *moral egoists*.

Moral egoism means that we seek moral order, but for self-interested reasons. When we articulate our purpose in life, our moral egoism is made explicit. Purpose is how we describe our individual significance in a morally ordered world. If the description is positive, it proclaims the goodness of self and imbues our daily struggles and desires with moral meaning.

I asked two women, "What is your purpose in life?" One said, "My children."[8] The other said, "Allah." These women are both African-American, both mothers, both married, both college educated, both working professionals, both charming, and both confident in their responses. They voice two common articulations of higher purpose: devotion to family and devotion to faith. The word "articulation" is important here, because purpose is first and foremost a system of meaning. It is how we conceptualize and express our moral significance.

Motherhood, the higher purpose of Woman 1, is something temporal and circumstantial—her children will eventually grow into adults. But motherhood evokes a deeper meaning; it describes not simply the actions of giving birth and raising children. Motherhood is imbued with higher purpose because it evokes a moral sensibility—the feeling that it is good to nurture, care, protect, and provide. Consequently, "mothers" can feel good about their lives, motivating them to suffer through the sleepless nights, rude retorts, maddening tedium, and deep anxieties that come with mothering.

Faith, the purpose of Woman 2, is also timeless and universal. Religions—especially the major monotheistic faiths—provide clear descriptions of higher purpose, including detailed narratives of how God and the self are related. The self in monotheism is at once nothing and everything. The self is nothing in comparison to God—you don't matter. Your purpose is to serve God selflessly. Yet, God loves *you*. Instantly, the self is made significant because it is the object of God's love—you matter greatly to God. Consequently, people of faith can feel good about their lives, motivating them to suffer through the deep doubts, sinful temptations, and public mockery that can come with faith.

Articulations of purpose show us why people feel *good* about themselves.

Most active and healthy people have no problem verbalizing why they feel good about themselves. Sadly, some cannot. An elderly woman told me that she "was nothing." She lives alone and works a thankless job for little money. She is without a sense of higher purpose and suffers congruently. She feels unneeded, unwanted, and uninspired. A middle-aged man told me how he worries that his grandfather, who just turned 90, has "lost all sense of purpose." "He just sits around and waits to die," he lamented, "he needs to find a reason to live."

These people lack a basic reason to feel good about themselves. They lack a sense of purpose. We all love to be loved, like to be liked, and need to be needed. In fact, having a sense of purpose is a direct measure of mental health. Feeling like you don't matter? You are depressed.[9]

As such, having a higher purpose is a core aspect of our psychological well-being.

The purpose industry addresses this need. Religions, political movements, moral philosophers, self-help salesman, streetwise prophets, and nefarious con artists all promise to help those without purpose find the good within themselves. They further promise that this deep inner good will transform the self, and thereby transform the world. And they are correct.

We are moral egoists, and when graced with the feeling of moral significance, our whole world is bathed in the light of goodness. In contrast, moral insignificance darkens the world in the shadow of meaninglessness.

At the end of the day,

we all strive to feel *good* about our *self.*

This is the micro-foundation of purpose. We yearn to be good. This yearning takes countless forms as a result of social circumstances that are beyond our control. In certain contexts, it leads individuals to commit horrific brutalities. In others, it produces amazing acts of kindness and self-sacrifice. The resulting variation in human purpose is the topic of this book.

Conversely, the topic of this chapter is non-variance—which is to say, what we all share. It is our deep desire to find *the good within*, which is at once selfish and selfless.

egoism

Franny complains,

> I'm just sick of ego, ego, ego. My own and everybody else's. I'm sick of everybody that wants to get somewhere, do something distinguished and all, be somebody interesting. It's disgusting—it is, it *is.*[10]

J. D. Salinger's Franny is lamenting our culture of narcissism. Her peers embrace it; they strive for success and distinction—to be people of social importance. In "the real world," personal significance is equated with wealth, power, and popularity. This is the reality of financial markets and status hierarchies. In this world, money defines significance and quantifies importance.

Franny finds the whole venture disgusting. Overachievers are such jerks. Can't we stop being such egoists and materialists? Can't we stop lusting after fame and fortune?

No, we cannot.

Our obsessive self-interest is evident and universal.[11] In the eighteenth century, Adam Smith stated it clearly: "It is not from the benevolence of the butcher, the brewer, or the baker that we expect our dinner, but from their regard to their own interest."[12] People don't sweat and toil for fun; they do it for personal gain.

The course of history seems to validate the idea that the human is a *Homo economicus*—"a being who inevitably does that by which he may obtain the greatest amount of necessities, conveniences, and luxuries, with the smallest quantity of labor and physical self-denial with which they can be obtained."[13]

If this is the driving impulse of human nature, we can consider our history one of great progress. We have produced massive financial markets, started countless businesses, and increased the standard of living for billions around the globe. Humans have mastered the real world. Game over.

But the game isn't over; a deep dissatisfaction lingers, even in places that aren't experiencing social unrest. We needn't look at the world wars and massive genocides that modernization made possible. A more mundane illustration of the downside of our real-world mastery will suffice.[14]

Picture an office worker sitting in her cubicle. Her life is one of comfort and security—air conditioning keeps her cool, an ergonomic chair prevents back pain, vending machines prevent thirst and hunger, hand sanitizers prevent disease, and a fourteenth-floor office prevents animal attacks. Her life is a pure wonder because her society has miraculously overcome the trials and tribulations that plagued humans for tens of thousands of years.

Yet, she stares at her computer screen wanting to be anywhere but in her cubicle. She is bored!

Why is *Homo economicus* driven to seek efficiency, convenience, luxury, and mastery over the real world only to feel unsatisfied when those goals are achieved? The Buddha warned us of the futility of egoism over two thousand years ago. Is our never-ending drive to have more stuff for ourselves some kind of cruel joke?

Happiness research suggests that it might be. We have long surpassed our self-interested need for more wealth and comfort. In *The Spirit Level*, epidemiologists Richard Wilkinson and Kate Pickett explain this well-established finding:

> The evidence that happiness levels fail to rise further as rich countries get still richer does not come only from comparisons of different countries at a single point in time . . . In a few countries, such as Japan, the USA and Britain, it is possible to look at changes in happiness over sufficiently long periods of time to see whether they rise as a country gets richer. The evidence shows that happiness has not increased even over periods long enough for real incomes to have doubled.[15]

This is a disappointing state of affairs. Put bluntly, personal gain only satisfies us for a while. And it may even have diminishing returns.

Figure 2.1 depicts this common wisdom. When we have nothing, we focus all our efforts on obtaining food, shelter, and security. Living under a bridge with no clear sense of where the next meal is coming from or whether it will be too cold to sleep is a recipe for certified misery. But once

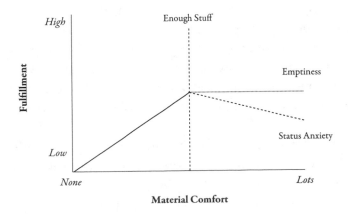

Figure 2.1 | Why the Real World Isn't Everything

we have attained enough stuff to fulfill these basic needs, there appears to be little or no benefit to getting more.

Once we have enough stuff, two things can happen. The first is a "ceiling effect" in which more stuff brings no more contentment but rather a sense of emptiness. The emptiness comes from an unconscious realization that all our toys, luxuries, and various diversions are not, in the long term, fulfilling. We may continue to seek out diversions to fill this void, but this process becomes a simple feedback loop in which doing and getting more leads us to want something else.

A person stuck in this feedback loop might never experience abject misery but, at the same time, will remain perpetually unfulfilled. Perhaps this is what the Buddha saw in himself when he was living a princely life of material splendor. Like him, we instinctively want more, but sadly, we have no real idea of what will satisfy us. Of course, the Buddha left his life of comfort and egoism and found contentment meditating in the unlikeliest of places—under a Bodhi tree.

A second possibility is even more distressing. In this scenario, more stuff actually creates more problems, responsibilities, and anxieties. The bitterest irony of bounty is that it will complicate life and also heighten our *status anxiety*—the absurd fear that we don't yet have enough, and the paranoid fear of losing it all.

Alain de Botton explains this phenomenon:

> Our judgment of what constitutes an appropriate limit on anything—for example, on wealth or esteem—is never arrived at independently; instead, we make such determinations by comparing our condition with that of a reference group, a set of people who we believe resemble us. We cannot, it seems, appreciate what we have for its own merit, or even against what our medieval forebears had. We cannot be impressed by how prosperous we are in historical terms.[16]

For instance, when we earn enough to move into a better neighborhood, we are immediately faced with bigger houses, nicer cars, and prettier lawns. The wealth and comforts of the new neighbors simply fuel our own sense of *relative deprivation*.[17] Keeping up with the Joneses—or the Kardashians—is a fruitless endeavor. There is always someone else with more money, more status, or more beauty.

The fact that we remain unsatisfied and even unhappy while enjoying the marvels of new technologies, the benefits of modern medicine, and even the good luck of personal success suggests that we all seek something more than fame and fortune. The economic assumption that humans always desire more stuff is accurate but fails to reveal a deeper longing—the lure of a reality more profound than "the real world."

Franny feels this in her bones. She is sick of egoists, overachievers, and more and more stuff. She yearns for something more real. Franny seeks a spiritual life, where her purpose and meaning transcend materialism, social achievement, and egoism. She yearns for the enlightenment of the Buddha and searches for it in the Jesus Prayer.

Franny wants a *higher purpose.* As do we all.

moral instinct

Having discovered the "pleasure center" of the brain, researchers subjected rats to a famous and devilish experiment.[18] They connected electrodes from a rat's brain to a lever that, when pushed, supplied the rat with a jolt of orgasmic pleasure. Sound good? It certainly made the rat feel good, until he died of exhaustion from pushing the lever over and over and over again.

Humans are not the only animals that seek pleasure. But unlike rats, we knowingly distinguish between types of desires, and that makes a huge difference. It means that we will not kill ourselves when hooked up to an "orgasmatron."[19] Why?

John Stuart Mill argued that we should always seek to maximize our pleasures.[20] At first, this sounds like the makings of a tragic rat experiment. If we only sought pleasure, wouldn't we turn into a bunch of heroin addicts and sex fiends? Of course, Mill recognized this problem. To clarify, he said that pleasures are of different orders—higher and lower. As you might have guessed, physical pleasures are lower, while "moral pleasures" are higher, which means, for Mill, that they actually produce more pleasure. Helping an old lady across the street will be more fun than snorting a line of pure cocaine or having raucous adulterous sex. While this may sound dubious, Mill is on to something. A cocaine high or illicit sex might be thrilling for a moment but can lead to deep feelings of regret and shame, elements of what we might call a conscience or moral compass.

Consequently, we don't just seek physical and material comforts; we also desire moral comforts. Sociologist Randall Collins calls this desire a need for "emotional energy." He explains:

> Emotional energy is what Durkheim called "moral sentiment": it includes feelings of what is right and wrong, moral and immoral. Persons who are full of emotional energy feel like good persons; they feel righteous about what they are doing. Persons with low emotional energy feel bad, though they do not necessarily interpret this feeling as guilt or evil (that would depend on the religious or other cultural cognitions available for labeling their feelings), at a minimum they lack the feeling of being morally good persons.[21]

Collins's concept of emotional energy is broad, but this is its strength. Just as brain scientists show that animals are driven by physical pleasure and economists theorize that everyone seeks material gain, Collins indicates that we all want *emotional energy*.

In general, our desire for emotional energy is greater than any yearning for sex or money, because if we lack a sense of moral goodness then we won't enjoy pleasures or luxuries. We simply won't feel *good* about them. Sex will evoke shame not enjoyment and riches will feel crass, not well deserved. Physical gratification and wealth acquisition only satisfy when imbued with emotional energy—that delicious feeling of rectitude. If believed to be virtuous, helping old ladies, snorting cocaine, and cheating on one's spouse will all feel great.

Edward Conard is a man who has achieved fulfillment. Conard was Mitt Romney's partner at the private equity firm Bain Capital. He wrote a book called *Unintended Consequences: Why Everything You've Been Told about the Economy Is Wrong*, in which he explains how growing wealth inequality helps society.

Conard made lots and lots of money at Bain Capital and felt extremely good about it. Would we expect anything else from Conard? Actually, it probably wouldn't surprise anyone to learn that Conard is secretly miserable or hopelessly depressed. But I expect this is not the case because Conard appears blessed with something that makes his earthly fame and fortune truly enjoyable—he sees it as having a higher meaning. He has turned real-world success into his purpose.

Conard believes that the concentration of wealth at the top should be twice as large as it currently is, because he thinks that we are all the beneficiaries of the super-rich and they actually deserve our gratitude.[22] Thank you, Bill Gates. Consequently, Conard's massive fortune and those of his peers are, he believes, more than well deserved. He feels himself to be a good person *because* he makes massive amounts of money. As a defender of free-market capitalism, he enjoys his bounty because he finds it righteous.

This is the upside of life's moral meaning. Armed with the belief that our gains are purpose driven, respectable, and important, the pleasures of success can be relished in full.

Ascribing moral significance to hardships also lightens the burden of failure. I met Adam, a recovering drug addict, at a mission shelter. He is an aging, broken-down, and disfigured man who leads a life that seems like the polar opposite of Conard's fairy-tale existence. Struggling to support himself and reconnect with his children (who have long since disowned him), Adam is surprisingly upbeat and optimistic—one might even say he is full of emotional energy.

What accounts for the bizarre disconnect between his circumstances and disposition? Adam tells me directly that it is his religious faith. Like Conard, Adam sees his life as one that is guided by a higher purpose. Adam cannot find fulfillment in riches, but he finds it in his struggle to become a better person. As a penitent sinner, Adam can appreciate the challenge of piecing together his shattered life because he finds it righteous.

Conard and Adam illustrate the moral power of a higher purpose. With it, one can feel good about obscene wealth or untold hardship.

Consequently, the real world is not the *most real* after all. Money and power alone do not satisfy. They need to be meaningfully associated with something more important—more real. That is why, even in a bull market, we need purpose. We are conditioned to look beyond moments of good fortune, those days when our stock is rising, to contemplate the bigger picture. What will be our ultimate fate? Where do we go from here?

These questions force us to take a longer view, one that looks past today, tomorrow, or even ten years down the road. This long view can continue indefinitely and we naturally follow it to its inevitable conclusion—death. What will my fortune or accomplishments mean after my death? Nothing. They will lack meaning because *I* lack existence.

There is a resolution to this dilemma. But it requires our full imaginative powers. We can imagine a higher order of existence, a transcendent order where moral universals provide meaning not just for today but for eternity. Transcendence is the natural resolution to our existential dilemma. As Christian Smith explains, "In order to make sense of the meaning of self, life, history, and the world, one has to get outside of them, to 'transcend' them."[23]

In order to validate *the good within*, our moral egoism seeks transcendent confirmation.

the transcendent

A woman rubs her amulet. Her request is simple—she wants to be a mother. Her friend made the idol from limestone. Her sister has one too; it hangs from her neck and she has nine children. Clasping her own necklace, the woman imagines a goddess, the mother of all mothers, and prays that she won't remain childless.

That may have happened 24,000 years ago, near the modern day village of Willendorf, Austria. The amulet was the Venus of Willendorf, a female idol with swollen stomach and breasts. Similar figurines have been discovered elsewhere and are believed to be fertility charms or perhaps stylized self-portraits.[24] But we have no real idea of the intent of the women or men who created these figurines, because they lived in prehistory, a time before humans recorded their thoughts. Still, upon seeing the Venus of Willendorf it seems natural to imagine a goddess and ponder the extent to which our imaginations match those of our ancient ancestors.

Evolutionary history provides us with some sense of the foundations of our ability to imagine something transcendent.[25] Anthropologists, historians, and cognitive scientists, while using varied terminology, tend to describe similar paths to the current "social brain" we all share. In *Deep History*, anthropologist Andrew Shryock and historian Daniel Lord Smail explain:

> Human brains have become bigger over time because natural selection has favored individuals who live in larger social groups, over those who live in smaller ones. To sustain larger groups, individuals need larger brains (to accommodate language capacity; because language in addition to grooming, is a means of creating social solidarity among humans).[26]

With the development of language (and apparently hygiene) came a complex social imagination.

We all benefit, and suffer, from our rich imaginations. The ubiquitous dream about appearing at a meeting in nothing but your underwear is an example of your social imagination turned wicked. We are able to conjure up all sorts of scenarios in which we are embarrassed, mortified, or cruelly shamed. We can thank our evolved social brains for these nasty images. In turn, we can also imagine being the object of untold adulation and adoration—"First of all, I would like to thank my parents" is how the fantasy acceptance speech usually begins.

Our brains have developed extraordinary faculties for conceptualizing our self in dreams, nightmares, and daily interactions. In the early twentieth century, the sociologist Charles Horton Cooley came up with the concept of the "looking-glass self" to describe how we come to envision ourselves through the eyes of others:

> A self-idea seems to have three principle elements: the imagination of our appearance to the other person, the imagination of his judgment of that appearance, and some sort of self-feeling, such as pride or mortification . . . The thing that moves us to pride or shame is not the mere mechanical reflection of ourselves, but an imputed sentiment, the imagined effect of this reflection upon another's mind.[27]

In other words, pride and shame are the ways we imagine what is going on in the minds of others. Do your acquaintances see you and glow with admiration or wince with disgust? What you imagine, whether accurate or not, is your self-image.

Today, some cognitive scientists argue that the rudimentary concept of the "looking-glass self" is the basis for imagining transcendence. Just as we constantly consider the perspective of others, we can easily conjure up the opinions of spirits that inhabit nature and space. I know that my house plants can cast some vicious looks when I have forgotten to water them. Similarly, a brutal winter sometimes seems like cosmic punishment for a beautiful summer. We often imbue consciousness and moral judgment not just to other humans but to animals, objects, and nature.

While quite alien to our scientific understanding of reality, ideas about the spirit world or the "thoughts" of nature come quite naturally to us. In such thoughts lie the origins of the gods. Todd Tremlin explains, "It turns out that thinking about gods, while requiring the complete brain system, actually pivots on just a handful of quite ordinary mental tools that are present at birth and mature in the first years of life."[28] Attachment, the earliest human social relationship that develops between a parent and infant, is the prototypical bond between a nurturing entity and a vulnerable being. As social skills develop, the infant begins the process of affiliation, first with family members, then with others, and finally with shared concepts and identities.

Empathy, or our brain's capacity to imagine the judgment and perspective of others, is another cognitive function that contributes to our capacity to invent transcendent entities such as gods. Complex social interaction requires us to picture the motivations of others. Humans logically began to imagine what motivates more abstract entities, like groups, and then nature, and finally, existence itself. Simply put, we invented gods (transcendent entities) as a result of tens of thousands of years of cognitive evolution.[29]

The very earliest works of art, such as the Venus of Willendorf, indicate a rich imaginative world. Cave paintings discovered in Chavet-Pont-d'Arc have been dated to between 27,000 and 35,000 years ago and depict creative visions of animals and people.[30] While clearly focused on issues of daily survival, these paintings appear to pay respect to wild beasts and, in one instance, an exaggerated female form—just like the Venus idol. These images are our only window into the minds of early humans.

Sociologist Robert Bellah argues that these ancient images reveal that the earliest people were deeply concerned with making sense of life within "a general order of existence"; in other words, Paleolithic people were philosophically minded.[31] They were striving for idealized self-representation and moral meaning—seeking to make sense of *it all*—even while crouched around a fire with an ear tuned to the sound of vicious beasts. They were driven by more than an instinct to survive; they were driven to understand the purpose of survival. Consumed with thoughts of daily threats and finding their next meal, early humans still pondered what the stones, the trees, the animals, and the gods thought. It's extraordinary and illustrates our universal urge to transcend material circumstance and imagine a world full of meaning.

Our social brain had procreative advantages. Our quest for meaning led to language and attempts to communicate abstractions (and groom and create gods), which led to better social cohesion and in turn to group strength and better survival. If the Venus of Willendorf *was* a fertility charm, her existence proves her power, because our ability to invent a goddess (a transcendent spirit) is tied directly to our capacity to survive. The advantages of a social brain seem apparent, given our unparalleled success (at least among mammals) in the evolutionary struggle.

The evolution of the human brain enables us to imagine transcendence. But, as economists assert, there are no free lunches. If one of the benefits of inventing transcendence is group solidarity based on a shared moral order, one of the costs is existential angst.

In 1849, Søren Kierkegaard wrote *Sickness Unto Death*. In addition to inspiring the existentialist branch of philosophy and predicting many of the basic themes of twentieth-century psychoanalysis, Kierkegaard came up with a very good title. The phrase "sickness unto death" explains what is universal to us all in three words. Our cognitive evolution has led unavoidably to the horrible realization that we are mortal. No other animal is saddled with this terrible demon. Kierkegaard called it "despair."[32] And it lingers, indeed, unto death.

Biologist Robert Sapolsky also explains how our social brains are to blame for prolonged stress and anxiety about the future:

For the vast majority of beasts on this planet, stress is about a short-term crisis, after which it's either over with or you're over with. When we sit around and worry about stressful things, we turn on the same physiological responses—but they are potentially a disaster when provoked chronically.[33]

Stress responses can be disastrous because we can worry and fret so chronically that it deteriorates our physical and mental health. The person who carved the Venus of Willendorf must have felt despair. And today we postulate that this idol was most likely a means to mitigate his or her despair by means of either artistic expression or spiritual quest.

Joseph Campbell, a popular analyst of comparative mythology, postulated that all myths of transcendence share common narrative elements that suggest the universality of certain fears, problems, and fantasies. Myth, according to Campbell, is primarily used to explain the general order of existence and provide moral directives for how to behave within this imagined transcendent reality.[34] All cultures create myths, gods, and narratives to produce moral meaning and, hopefully, mitigate despair. Myth mitigates despair by inspiring creativity and spirituality.

A sense of place, meaning, and purpose within a world full of death, disappointment, and futility enables us humans to feel at peace with ourselves and our fate. The process is circular. Our social brains help us to survive but also subject us to the realization of our mortality. In turn, our social brains invent new ways to transcend death. The urge to transcend the material world leads first to real-world mastery and second to the mitigation of despair.

Kierkegaard's suggested instrument to mitigate despair was God, and his suggestion is, by far, the most popular in the world today.[35] Rodney Stark argues that the God of Kierkegaard was the result of a "master trend" in human history. While diverse, conceptualizations of the supernatural tend to shift in predictable ways. Stark argues that

1. Humans will prefer Gods to unconscious divine essences.
2. Human images of God will tend to progress from those having smaller to those having greater scope.
3. Humans will prefer an image of God(s) as rational and loving.[36]

These preferences are widely shared because they are grounded in basic logic. Why would anyone prefer an evil spirit to a loving one? Why would people prefer a weak and whiny spirit to a powerful and confident one?

In the end, Stark concludes that "these preferences lead to a conception of God as a loving, conscious, rational being of unlimited scope who created and rules over the entire universe."[37] It took tens of thousands of years, but we eventually came up with the everyday version of God many of us know.

This *One True God* (to borrow the title of one of Stark's books), the God of monotheism, is a wonderful balm for despair.[38] He is omnipresent, omniscient, reasonable, loving, and—most importantly—cares about you. What is left to despair about? Everything is in its place and there is a place for everything, including you. As Stark explains it, the advent of the One True God is predictable because he is the most efficient way to alleviate all sources of despair—the uncertainty, the fragility, the injustice, the disappointment, and the overwhelming purposelessness of life dissolve in his presence.

Monotheism is a predictable outcome of moral egoism. One True God gives us a morally meaningful life and self. Thank God.

And then, we kill him. Not really, but here is how Friedrich Nietzsche first and famously explained it in 1882:

> After Buddha was dead, people
> showed his shadow for centuries afterwards in a
> cave,—an immense frightful shadow. God is dead:
> but as the human race is constituted, there will
> perhaps be caves for millenniums yet, in which
> people will show his shadow.—And we—we have
> still to overcome his shadow![39]

Like Stark, Nietzsche describes an evolution in belief, in which our urge to transcend the world takes on new and improved moral meanings. If monotheism was once an improvement over polytheism in terms of mitigating despair and creating moral order, then won't God also be replaced by something new? This is what Nietzsche pondered in the latter half of the nineteenth century, and it is what we still ponder today.

But even without God, humans continue to invent and ponder transcendence. Nietzsche understood that "it is a *metaphysical faith* upon which our faith in science rests ... we godless anti-metaphysicians still take our fire from the flame lit by a faith that is thousands of years old."[40] Higher purpose can take religious and secular forms, but they both position the self within a distinctly moral universe.

Secular philosophies and ideologies still speak of universal conceptions of "Good and Bad," "Truth," "Justice," or a "moral sense." James Q. Wilson explains:

> To say that there exists a moral sense (or, more accurately, several moral senses) is to say that there are aspects of our moral life that are universal, a statement that serious thinkers from Aristotle to Adam Smith had no trouble in accepting. In this view, cultural diversity, though vast, exotic, and bewildering, is not the whole story.[41]

For Wilson, humans have a deep moral sensibility that can be found not just in religion but also in logic, science, and even social science.[42] In fact, the history of secularism in the United States indicates that atheism didn't become popular until nonbelief advanced its own transcendent moral framework with a secular vocabulary.[43] The moral certitude of many within the New Atheism movement illustrates this phenomenon today.[44]

Our moral instinct leads to articulations of transcendent ideals, in both religious and secular language. And these ideals—God, Justice, and Goodness alike—provide a way to transcend the self and define it as intrinsically meaningful. They allow you to say with confidence, "I am just," "I am fair," and "I am a good person."

Our moral egoism drives this process. But our definitions of *good* and *self* vary greatly. This variation has little to do with biological differences, although chemical imbalances and distinctive brain structures play a role; it is mainly the function of social differences.

Social context provides the concepts, metaphors, and ideals through which we understand transcendence and articulate higher purpose. While we all seek the good within, social differences have generated no singular conception of transcendence from which to draw our moral significance. As Max Weber asserted, "The ultimate possible attitudes to life are irreconcilable, and hence their struggle can never be brought to a final conclusion."[45]

So is there no meaning to life? No, there are countless meanings. They not only determine whether you will find the good within, but more fundamentally what "self" and "the good" mean.

the problem of meanings

In response to media reports that atomic physicists were seeking the meaning of the universe, Billy Bragg wrote the song, "No One Knows Nothing Anymore." He sings:

> But what if there's nothing?
>
> No big answer to find?
>
> What if we're just passing through time?[46]

We are just passing through time. But there is something to find, and we keep finding it over and over again. That something is meaning. Meaning "makes what would otherwise be mere sounds and inscriptions into instruments of communication and understanding."[47]

Physicists built the Large Hadron Collider to spin atoms round and round in search of the "God Particle," an elementary particle used to confirm the existence of a force field that is thought to give structure to the universe. One of the coiners of this provocative nickname for the *Higgs boson* particle explained: "The publisher wouldn't let us call it the Goddamn Particle, though that might be a more appropriate title, given its villainous nature and the expense it is causing."[48]

The publisher knew that "Higgs boson" was a meaningless inscription, a mere sound to us non-physicists. Calling it the God Particle turned it into an instrument of communication.[49] And the media became interested, for a moment, in theoretical physics.

Still, the universe's meaning was not found in a particle accelerator. Or maybe it was, for the physicists engaged in a decades-long search for the God Particle. That was their purpose, the meaning of their professional lives. Finding the Holy Grail of Higgs field theory most likely blessed these researchers with the euphoria of revelation and a confirmation of self-worth.[50] The God Particle still left Bragg and many of us unenlightened.

I spoke to a woman who has a very different method to resolve the mysteries of the universe, one that does not require billions of dollars and hundreds of advanced degrees. She just needs the Bible. When she wants to know something, she opens the Bible at random, closes her eyes, and places her finger on the page. She is convinced that the selected passage will contain the answer she seeks.

While this method of enlightenment will sound dubious to many, it is a common technique within this woman's community. She is married to a pastor of a small rural church. Members of her congregation are self-described biblical literalists and look to the Bible to explain all of life's mysteries. For them, the Bible defines what is meaningful. Their sense of reality is based not on the logic of the text but rather on their shared faith that the text is True. Guided by faith, this tightly knit community transforms random Bible verses from mere sounds and inscriptions into instruments of communication and understanding. But the Good Book still leaves many unenlightened.

Particle physicists and biblical literalists have different revelations because they have different sources of meaning. Social theorist Peter Berger describes these sources as "plausibility structures." He explains:

A plausibility structure is the social context in which any cognitive or normative definition of reality is plausible. It is plausible in Boston today for a woman to speak of another woman as her spouse. It was not so in Boston a few decades ago. It is definitely not so today in Pakistan (where the implausibility can quickly be ratified by lethal violence).[51]

Culture, history, and community destroy and create plausibility structures. While one might think of biblical literalism as a carryover from some bygone era, it is actually a relatively new phenomenon. Without the printing press or the ability to read, average citizens from past eras could not *be* biblical literalists. Literalism requires a text and the skill to decipher its markings. For this reason, biblical literalism is modern, based on historical developments and community dynamics that made the Bible an accessible source for Truth.

The modern world has created space for all sorts of new plausibility structures that can generate conflict within individuals and societies.

Groups can fight over the definition of marriage as well as over whether the God Particle undermines the God of the Bible. These public disputes reflect the incompatibility of certain plausibility structures. In turn, people can internalize these disputes and feel confused about what "marriage" or "God" really means.

One fear is that the modern world is so crowded by competing plausibility structures that we no longer know what to believe. The onslaught of opposing Truth claims and confusing language is creating a world of full of meanings but lacking in any shared meaning.

For example, film and television have transformed our visual experience of the world. Today, children are routinely exposed a dizzying array of moving pictures and images. Many, including the film director Martin Scorsese, are concerned about the social and personal ramifications of this. He writes:

> We're face to face with images all the time in a way that we have never been before. And that's why I believe we need to stress visual literacy in our schools. Young people need to understand that not all images are there to be consumed like fast food and then forgotten—we need to educate them to understand the difference between moving images that engage their humanity and their intelligence, and moving images that are just selling them something.[52]

Scorsese worries that visual imagery is so powerful and so fragmented that we will fail to make anything meaningful out of all this new information. He recommends teaching visual literacy to help people find their way in a universe teeming with conflicting and confusing images.

The visual onslaught of television and film is just one obvious indicator of a deeper shift in how modern humans experience an ever-increasing barrage of messages. Modern life presents endless ideas, metaphors, and images to contemplate. Somehow we must navigate this chaos to find some moral clarity. We have to cut through all the noise if we are to attain a clear purpose in life.

Has modernity made the possibility of finding a purpose less likely? Or does having access to more options increase the odds of finding a purpose that rings true? The next chapter weighs these possibilities.

3

the reality
of meaninglessness

What does nihilism mean? That the highest
values devaluate themselves.

Friedrich Nietzsche

What is your purpose in life? Do you lack one?

People slip into lives that lack meaning. They feel they have no intrinsic value. Some feel directionless or confused. These feelings are often tied directly to mental health problems, like depression and anxiety. A few people even come to embrace a bleak worldview that is less a psychological disorder than a philosophical position: nihilism.

Nihilism is the belief that life has no purpose. It is not simply that one cannot find a purpose, but rather that none exists to be found. If you believe your life has a purpose, the nihilist would argue that it is a mere delusion, a product of wishful thinking, an attempt to avoid the grim realities of a meaningless universe.

The pure nihilist is a social outlier and yet a popular character in fiction. In the 1861 novel *Fathers and Sons*, Ivan Turgenev supplied us with the radical nihilist Yevgeny Bazarov, a young man bent on devaluing the highest values of his society. His cynicism is ruthlessly aimed at religion, art, political authority, and the most universally embraced purpose of all—love. Bazarov scoffs, "And what about the mystic relationship between a man and woman? . . . That's all humbug, rot, art!"[1] A Russian critic at the time lamented that "what is characteristic of Bazarov is scattered throughout the masses."[2] Nineteenth-century Russia was thought to be descending into a culture of nihilism, in which love, religion, and traditional values had lost all potency.

That fear haunts us today. The nihilistic teen who marches into his school and kills indiscriminately is a phenomenon well known in our time. He has lost sight of the value of human life and even the value of his own. Frustration, rage, apathy, and boredom coalesce to create an unfeeling monster; he kills children like he is playing a video game. He sees no point to it all.

Luckily, very few people slip into the extremes of cold-hearted nihilism (which suggests a psychotic break with reality). Yet from time to time we can feel that there is no point to it all. Despair and misanthropy are common frustrations. The band King Missile gives voice to a hipster nihilist in the song "No Point," which blithely asserts:

> There is no point in needing someone and no point in being alone. There is no point in doing nothing and no point in not doing nothing.

The song is funny, but many cultural expressions of nihilism are cruel—openly misogynistic lyrics, homicidal video games, torture porn. These are all conspicuous signs of a disaffected age in which violence is routinely and casually used for entertainment and compassion marks one as a fool. What those romantic fools think is good and meaningful becomes just "rot, art!"

Philosophers, sociologists, and cultural critics have examined the rise of nihilism for decades, if not centuries. For them, purposelessness is an epidemic. In 1953, Rollo May announced:

> The chief problem of people in the middle decade of the twentieth century is *emptiness*. By that I mean not only that many people do not know what they want; they often do not have any clear idea of what they feel . . . Thus they feel swayed this way and that, with painful feelings of powerlessness, because they feel vacuous, empty.[3]

Cultural nihilism had become a mental health diagnosis. The notion that nihilism can spread casts it as a social problem and not just a personal defect. What is causing people to lose a sense of life's meaning? Different commentators identify different sources. The religiously faithful decry the encroachment of secular immorality; social critics lament the emptiness of consumer culture; and political pundits criticize us for lacking civic commitment.

These varied woes have a common source: modernity. It is a force that supposedly secularizes, commercializes, disenchants, depraves, and cheapens our highest values. The result is a complete breakdown in moral order and even a loss of faith that there could even *be* a moral order.

Nietzsche spoke of nihilism as a social phenomenon. Krzysztof Michalski explains:

> The nihilism that Nietzsche has in mind is first of all something that happens and not something that we, correctly or incorrectly, think about reality. Nihilism is therefore an event, or a chain of events, a historical process—and only secondarily, if at all, an attitude, an outlook, or position.[4]

Nietzsche's nihilism is an extreme version of Emile Durkheim's *anomie*—a social condition in which shared norms and values no longer hold communities together.[5] In 1897, thirty years after Turgenev wrote *Fathers and Sons*, Durkheim showed how urbanization and the corresponding loss of bucolic villages set people adrift from close friends, family bonds, and clear moral obligations. His central measure of an anomic culture was suicide rates—the logic being that if more and more people kill themselves then moral order has broken down.

An increase in the percentage of people who feel they have no purpose is another indicator of a culture that has lost its values.[6] Life without purpose is the cruelest of cultural changes.

The idea that modernity produces anomie is ironic. We have made tremendous advances in technology, health, education, communication, standards of living, and transportation, only to produce an overwhelming sense of meaninglessness in the world. It appears that our material worth comes with existential costs.

So who pays these costs? The answer is complex because there are two different trends at work. They are the topic of this chapter.

The first trend confirms what Nietzsche, Durkheim, and countless other thinkers have argued: more developed societies contain a higher percentage of people who say they have no sense of meaning in life. It is the wealthy countries that show the clearest signs of existential despair. While the populations of the developing world clearly suffer tremendous hardships, they seem resilient and focused in their will to survive. The poorest of the poor still cling to a meaningful life.

It is modernity that enhances meaninglessness. We get to have all these wonderful conveniences, like air-conditioning, dishwashers, and iPhones, but we lose our moral foundations. Does that sound like a good trade? Yet, it is *not* the people with the most luxuries who are most threatened by despair. It is the poor and elderly *within* wealthy countries who fall prey to emptiness. They may enjoy material advances unknown to the poor of the developing world, but they are the ones who pay the existential costs of these comforts. This is our second trend, namely, that meaninglessness is unequally distributed within advanced societies. In meaning, just as in wealth, we are living in an age of inequality.

The rich have a stronger immunity to life's emptiness. They have found the means to rise above the weakening of traditional values by creating values unto themselves. They *lean in* and snatch meaning from the abyss. They have embraced a new sacred value—the sovereignty of the self. Daniel Haybron describes this modern ethos thusly: "What's best for me depends on what I care about, and on such matters I am sovereign."[7] It is an attitude that paradoxically arose from the psychotherapists who initially documented the onset of nihilism. They provided the language and philosophical outlook from which a new sacred world emerged. They created and legitimated moral self-discovery for the modern individual.

Armed with this modern ethos, the individual creates moral order out of chaos, because she believes she has the autonomy to do it. A culture based on therapeutic language and a self-help philosophy endows the individual with tremendous moral authority. Those in a position to act on this are the purpose-driven people of the modern world. They exercise, enjoy their toys and vacations, are dedicated careerists, find love, and feel they have purpose.

For the less fortunate, modernity has made despair a reality. The modern ethos of self-discovery adds insult to the injury of relative deprivation. The poor not only have fewer toys, vacations, and career opportunities, but they also feel an emptiness inside. They are victims of cultural change; while modern life is a bounty of new meaning for many, a purposeful life is no longer guaranteed.

purpose guaranteed

Life as a moral egoist is so much easier within a clear moral order, provided it is not too oppressive. It offers a distinct roadmap to feeling good about yourself. The best guidelines are ones that need no proof. Their Truth is assumed because they are communicated and embedded within a moral culture.

David Foster Wallace gives us a succinct definition of culture in the form of a joke:

> There are these two young fish swimming along and they happen to meet an older fish swimming the other way, who nods at them and says, "Morning, boys. How's the water?" And the two young fish swim on for a bit, and then eventually one of them looks over at the other and goes, "What the hell is water?"[8]

Water is culture. It is so ubiquitous and "taken for granted" as to be invisible to us most of the time.[9] The old wise fish sees the water, but the young'uns do not. It takes experience and reflection and wisdom to see our own culture because it is so embedded in how we think and live. Strong moral cultures instill purpose even without our knowledge—we *feel* what is right and wrong, just like the fish feels the water.

Peter Berger and Thomas Luckmann explored the process of deep socialization in *The Social Construction of Reality*, and their title became a common phrase in both academic and casual conversation. The idea that *reality* is constructed may strike us as an overstatement. Most of our perceptions of reality seem to come quite naturally, without needing any reconfiguring. The old fish didn't *construct* the water—he simply recognized it. Similarly, I don't *construct* the oppressive heat of an Austin summer or the rumblings of my stomach come dinner time—I simply notice these things.

English writer Samuel Johnson famously disputed philosopher George Berkeley's assertion that the material world is imaginary (a construction of our minds) by kicking a stone and declaring, "Thus I refute Berkeley!"[10] See, the stone hurting his foot proves the stone is no mere figment; it is concrete reality. But the "social construction of reality" is not about denying the existence of material things or questioning the accuracy of human cognition. Rather, it is about how cultural and social circumstances lead us to *interpret* the same facts and the same sensations differently.

The young fish fail to recognize the fact that they are in water because they never thought about it, they never learned about it in school, and they never heard anyone say the word "water" before. That is how reality is socially constructed—our attention to facts and our naming of facts and the importance we give to facts are products of our socialization.

Modernity changes culture. It affects how we perceive reality in the deepest of senses. In turn, this shifts how we understand our purpose in life. Social theorists posit that purpose and moral order were much simpler when societies were simpler. Peter Berger uses the term "sacred canopy" to describe a premodern society in which shared ideas, symbols, and concepts are so ingrained as to go unquestioned. It is a wonderfully evocative image—a protective covering of meaning that shields us from doubt and shrouds us in a common faith and communal purpose. Berger explains that the sacred canopy lessens the prevalence of existential crises. For him, the "nomos," a shared sense of reality provided by the sacred canopy, can restore and invigorate the individual. He writes that a person

> may "lose himself" in the meaning-giving nomos of his society. In consequence, the pain [of mortality] becomes more tolerable, the terror less overwhelming, as the sheltering canopy of the nomos extends to cover even those experiences that may reduce the individual to howling animality.[11]

The sacred canopy serves up moral meaning on a platter—it's clear and obvious what's good and bad. Everyone goes about their roles in the context of coordinated rituals, routines, worries, and aspirations. Moral order and individual purpose are in sync and unquestioned.

Modernity popularized cynicism. No sacred object was beyond critique. As Bob Dylan sang in 1964, "It's easy to see without looking too far, That not much is really sacred." Complaints that we have entered a cynical age have become constant over the past century—often for good reason. A clear example of something universally *sacred*—a value, concept, or authority that stands above ridicule—is difficult to find today. Our leaders are routinely derided in the media. Our celebrities seek little more than fame. Consumer culture crassly panders to our basest needs. And cynics scoff at the moral simplicity of devoted believers and positive thinkers. It is remarkably easy to see that not much is really sacred anymore.

Modernity boosts our physical security only to enhance our existential confusion.[12] Now, we have the time and the intellectual space to become nihilists—or at least to be wracked by despair. In sum:

Modern culture increases the likelihood that an individual will lack purpose.

We can test this hypothesis, to some small degree. The Gallup World Poll contains social survey data from over 150 countries, making it representative of 95 percent of the world's adult population.[13] Gallup calls it "a window into the minds of 6 billion people."[14] As such, it provides a global picture of public opinion like no other.[15] And luckily, it asks, "Do you feel that your life has an important purpose or meaning?" The data provide a glimpse of global differences in how people feel about the meaning of life.[16]

If modernity leads to emptiness, we would expect people in more technologically and economically developed settings to be less likely to find life meaningful. Map 3.1 provides a sense of global inequality at a glance. A nation's shade indicates its per-capita GDP—darker means wealthier, and lighter means poorer.

Per-capita GDP is highly correlated with other measures of modernization such as political democracy, public education, advanced health care, technology, and transportation. It is also negatively correlated with corruption, violence, and suffering.[17]

Compare Map 3.1 to Map 3.2, which depicts a nation's average response to the question about life's purpose. Darker shading indicates

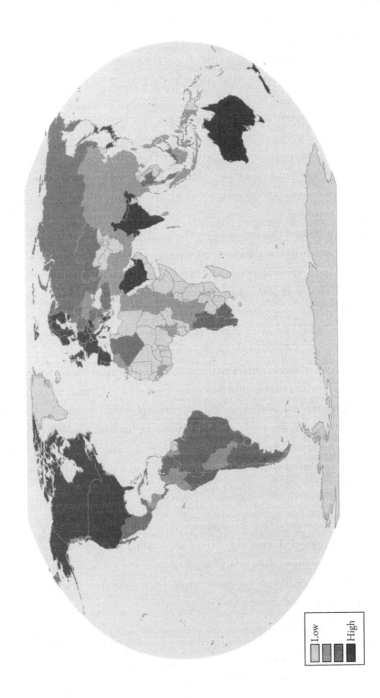

Map 3.1 | Levels of Per-capita GDP

Low
High

that many of a nation's citizenry feel that they have an important meaning in life, while lighter shades indicate an aggregate lack of purpose.

The purpose map looks like the reverse of economic development map.[18] These maps provide some initial confirmation of our hypothesis. More modern countries do tend to have fewer people who feel their life is purposeful. Isn't that a no-brainer?

When I first looked at these data I mistakenly got the purpose data backward.[19] Overlooking this fact, I "discovered" that poorer countries had more people that said that their lives lacked any purpose. It seemed obvious that people living in the worst conditions would find their lives devoid of meaning. Consequently, my error was not clear to me at first.

When I corrected the error I got the finding presented above—that more developed countries also lack meaning. It seems that, overall, desperate times create very purpose-driven people, or at least people who are not worried about the meaninglessness of it all. Why? The life of one woman in the developing world provides some insight.

Black Diamond (a nom de guerre) lives in Monrovia, the capital of Liberia. In 2000, during a civil war, her parents were killed and she was gang-raped. Many of her countrywomen suffered similar fates. She somehow survived and now is the sole provider for five children, two her own and three orphaned by violence. She is unemployed, regularly hungry, and routinely plagued by malaria. Interviewed by *The Guardian* about her time fighting with the Women's Auxiliary Corps, a predominantly Muslim group affiliated with the Liberians United for Reconciliation and Democracy (LURD), Diamond explained,

> Before the war, rape was almost unknown in our country. When the rapes started, I and the other girls who fought were determined not to be victims. We wanted to fight back to show our attackers they couldn't get away with such things and that they, not we, should feel shame for the rapes.[20]

The Republic of Liberia is in West Africa, bordered by Sierra Leone, Guinea, Côte d'Ivoire, and the Atlantic Ocean. It is one of the poorest nations in the world. The World Bank estimates that only 17 percent of

Map 3.2 | Levels of Purpose
Purpose data unavailable for Algeria, China, The Congo, Iraq, Libya, Oman, Somalia, Syria, Turkmenistan, and Tunisia.

Source: Gallup World Poll

Low

High

Liberians have access to "adequate sanitation facilities," and over 20 percent of children under the age of 5 are malnourished. Life expectancy is fifty-seven years and approximately 40 percent of Liberians cannot read or write. The country has experienced civil unrest for decades and tens of thousands of citizens have been displaced from their homes as a result of ethnic conflict and violence. Life in Liberia seems to be as dismal as it can get.

But when we look at purpose by country, Liberians rank number one in the world. Black Diamond is like a lot of Liberians. She survived an unimaginably horrible experience and lives in dire poverty, but she is miraculously buoyed by purpose. She feels empowered, important, and resolute.

In fact, of the 1,000 Liberians surveyed by the Gallup World Poll in 2007, *none* indicated that they felt unimportant or without purpose.[21] What does this astounding finding tell us? First, it tells us that a desperately poor Liberian is as likely as a relatively well-off Liberian to say she has purpose. No social or economic or demographic distinctions matter in how a Liberian will respond to the question, "Do you feel that your life has an important purpose or meaning?" They will all say "Yes."

And they are not alone. Ninety-nine percent of citizens of Congo Kinshasa, Ghana, Mali, Nigeria, and Togo say their lives have an "important" purpose. All of these countries are either poor or corrupt or war-torn or all of the above.

Black Diamond feels her purpose in her bones. She became a colonel in an army of women bent on avenging their abuse. Her behavior is admittedly desperate, but it is hardly meek or passive, nor is she naively sanguine about her lack of political power. And her countrywomen and countrymen share her purposefulness regardless of whether they were victims of abuse, perpetrators of that abuse, or simply lucky enough to avoid the whole terrible mess. What Liberians share is a culture where to be purposeless is unthinkable.

First, Liberian culture is fraught with existential urgency. You either fight to survive or you die.[22] Humans are excellent survivors and our ability to construct meaning in the world is the key to our success. Liberians, in many ways, display our innate talents for constructing purpose in response to crisis. In fact, crisis often instills a strong and immediate sense of purpose because the individual taps into her inborn ability to make sense of it all.

Modern people in crisis also experience this. I spoke with Patrick, an American veteran who served in the war in Afghanistan and witnessed the death of many of his comrades. His experience was traumatic but didn't result in despair. When I asked how it affected his purpose in life, Patrick explained:

> The loss of my friends who were really close to me gave me a sense of purpose. Once you see life taken from you first-hand, you do wonder why wasn't that me. Is someone looking out for me? I remember plenty of instances when I thought this. More so taking life is troubling because you are the decider of life. Talk about power no man should have. Everything is different in the sense of my purpose now versus six years ago.

Patrick was humbled by his ordeal and came away with a renewed sense of the preciousness and importance of life. He interpreted his implausible survival as something of a moral calling. Existential urgency produced in him a powerful moral directive to find a way to live in service to others. Now, he is pursuing a master's degree in social work.

Modern cultures lack the existential urgency found in developing countries.[23] We have higher life expectancy, better health care, and much greater access to all the toys and comforts that the postindustrial world has to offer. This may explain why modernity has increased the likelihood that someone will find life meaningless; perhaps we simply have too much time to ponder the possibility.[24]

In addition, modern cultures have outgrown their sacred canopies, while most developing regions have strong religious cultures. Liberians still have a sacred canopy of sorts. Around 40 percent of Liberians are Christians and 16 percent are Muslims, but the majority of Liberians (44 percent) are "ethnoreligionists."[25] Ethnoreligions are expressions of folk and shamanistic beliefs that are attached to distinct ethnic or tribal groups. As such, they are extremely insular and exclusive religious faiths. In many ways, an ethnoreligious culture provides one of the best contemporary examples of a sacred canopy. Ideas about ethnicity, spirituality, tribal loyalty, and the sacred are fused to the point where the individual feels them in her skin. One cannot easily shed this kind of sacred purpose because it is the water in which Liberians swim.

In fact, a strong religious culture is the best predictor of a purpose-driven population. Map 3.3 depicts the overall religiosity of different nations. Lighter shaded countries are more secular. This map resembles the purpose map. Specifically, the religiousness of a nation is positively related to the percentage of citizens who feel purposeful.[26] In addition, religiosity is negatively related to per-capita GDP.[27]

Here are the blunt findings:[28]

- Wealthier countries, on average, contain fewer purposeful people.
- Wealthier countries, on average, contain fewer religious people.
- Countries with a lot of religious people, on average, tend to have a lot of purposeful people.

These relationships are strong but never perfect. Some very religious countries, like Poland, have many people (16 percent) who lack any sense of meaning in their lives. The cases of Poland and other counter-examples indicate that the growth of meaninglessness is not simply a story of secularization. Secular cultures can be purposeful and religious cultures can drift toward despair. Rather, the process of modernization has created cultural space for both outlooks. They are correlated but not synonymous.

Sacred canopies and existential urgency almost guarantee a meaningful life. In contrast, modernity made survival easier and moral order more complicated. For these reasons, the modern individual ponders the meaning of her life with different concerns and considerations. She sees that multiple paths are available. Among them is the threat that life will have no meaning.

But that is the individual's problem, because in a modern moral culture the meaning of life is not ordained. You must select from competing moral realities. You are seemingly *free* to become a Christian, a Muslim, a Buddhist, a New Ager, a secular humanist, a New Atheist, a careerist, a lover, an artist, and even a nihilist.

Purpose is no longer guaranteed, so now you must discover one for yourself.

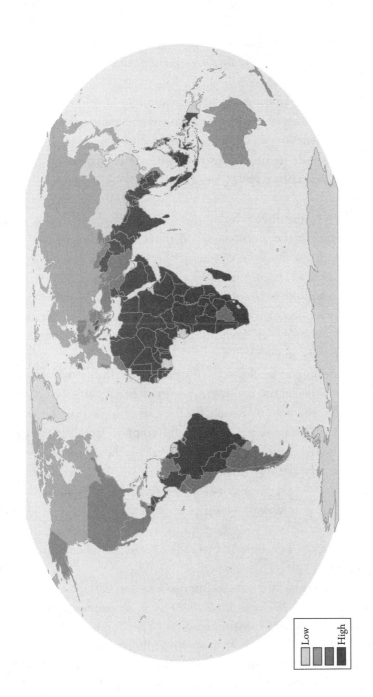

	Low
	High

Map 3.3 | Levels of Religiosity

Source: Gallup World Poll

purpose re-discovered

Fyodor Dostoevsky imagined that the devil privately envies those who have clear moral outlooks. In *The Brothers Karamazov*, the devil laments:

> What I dream of is becoming incarnate once, for all, and irrevocably in the form of some merchant's wife weighing eighteen stone, and of believing all she believes. My ideal is to go to church and offer a candle in simple-hearted faith, upon my word it is. Then there would be an end to my sufferings.[29]

We should all envy the merchant's wife for her modest, direct, and unquestioned belief in the sunniest of all moral orders—a loving and all-powerful God. Even the devil covets her certainty. Sadly, we are told that modernity has made us, along with the wretched devil, deeply cynical, placing us beyond the reach of this simple faith.

Nostalgia for some lost era of sacred devotion is common. Wouldn't it be simpler and nicer if we all lived under the moral security of a sacred canopy? It all depends on who you are.

Sacred canopies can be downright oppressive. They muffle voices of dissent. In fact, the sacred canopy is the greatest of censors because it creates a moral universe in which the language of opposition simply does not exist. Totalitarian societies attempt to create this very situation.[30] The Soviet Union famously altered the language of public discourse so that any critique of Marxist-Leninism was predefined as counterrevolutionary.[31] Oppressive rulers lust for the kind of monolithic moral legitimacy a sacred canopy supplies—the divine right of kings and the science of socialism provided undisputed legitimacy for those in power. Their might was ordained by God or Nature—who would dare question either?

Today, North Korea attempts to impose a sacred canopy on its citizenry. Beginning in the 1970s, ruler Kim Il Sung developed a religious system that proclaimed him spiritual leader of his people. His supernatural aura was fostered in North Korean mythology and handed down to his son and now his grandson. The purpose of this all-encompassing religious-political ideology is to create a faith in a godlike leader. The supreme leader seeks to become his people's sacred object—someone who is beyond ridicule and provides a foundation for moral order. The result is an oppressive and brutal sacred culture. The collapse of the North Korean regime would release its people from a great *moral* tyranny (in addition to many other kinds of tyranny).

The collapse of sacred canopies can be liberating. Moral ideals can lift people out of meaninglessness but they can also bind people in servitude. Modern women can celebrate their victories over oppressive patriarchal values. And while racism still persists, non-Whites in the United States enjoy the demise of an omnipresent moral system bent on their subjugation. Today, we are witnessing a similar change in how Americans understand sexual morality. Some see same-sex relations and marriage as the height of profanity—a violation of sacred sexual codes. Yet public opinion is dramatically shifting on this topic. In many communities throughout the United States, gays and lesbians openly pursue a universal purpose—love for another—that was formerly denied them.

This is the moral upside of modernization. It provides space for diversity of purpose and frees the individual to follow a purpose of her own choosing. Overarching ideals, both religious and secular, are not gone; they are just no longer universal.

Charles Taylor explains that modernity is "a move from a society where belief in God is unchallenged and indeed, unproblematic, to one in which it is understood to be one option among others."[32] In premodern times, anyone challenging the existence of God would be met with blank stares. Today, Nietzsche's famous proclamation that "God is dead" doesn't shock. We are accustomed to debates about God's existence and seem to even relish them. The moral and philosophical arguments of New Atheists routinely top the bestseller lists; in turn, religious believers are inspired to produce new books attesting to the reality of God.

The fact that faith in God is only one option among others does not mean that everyone will opt out.[33] Indeed, the percentage of Americans who identify as Christian (around 80 percent) would shock many nineteenth-century theorists who predicted the demise of religion. What these theorists missed was the extent to which God can modernize. Images of God are in a constant state of revision, adjusting to scientific and cultural change.

In the 1950s, theologian Paul Tillich felt that traditional theism was in dire need of change.[34] Tillich argued:

> God appears as the invincible tyrant, the being in contrast with whom all other beings are without freedom and subjectivity. He is equated with the recent tyrants who with the help of terror try to transform everything into a mere object, a thing among things, a cog in a machine they control . . . This is the God Nietzsche said had to be killed . . . It is an atheism which is justified as the reaction against theological theism and its disturbing implications.[35]

While Tillich remained a Christian, he felt that too many people saw God as a fascist dictator—a ruler who subjects us to his whims, which are maddeningly inscrutable or devilishly cryptic. And at a time when fascist tyranny was hardly a phenomenon of the distant past, Tillich believed we had to overcome this kind of thinking in order for us to become free and enlightened.

A newer, less tyrannical God was needed, and American Christians appear to have found him. They now worship a God who would be unrecognizable to earlier generations. Their God is intimately involved in their emotional lives, daily struggles, and intimate thoughts.[36] God doesn't even appear bored by it all; in fact, he is as engrossed and interested in the believer as the believer is in him. An engaged God is a thoroughly modern God—he is a life partner, self-help consultant, and psychoanalyst rolled into one. Fire and brimstone is so old-fashioned.

Psychological anthropologist T. M. Luhrmann looked closely at how American evangelicals foster such an intimate and engaged image of God. She explains that believers

> must scrutinize their spontaneous thoughts and their mental images, their perceptions and their feelings, looking for moments that might be God. They are asked to create elaborate dialogues in the imaginations, and to get emotionally involved in those daydreams (or God-dreams).[37]

Through an intentional and repetitive focus on "God-dreams," the believer personalizes her God. Intensive self-reflection yields a God who feels as real as one's most private thoughts; in fact, the two become indistinguishable.

Interestingly, this kind of spiritual self-discovery is popular among wealthy, cosmopolitan, and well-educated Americans—the very people modernity was supposed to secularize. Luhrmann reflects that "this high-maintenance, effortful God may appeal to so many modern people precisely because the work demanded makes the God feel more salient. More real."[38]

The "work" is self-analysis. The modern believer no longer relies on the blessings of a king or the authority of the church or the magic of a shaman. Instead, she is embedded in a culture that stresses individual freedom and self-discovery. A self-discovered God requires no further legitimacy beyond the high-maintenance efforts of prayer, meditation, and inner dialogue.

Sociologist Christian Smith describes this phenomenon as a "sacred umbrella":

> In the modern world, religion does survive and can thrive, not in the form of "sacred canopies," but rather in the form of "sacred umbrellas." Canopies are expansive, immobile, and held up by props beyond the reach of those covered. Umbrellas, on the other hand, are small, handheld, and portable—like the faith-sustaining religious worlds that modern people construct for themselves.[39]

Believers construct sacred umbrellas from tools modern culture supplies. Paradoxically, these tools arose out of an intellectual tradition that had no use for religion. It was premised on tearing down the anachronistic and superstitious values of an unscientific age. The psychologists of the twentieth century created a new language and system from which to understand individuals, beliefs, and reality. Contemporary Christians speak this language and so does their God.

Social theorist Philip Rieff called it the "triumph of the therapeutic." The ideas of Freud—and psychotherapy in general—became not only mainstream but predominant in moral discourse. In 1966, Rieff pointed out that "in the age of psychologizing, clarity about oneself supersedes devotion to an ideal as the model of right conduct."[40] A therapeutic culture privileges self-discovery over commitment to a shared sacred.

Rieff feared that excessive self-analysis would leave society directionless, without any "communal purpose."[41] But therapeutic language and techniques proved compatible with the modern need for purpose, both personal and communal. The modern American Christian doesn't so much let her devotion to self-discovery supersede her devotion to God as rolls these two projects into one. By combining old sacred ideals with new therapeutic strategies, she creates a modern faith that can easily weather the storm of a cynical age. When the idea of God is openly under fire, the believer relies not on the authority of science or reason but rather on a systematic investigation of her "God-dreams." Reality is what she feels within herself, not what the skeptics tell her.[42]

So how do you feel about this?

The therapeutic culture is premised on *that* question. We all have a strong sense that our inner emotional states are of prime importance and we need to analyze, critique, and understand them in order for them to be, well, therapeutic. Therapeutic discourse turns our natural tendency toward self-interest into a moral obligation to self-discover. Self-discovery is supposed to make us more efficient, more balanced, more sociable, and more creative. Most importantly, we are supposed to feel better about ourselves.

As therapeutic language became a part of the "water" of modern culture, it elevated self-discovery and all the purposes that emerge from it: religious, secular, and nihilistic. Sociologist Eva Illouz points out that

> not only has almost half of the entire population [of the United States] consulted a mental health practitioner, but even more critically the therapeutic outlook has been institutionalized in various social spheres of contemporary societies (e.g., in economic organizations; mass media; patterns of child rearing; intimate and sexual relationships; schools; the army; the welfare state; prison rehabilitation programs; and international conflicts).[43]

Positive psychology, self-help, spiritual quests, business ethics, creative endeavors, and relationship guidance bleed into one another within the therapeutic culture. They all seek emotional clarity and deep self-analysis. The goals may be very different, but the techniques are the same.

In fact, therapeutic culture is premised on an avoidance of prescriptions of a narrow and universal purpose. The medium is the message. God is found, not imposed. Love is discovered, not arranged. Bliss is followed, not foretold. In this way, therapeutic culture casts off the oppressive dogmatism of the sacred canopy. You are free to discover your purpose, your meaningful life, and your sacred umbrella.

Yet the old sacred ideals linger in the modern age of self-discovery. God, country, and tribe are reconstituted as modern purposes. For instance, family remains a key source of purpose and moral commitment, but not a sacred obligation that supersedes autonomy. Illouz explains that a family narrative is "what family genealogy might have been to our ancestors . . . but with one crucial difference: the therapeutic persuasion not only defines and explains the self in terms of its family history but also claims to free it from its repressive yoke."[44]

In other words, we critique our parents and families in ways that wouldn't make sense in a premodern culture. Our mothers, our fathers, our communities, our religions, and our cultures become separate things that can be objectified, critiqued, and then either embraced or discarded. As such, the self has autonomy and freedom and, most importantly, the choice to accept or reject sacred ideals. Therapeutic language does not deny the power of our cultural context, but provides a vocabulary to talk about overcoming it.

Modern faith is premised on self-discovery—what feels real becomes our sacred umbrella. The fear of nihilism is the fear that we will all start to feel that nothing is real, that nothing is meaningful, and that nothing is sacred.

But modernity and the therapeutic culture *have* provided a new source of sacred meaning. The self is sacred. Our emotions are sacred objects, not to be ridiculed but to be investigated seriously with the faith that this effort will yield great meaning. So forget about sacred canopies; the modern question is: which sacred options appeal to you the most? Discover those and you can open your personal sacred umbrella.

The purpose industry is built on this promise. Purveyors of purpose offer techniques for self-discovery and self-actualization. The unquestioned assumption is that there is something wonderful to find, and once you tap it you will achieve both moral significance and delightful efficiency.

The assumption is misleading. Dostoevsky's devil envied the merchant wife's faith in God, yet he was unable to make it his own. His preference for a simple belief didn't match his suspicious mind. He was too world-weary to accept God wholeheartedly, and he suffered accordingly. Similarly, we might have the freedom to discover our purpose in life, but we are not free to make it anything we please. We are still bound by our experiences, knowledge, and context.

As moral egoists, we all yearn to find the good within. Sadly, some modern circumstances produce individuals who will never find it. They have no existential meaning to bolster them, and it is beyond their power to acquire it. Life feels worthless. These lost souls tend to subsist at the bottom of a stratified system—an existential hierarchy that rewards some with meaningful lives and punishes others with emptiness.

purpose stratified

Where are these empty people? Everywhere. But they are distributed unequally, across the globe *and* within countries. While great tragedy might befall those in developing and war-torn societies, they tend to have common sacred ideals that make their lives feel meaningful even in the face of tragedy, and perhaps more significant *because* of their circumstances. By contrast, those most afflicted by despair tend to live in relative safety within modern pluralistic societies.

Meaninglessness is no longer a marginalized perspective; it now can be openly and acceptably proclaimed. In fact, the proclamation that "everything is meaningless" is common fare and can be understood as a bratty complaint or a tragic admission of deep mental pain. Modernity popularized both meanings.

Around the world, the people most likely to say that their life has no meaning are the Dutch (see Figure 3.1). This follows some expected patterns. The Netherlands is a highly modern and pluralistic country. It has long history of liberalism and openness to new ideas, and it is currently one of the ten richest countries in the world. Secular, check. Wealthy, check. Open to newness, check. Seems like a perfect hot house for meaninglessness.

Figure 3.1 | Percentage of Population with NO Purpose

Source: Gallup World Poll

And it is a hot house. If you ask someone from the Netherlands, "Do you feel that your life has an important purpose or meaning?," 27 percent of them will say "no!" Only 6 percent of Americans say the same.

What specifically makes the Dutch so despairing? Is it their secularism? The Netherlands is certainly more secular than most countries.[45] But there is only a weak correlation between national levels of religiosity and levels of meaninglessness; very secular cultures don't necessarily lead to emptiness. Education also tends to be negatively related to meaninglessness, suggesting that philosophical sophistication does not produce pessimism. Put simply, educated secular people tend to have a strong sense of purpose.

Within the Netherlands and other modern countries, it is mainly the poor and the elderly who feel life is meaningless. In demographic terms, the most likely person in the world to feel that life is without purpose is an older person who is not personally wealthy but lives in a wealthy country. Remember the merchant's wife who was envied by Dostoevsky's devil? She matches the demographic profile of modern meaninglessness, with one notable difference—she kept her faith in God. This same woman in today's world does not believe in anything. She is no longer to be envied because she now shares the devil's deep cynicism about the reality of any higher purpose. Many of the poor, the elderly, and the less educated have turned away a sunny theology and now gaze upon a world in which nothing really matters.

This upends the stereotype of the nihilistic sophisticate sipping espresso in a European café while pondering being and nothingness.[46] Europeans who lead meaningless existences aren't the ones sitting in cafes reading nihilistic philosophy; they're the ones sitting at home reading nothing. They're the ones who pay the existential costs of modernity's material bounty.

Three factors explain this development. First, modernity made this possible. Dostoevsky's merchant's wife never considered that God might be a fiction or that that life could be meaningless. This is why the devil so envies her. She lives under the security of a sacred canopy. But in today's world, a believer must work for his faith, carefully fostering a religious community with its own set of self-discovery techniques. This kind of work is necessary because the possibility of meaninglessness looms large in our cultural ether. The work of faith requires energy, commitment, and resources. Some people are simply not up to the challenge and drift into existential hopelessness.

Relative deprivation also plays a role in increasing levels of purpose-lessness. Europe's economic recession has created growing inequality, frustrating middle- and working-class people who are finding it more difficult to get by.[47] Citizens of the postindustrial world have grown to expect certain comforts in life; in fact, the modern ethos suggests that things should always get better. Economist Timur Kuran notes, "Where a medieval peasant saw the social future as ordained, the modern urbanite sees it as manipulable."[48] This belief can inspire incredible innovations. But economic recession undermines this faith. A culture that celebrates self-empowerment suggests that your fate is your fault.[49]

Third, age is related to meaninglessness. Within a rapidly changing economy that demands ever new skills and a culture that stresses individualism over family obligation, many elderly people find themselves adrift. They feel they have little to contribute and that they receive little attention or care. Without God or some other deep faith to cling to, the solitary senior can easily lose sight of any purpose in living or dying.But this is not the fate for most in the postindustrial world. The sovereignty of the modern self turns the confusion of so many sacred options into a generous buffet—a buffet kept stocked by the purpose industry. Psychologists, self-help experts, life coaches, and clergy offer assistance in building a better, happier, and more purpose-driven life. We can pick whichever option looks most appealing. It requires effort, but the strain is well rewarded. Self-discovery produces good feelings.

With the purpose industry in place and our innate moral egoism in force, there is little reason to fear that despair will spread to epidemic levels. Hopelessness is the plight of those who lack the means to make their lives meaningful; they are victims of cultural pluralism, relative deprivation, and social obsolescence.

the importance of water

Are we losing sight of life's purpose? It depends on the water.

Water is cultural context. For people in premodern communities, it takes the form of a sacred canopy—universally shared assumptions that produce an unquestioned sense of meaning in the world. A tragic life will be understood as part of some larger undisputed moral order. We might ask, "Why did God abandon me?," but we won't abandon God.

For people in the modern world, the water is our faith in self—the idea that our inner states and feelings reflect a deep reality. But within this water, a host of possible sacred options emerge—religious, secular, or nihilistic realities. Individuals can easily abandon God. Their deepest question becomes, "Who am I?," rather than, "Who is God?"

Is this sea change good or bad? It depends.

Worriers of various persuasions feel that technology, urbanization, and globalization have heightened our moral and existential troubles. Some think we have lost our connection to God, while others feel we have lost our connection to nature, and still others feel we have lost our connection to each other (or maybe all three of these simultaneously).[50] All of these pessimists tell a story of moral decay and cultural decline.

Their opponents offer a brighter vision. Cultural change has enhanced our ability to lead lives freed from the weight of past hatreds and superstitions. We are able to explore our own senses of morality. These changes make it possible to find moral significance where none existed before. We are free to become who we *really* are. It is a story of moral evolution and cultural growth.

Both stories are true, to a certain extent. Modernity does show signs of moral decay; modern people are much more likely to feel that life lacks any purpose and modern European societies are less religious than they were in the past. Modernity also shows signs of moral progress; our understanding of well-being and our respect for diversity have improved in marked ways. The modern individual is now freer than ever to pursue her own purpose in life.

These contradictory stories meet in the realization that it is the disenfranchised and socially forgotten who feel most worthless in the modern age. One camp blames the fact that many communities and families have abandoned their traditional togetherness and obligation to family; the other points the finger at inequality and injustice.

The solution likewise depends on one's perspective. Some see "religion" and "traditional values" and "character building" as our salvation.[51] Others call for "tolerance" and "inclusion" and "equal opportunity."[52] Both approaches have empirical support. How a society might legislate or enact either of these hypothesized solutions is one of modernity's central political conflicts. Some hope to turn back time, while others seek to shake off the past.

In truth, cultural change is above such manipulations.[53] The sociologist Pitrim Sorokin believed that our existential health fluctuates with large-scale historical currents.[54] Most ambitiously, he attempted to map fluctuations in existential "systems of truth" from 600 BCE to the twentieth century. Like Rieff, Sorokin noted that the twentieth century was an era in which the self had become a sacred totem. He called it the rise of "singularism," the idea that the individual is the only social unit that matters and the only judge of ethical value.[55]

Self-discovery becomes the modern goal. Carl Jung understood that

> the serious problems of life are never fully solved. If it should for once appear that they are, this is the sign that something has been lost. The meaning and design of a problem seem not to lie in its solution, but in our working at it incessantly. This alone preserves us from stultification and petrifaction.[56]

Jung suggests that life's meaning is about searching for life's meaning. Purpose becomes a never-ending quest to discover who we really are and what we really want. As philosophers Hubert Dreyfus and Sean Kelly note, "the [modern] project, then, is not to *decide* what to care about, but to *discover* what it is about which one already cares."[57]

You must discover yourself. So how do you discover this *self*?

4

self-enchantment

Just a perfect day, you made me forget myself.
I thought I was someone else—someone good.

Lou Reed

What is your purpose in life? Can it be found within you?

Way back in 2014, a television ad showed people in exotic locales using the iPad Air, accompanied by these words:

> O me, O life of the questions of these recurring. Of the endless trains of the faithless. Of cities filled with the foolish. What good amid these, O me, O life? Answer: that you are here. That life exists and identity. That the powerful play goes on, and you may contribute a verse.
>
> That the powerful play goes on, and you may contribute a verse.[1]
>
> What will your verse be?[2]

What good are you amid the vast universe? The Apple Corporation, borrowing the words of Walt Whitman via Robin Williams, suggests that your existential worth is tied to creative expression. It promises that some poetic verse lies within us and that stylish technology can help bring it out.

The commercial's sentiment is uplifting, inclusive, and connects two things that have historically been thought to be in opposition: modern technology and existential meaning. Max Weber famously argued that advancements in technology, science, and rational thinking would create an "image of a cosmos governed by impersonal rules," which, in turn, would rob society of its "meaning," of its spiritual and mystical "enchantment."[3] He saw modernity as a process leading to "the disenchantment of the world."[4]

There is much evidence to support Weber's idea. Globalization collapses the sacred canopies of old. Countless ancient totems are now just dust. Science and rational thinking coldly quantify our mental health, our aptitudes, our earning potentials, our mates' compatibility, and our life expectancies. New and engaging technologies easily draw us away from human intimacy and the wonders of nature—we stare more and more at screens. Life has become secular, scientific, and digital. Where is the magic and poetry?

Well, the postindustrial world offers lots of fantasy, at least fantasy entertainment.[5] It also offers a kind of freedom to think and explore and self-invent in ways that our ancestors could never have imagined. These myriad possibilities provide a different kind of magic and poetry. Perhaps we no longer stand in awe of a demon- and spirit-haunted world, but we still see mystery in life.

That mystery now lies within—the self has its own demons and spirits. The lure of self-discovery titillates with the prospect that you just might find something wonderful, miraculous, and unexpected in yourself. You will compose a poetic life, a verse in that powerful play that goes on.

This is how modernity re-enchants the world; it promises *self-enchantment*, the satisfying feeling of a beautiful and powerful moral purpose deep within oneself. This inner goodness provides a lasting sense of self-worth, confidence, and belonging. If we pay close enough attention to it, it will whisper to us the True meaning of life.

The possibility of self-enchantment is premised on a modern faith, the belief that we have the power to shake off the meaninglessness, cynicism, and commotion of the postindustrial age to become whomever we want to be and believe anything we want to believe. We are free to discover our own God, our own science, our own news, our own Truth, and our own verse. As Randall Collins put it, the self is now "treated as if it were a little god."[6] We can become the creators of our own reality.

Yet we are not little gods and we are not free to create whatever reality we wish. Self-enchantment is elusive; it requires social support, constant effort, and a lot of luck. The dogged pursuit of self-discovery does not guarantee that we will like what we find. And what we find is not some objective core self. The self we find is as much a fantasy as the enchanted world turned out to be, because the self, just like all the sacred totems that preceded it, is an illusion.

The forces of modernization that Weber feared would imprison us in an "iron cage" of scientific dispassion and cold technology are still at work. But this rational scientific culture also produced the therapeutic language that breathes meaning into self-affirming spirituality, self-help strategies, and positive psychology. This chapter discusses these competing social forces, which simultaneously work to disenchant our existence by reducing us to test scores, genetic dispositions, and economic metrics, while also offering to re-enchant our existence with the beguiling promise that we can maintain a positive self-image over the course of a life.

Self-enchantment is what modern people desire. It gives purpose to life within a disenchanted world. We want to transcend all the roles, identities, predictions, calculations, rankings, and assessments that the modern world assigns us and feel like we are someone transcendently good.

self-discovery

Fifty-seven percent of all Americans say, "I desire to discover who I really am" (see Figure 4.1). Young, urban, and educated people are the most likely to say this, but the fact that over half of America wants to find their *True* selves indicates that this desire crosses racial, religious, and class divides. In fact, most Americans think about the meaning of life often and feel that developing a "philosophy of life" is of prime importance.[7]

What does it mean to discover who you are? Rene Descartes famously began his logical proof of *all* existence by pronouncing, "I think therefore I am."[8] He wanted to begin theorizing from the only self-evident thing he could think of, and the first thing he thought was . . . *himself.*[9] The self is one of the most present objects in our consciousness; it also turns

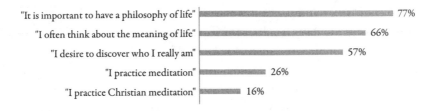

"It is important to have a philosophy of life" — 77%
"I often think about the meaning of life" — 66%
"I desire to discover who I really am" — 57%
"I practice meditation" — 26%
"I practice Christian meditation" — 16%

Figure 4.1 | American Attitudes on Self-discovery
Source: Baylor Religion Survey, Wave 3

out to be one of the most inscrutable. This is probably why over half of Americans, even those with relatively happy lives, are still searching for themselves.

Being modern individuals, we often utilize the most scientific means to solve the puzzle of self. In 2013, the Obama administration dedicated $100 million to the Brain Research through Advancing Innovative Neurotechnologies (BRAIN) Initiative, a multifaceted project intended to map the activity of every neuron in the human brain. This research is expected to yield better treatments of brain injuries, disorders, and diseases. Yet it is unclear what it will tell us about our true selves. In fact, the latest findings in neuroscience indicate that our popular notion of self is "an illusion."[10]

The "self-illusion" refers to that deep feeling we have of a unified personal essence, a core being that can be "discovered." This strong intuition is a product of our imagination. We imagine something—*the self*—that cannot be scientifically observed in the chemistry or structure of our brains. As Susan Blackmore describes it, "the illusion of continuity and separateness is provided by a story the brain tells, or a fantasy it weaves."[11] In other words, I think therefore I imagine a self.

How does one imagine a self? One way to observe the construction of self in action is to meditate. More than one-quarter of Americans say they meditate. And, similar to those who say they want to discover who they really are, such people tend to be more educated. In addition, many meditators describe themselves as "religious," which may seem odd in a predominately Christian society. But 60 percent of meditators in the United States say they practice a form of "Christian meditation."[12]

Meditation—and there are countless versions of it—is a means of becoming more self-aware. Bhante Gunaratana describes the Vipassana technique, attributed to the Buddha himself:

> Meditation is participatory observation: what you are looking at responds to the process of looking. In this case, what you are looking at is *you*, and what you see depends on how you look . . . just sit back, and see what happens. Treat the whole thing as an experiment.[13]

You are supposed to sit down, be quiet, breathe, and observe what is going on in your head.[14] While meditation originated centuries ago, its rational, efficient, and systematic procedures fit perfectly with a modern perspective. The activity is openly scientific; you are conducting an experiment of participatory observation. All you need is yourself and some time. In the end, Gunaratana says, we will "learn to listen to our own thoughts without being caught in them."[15]

The therapeutic benefits of meditation are widely reported, and medical studies largely confirm these claims, although there is some disagreement about the specific benefits.[16] As many meditators will tell you, the only way to see what meditation will yield is to do it yourself.[17]

To gain further insight, we can also look to the testimonies of serious-minded meditators. The Hindu prince Siddhārtha and the Scottish philosopher David Hume are good places to start. Bruce Hood describes their experiences:

> Three hundred years ago in a dull, drizzly, cold, misty, and miserable (or *driech* as we Scots love to say) Edinburgh, Hume sat and contemplated his own mind. He looked in on his self. He tried to describe his inner self and thought that there was no single entity, but rather bundles of sensations, perceptions, and thoughts piled on top of each other. He concluded that the self emerged out of the bundling together of these experiences. It is not clear whether Hume was aware of exotic Eastern philosophy but in the sixth century BC, thousands of miles away in much warmer climates, the young Buddha, meditating underneath a fig tree, had reached much the same conclusion with his principle of *annata* (no self).[18]

Interestingly, the testimonies of Hume and the Buddha fit closely with the findings of neuroscience; specifically, that there is no center of activity in the brain—a core self is something we imagine.[19]

The struggle to meditate, "to listen to our own thoughts without being caught up in them," tells us something about how we imagine self and purpose.[20] We are assaulted daily by worries and obligations that are nearly impossible to observe with complete detachment. It is difficult to get beyond these immediate concerns and unearth a state of being in which we are free from the anxieties, stresses, and insecurities of life. The paradox of self, so clearly observed in the teaching of the Buddha, is that to overcome suffering we must rid ourselves of the imagination of self. But this does not come easily or often.

The inner struggle that comes with meditation reflects one of the most fundamental obstacles to composing a purpose-driven life: the turmoil present in the imagined *self*. All of the major religions ponder the reality of inner conflict and the need to overcome it. While the term *jihad* sometimes refers to religious crusades and holy wars, it can also describe a personal struggle to become the best human you can. When asked what is the greatest jihad of all, the Prophet Muhammad replied, "To fight against one's inner passions, against the evil tendencies within oneself."[21] Countless paths to self-discovery seek to help us tame our inner conflict.

We fight to transcend those aspects of self that are considered evil, unproductive, unattractive, and restrictive. The goal is self-enchantment, to find a virtuous core. Traditional religions offer different visions of what that is and how to achieve it. For Buddhists, self-discovery leads to the realization that self is really part of a cosmic Oneness; for Christians, self-discovery leads to an everlasting enchantment in the form of eternal salvation; for Muslims, self-discovery leads to a conscious and consistent submission to Allah.[22] All of these visions promise a self finally released from suffering and sin.

Secular modern culture, just like the religions of old, has its own version of self-enchantment. It is the faith that self-discovery is ultimately therapeutic and will lead to a healthy, morally secure, and purposeful self. Our therapeutic culture encourages us to put in the time and effort needed to find the good within but, unlike religions, provides few indications of what ultimate reality we will find.[23] People around the globe find very different things. Monotheists find God; spiritualists find cosmic unity; secularists find inner goodness and moral universals; and nihilists find nothing at all. Who is correct and who is simply fooling themselves?

We are *all* fooling ourselves.

This assertion is not as radical as it seems. Even conservative religious traditions have long recognized the weaknesses of human imagination. An Islamic adage states this clearly, "Whatever comes to your mind about His nature, God is different than that."[24] This suggests that Allah is a metaphor, just like *Oneness* and *the true self* are metaphors—they dimly represent our deepest hopes and feelings, which are too vast to concisely articulate. Absolute self-discovery is futile because what we find *within* can only be articulated by an imperfect metaphor. And we all know the metaphors are insufficient.

Faith is the belief that behind our metaphor lies a real Truth. It enchants us. We feel the presence of Allah, or God, or Oneness, or moral goodness, or human potential deep in our bones. But this kind of faith requires effort and luck. It requires a cultural context that supports and promotes this faith, and a community that establishes the day-to-day truth of it.

One's own goodness is an imagined reality that always exists alongside a social reality—that is, how others see us. In the best-case scenario, social interaction continually confirms our positive sense of self and happily affirms our purpose in life. But in worst-case scenarios, social interaction undermines a person's self-worth and opens up the possibility that everything in the world is rotten, even one's self.

Most of us fall somewhere in the middle. We experience some combination of positive and negative social interactions. We *need* to feel good about ourselves in order to establish a meaningful life, but social forces seep into our souls. We can only pray that these forces are benevolent because their power is unassailable.

self-consciousness

You are standing in front of strangers in your underwear. How do you feel? Unless you are an underwear model or an eager exhibitionist, you probably feel self-conscious. *Public self-consciousness* is an acute awareness that others are assessing us.[25] We don't like this feeling and want to ignore it; it creates embarrassment and shame. Clearly, it feels *better* to be less inhibited and less dominated by the pettiness and prejudices of others. You know, we just want to be *ourselves*. We want to express our beautiful verse in the powerful play that goes on—just like Apple tells us to.

One hundred and thirty years before the iPad Air, Walt Whitman published *Leaves of Grass*. As a gay man in a puritanical culture, Whitman must have felt self-conscious.[26] Yet his poems express deeply personal and intimate feelings to a public that would have been hostile to his private sexuality. The first poem in the book is "Song of Myself." Here is how it begins:

I celebrate myself, and sing myself,

And what I assume you shall assume,

For every atom belonging to me as good belongs to you.[27]

Whitman's poem is now hailed as visionary, both artistically and conceptually. The first three lines alone say something profound about how to imagine the self.

"I celebrate myself" suggests a radical individualism, unafraid of public opinion. The self is not something to hide or be ashamed of but rather something to acknowledge and praise. Celebrating myself ascribes terrific power and importance to me—I become my own sacred object. Whitman gives voice to this modern ideal.

Whitman did not worship the self as a little god but rather hoped to release it from the bonds of repression. It was his dream of self-enchantment; he proclaims a universal oneness, asserting that "every atom belonging to me as good belongs to you." We are all tied together and interconnected; all our little gods combine to create a unity.

Whitman unites two conceptions of self in one stanza—the self as autonomous and creative (a Western trope) and the self as an aspect of unity (an Eastern trope). Research suggests these East/West stereotypes correspond to geographic and ethnic categories. Specifically, Americans are more likely than Japanese to think of the self as some private object unaffected by others, and Asian-Americans place more importance on collective identities than European-Americans.[28] This suggests that the self that one ultimately "discovers" is partially defined by one's culture. Eastern mystics tend to find unity, while Western seekers discover individuality.

Americans seem to be especially captivated by the idea that each self is unique—in this we are all alike. Following Whitman's lead, Americans also want to celebrate themselves. When asked directly about their personal characteristics, almost all Americans say they are "dependable" and "giving" and "sympathetic" (see Figure 4.2). Interestingly, three-quarters of Americans declare themselves "humble." Very few Americans (17 percent) say they are "uncreative," one of the most self-effacing and un-American adjectives on the survey.

These self-descriptors say less about individuals than about how they want to be seen (see Table 4.1). For instance, women are more likely than men to say they are "giving," "sympathetic," "upbeat," and "humble."[29] Religious people also tend to favor these descriptors. Older people are

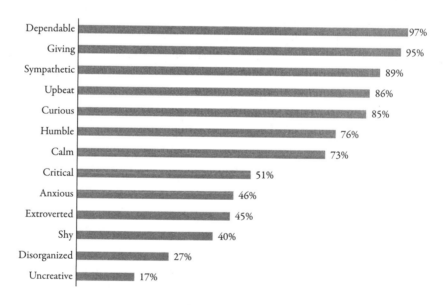

Figure 4.2 | How Americans See Themselves

Source: Baylor Religion Survey, Wave 2 and Wave 3

Note: Some of these characteristics are measures of Big-Five factors; they are dependable, sympathetic, calm, critical, anxious, extroverted, disorganized, and uncreative. Instead of factoring scores into a Big-Five schema, I let the terms stand alone for conceptual clarity. You can see the actual response rate to each item.

more likely to say they are "dependable." The wealthy are self-assuredly "upbeat" and "extroverted."

Why do different groups use different words to describe the self? George Herbert Mead pioneered our modern understanding of how culture creates self. He argued that "the self arises through taking of the attitudes of others."[30] The ways others feel about us are communicated in language, facial expressions, and gestures that differ from group to group and from situation to situation.

While many people work under the assumption that self-descriptors identify distinct personality types, Mead offers more a plausible critique of their source, namely, that groups establish different ways to talk about the ideal self. For instance, women are supposed to be more "sympathetic" than men, and religious people are supposed to be more "humble" than secular people. The fact that self-descriptors map onto cultural stereotypes about gender, religiosity, and age supports Mead's idea of a socially constructed self.

Table 4.1   Demographic Characteristics Correlated with Self-descriptors

	FEMALE	AGE	EDUCATION	INCOME	RELIGIOUS
Dependable		+		+	
Giving	+	+	–	–	+
Sympathetic	+	+			+
Upbeat	+			+	+
Curious			+		–
Humble	+		–	–	+
Calm				–	
Critical	+	+	–	–	
Anxious	–		+	+	
Extroverted			+	+	
Shy		–		–	
Disorganized		+	+	+	
Uncreative		–			

SOURCE: *Baylor Religion Survey, Wave 2 and Wave 3*

NOTE: *Only significant correlations reported; + means a positive correlation; – means a negative correlation.*

The other day I saw Justin, a ten-year-old boy, playing left forward in a soccer tournament.[31] His position on the team dictates that he takes shots on the goal. But Justin never does this; he runs away from the ball and stands in the wrong place. His teammates yell, "What are you doing?!" His coach shouts orders. Justin leaves the field in tears and asks to be allowed to quit.

Soccer should be simple because it has clear rules and roles. Each player has a designated position that prescribes his purpose in relation to everyone else. The team functions only to the extent that all players understand their roles from the perspective *of* the team—this is the essence of teamwork, and the adage, "There is no *I* in team."

Teamwork requires a *generalized other.* Mead argued:

> The organized community or social group which gives to the individual his unity of self may be called "the generalized other." The attitude of the generalized other is the attitude of the whole community. Thus, for example, in the case of such a social group as a ball team, the team is the generalized other.[32]

Each player understands what the team wants, not because they are yelling at each other but because they all share the same understanding of the rules and strategies of the game.

Justin is not a team player. But he is not a selfish player. He is simply unable to perform what little of his position he understands. Justin plays a role, just not the one he is officially assigned. He is thrown into the unofficial role of a "bad" player, which Justin is beginning to understand very well.

As players learn their positions on the field, they also learn their social positions on the team. There are stars, leaders, jokers, showboats, bullies, and bad players. Teammates are told they are these things and very soon they begin to tell it to themselves. This process—*labeling theory*—illustrates how the generalized other operates.[33] You perceive how others see you and then you come to believe their assessment. After some time you don't even have to think about it; it becomes second nature. The generalized other is ever-present in Justin's head, repeating over and over, "You stink." And Justin comes to believe it.

Justin cannot "celebrate" himself because he is not celebrated by others. His only hope is to rely on alternative evaluations of self. If he is "good" at something else, this can become a new source of self-esteem. Ultimately, Justin will want to move beyond being good *at things* and simply want to know that he is good *inside*. If he is lucky, a teacher might one day assign Whitman's *Leaves of Grass* and Justin will transcend his earthly lot and discover a self to celebrate forever. In short, he could self-enchant.

Self-enchantment—that feeling of eternal goodness within oneself—is often and ironically fleeting. Enchantment continually competes with disparaging social messages. The critical gazes of others can rob us of our positive self-image. We no longer feel as "dependable," "giving," and "humble" as our survey responses indicate. And as Mead argued, the critical gaze of others becomes internalized.

Leo Tolstoy experienced this kind of self-conscious confusion during his mother's funeral. He recalls peering into her coffin as a small boy:

> As I gazed . . . for a time I lost all sense of existence, and experienced a kind of vague blissfulness which though grand and sweet, was also sad . . .
>
> The door creaked as the chanter entered who was to relieve his predecessor. The noise awakened me, and my first thought was that, seeing me standing on the chair in a posture which had nothing touching in its aspect, he might take me for an unfeeling boy who had climbed on to the chair out of mere curiosity: wherefore I hastened to make the sign of the cross, to bend down my head, and to burst out crying . . . this egotistic consciousness completely annulled any element of sincerity in my woe.[34]

This short passage is rife with emotional complexity. First, Tolstoy is captivated by the oddity of facing his dead mother—the swirl of emotions is dizzying, alternating "sweet" and "sad." An emotional catharsis entrances him. Time and existence lose their meaning and he communes with a transcendent reality.

When another person enters the room, Tolstoy becomes aware of his own appearance and immediately strikes an emotional pose he thinks is more appropriate. A moment before, his generalized other offered a damning critique of self—it said, "You don't look sad enough." His reflexive self-consciousness disenchanted him.

Tolstoy ironically feels guilty about sobbing at his mother's funeral, because it feels insincere. But he is too hard on himself. Emotional performances are not necessarily false; in fact, we can never fully determine what parts of feelings are instinctual and what parts arise from social norms.[35] Emotions—both their outward expressions and cognitive interpretations—reflect the interconnection of physical arousals and social expectations. Jonathan Turner and Jan Stets explain this complex relationship:

> Emotions are ultimately aroused by the activation of body systems. This arousal generally comes from cognitive appraisals of self in relation to others, social structure, and culture . . . No one element—biology, cultural construction, or cognition—is solely responsible for how emotions are experienced and expressed.[36]

The physiological aspect of emotion requires no great proof. We feel it in our bodies. Sadness, anger, joy, and fear percolate in our senses and emit involuntary reactions. We sob, tremble, or grin involuntarily. Quite clearly, emotion is bodily and reflexive.

The cultural and social aspects of emotion are more difficult to pin down. While certain "primary emotions" are thought to be universal, the ways in which we express these basic feelings are socially shaped. Furthermore, many emotions are directly tied to how we imagine the meaning and the ramifications of social life. While social norms—rules of behavior and codes of conduct—vary greatly between cultures, they become immediate in our reaction to the world. Moral psychologists now better understand that "norms are encoded in the human mind"; they call the bundling of arousals and norms a *moral emotion*.[37] It comes without our willing it.

A *moral emotion* imbues a physical reaction with meaning.[38] One of the central struggles of true self-discovery is that we experience competing moral emotions. Some evoke the bliss of self-enchantment while others undermine it. Tolstoy felt this tension acutely. His vision of an ethereal world beyond time *as well as* his self-conscious sobbing were, in part, socially constructed. Mystic visions of ghosts and the supernatural were well known in Tolstoy's time. Similarly, the need to appear sad at a funeral is a universal norm.[39] In the end, Tolstoy's feeling of transcendence was no more or less real than his feeling of guilt and embarrassment. The trick is to hold on to the positive moral emotion for as long as possible—which throughout Tolstoy's life proved maddeningly elusive.

Religions, support groups, and positive social interactions help to keep feelings of transcendence alive. Faith in transcendent ideals can anchor the moral goodness of self even when circumstance and emotion shake it. This is the ongoing struggle of self-discovery, the inner jihad waged by us all. We want to experience an inner peace that is supposed to come with being a good and purpose-driven person. Yet we are assaulted by real world struggles, obligations, and cruel assessments that appear to undermine this experience.

cruel assessments

Americans have, for centuries, called each other horrible names. The list of cruel and abusive labels is long. Hopefully, those who have suffered public castigation and humiliation can find ways to shake off the anger and derision aimed at them. Some find solace in communities that offer love, religions that offer self-esteem, and visions of a kinder world that offer hope. Still, such cruel assessments are not so easily tossed aside. They tend to push people in dark directions.

The modern world offers lots of ways for us to feel inadequate or like nobodies. The possibility of failure looms at work, at home, in bed, at play, in worship, and in self-discovery. It looms at every turn, because we have become hyper-aware of all the winners in our midst. Advances in information, communication, and technology remind us constantly of how far we fall short of the frontrunners. How do we stack up to the beautiful, wealthy, successful, and adored people of the world? Not terribly well.

Parents have access to magazines and blogs dedicated to showing them what "good" parenting is. Can they live up to these expectations? Look at all the fabulous, high-paying careers depicted on our television screens. So many people appear to have jobs that satisfy their financial and creative needs. Where are all these cool jobs? What about that verse you were going to write once you finally bought the iPad Air? Don't bother; it will just sound trite compared to Whitman and Tolstoy.

There are millions of ways *not* to live up to your potential. Modern consumerism only exaggerates these anxieties. Businesses sell products that will supposedly help us achieve our full potential and become important and respected. Who is the smart person? The one who has H&R Block do her taxes. Who is the best mother? The one who buys Pampers. Who is the sexiest? The one who uses Axe body spray. Who loves his spouse the most? The one who goes to Jared. Who is the best steward of the environment? The one who drives a Prius. Consumer culture tells you what you should be doing in order to be a happier and better person.

While most of us can see through the obvious contrivances of commercial culture, as a whole it produces an overwhelming set of messages that convey ideals of self. Commercialism becomes a generalized other. Over and over, we see who is ridiculed and who is lionized. We can fast forward all we want, because the ads are now playing in our heads. They are not overtly cruel, but they can evoke despair by showing us the innumerable things we have yet to achieve, acquire, and conquer.

For instance, the hyper-sexualized images that are so common in commercials, television, and film have powerful ramifications for how viewers understand the norms and expectations of sexual expression. I interviewed groups of men suffering from erectile dysfunction. They felt the sting of sexual failure acutely.[40] My research took place before the introduction of Viagra and similar drugs that, in theory, would have turned these men into happy consumers. But at the time, they felt like sexual failures. They described how our culture's sexual ideals filled them with shame and disgust. This is nothing new; ideals of beauty have been making women feel like failures for centuries. The modern world just makes the ideals more and more unattainable, thereby increasing the percentage of people who fail by comparison.

At the end of each interview, I asked some common demographic questions.[41] Please tell me, "How old are you?"; "How would you describe your race?"; "What is highest level of education you have completed?"; and finally, "What is your approximate income?" At this last question I was often eyed suspiciously and queried, "Why exactly do you need to know that?"

Men who had told me painful details about their sexual lives didn't want me to know how much money they made. Their feelings of sexual failure had been laid bare, so why were they so secretive about their paychecks? They knew that their income would be just one more marker of failure. This is the reason why revealing your financial worth is an act of solemn intimacy.

It is no coincidence that wealth is often referred to as one's *worth*. And unlike sexual failure, which can be hidden in the confines of the bedroom, professional and financial failure is one of the most public expressions of self-worth. William James explained that

> a man's Self is the sum total of all that he can call his, not only his body and his psychic powers, but clothes and his house, his wife and his children, his ancestors and friends, his reputation and his works, his land and horse and yacht and bank account.[42]

What we own are not things we demurely admit, but things we boast about. Americans wear their wealth on their sleeves, sometimes literally. Cufflinks, cars, and houses announce the status of individuals. Our economic hierarchy, which is getting more and more rigid by the day, functions as a constant assessment of self. For some it can be cruel and for others quite generous. How can corporate CEOs possibly *deserve* their lucky fortunes? We are told that they work hard and are brilliant. Of course, the implication of this justification is that the rest of us don't work hard and are not brilliant.

Many Americans think that the economic hierarchy of the United States is fair; in fact, Americans who make under $20,000 a year believe in the American Dream as much as those who earn over $150,000 (see Figure 4.3). The vast majority agree that anything is possible with hard work and that success reflects ability. With widespread belief in the American Dream, one's salary and wealth are easily equated with one's ability and work ethic, thus establishing a moral universe in which one's worth as a person can be easily quantified. Poor people are seen as being "bad" at life and their economic worth fuses with their self-worth.

Beth, an elderly woman in the midst of a health and housing crisis, told me, "The system is working against me." She is correct; the system torments her by taking away her home, her medicine, and her self-worth. Her sense of alienation has led her to see herself as a perpetual victim, a social pest, and someone of no consequence to her larger community.[43] People who feel alienated often slip into a state of "learned helplessness."[44]

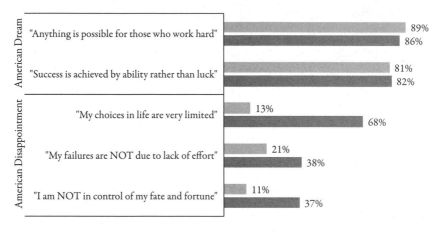

Figure 4.3 | Dreams and Disappointments

Source: Baylor Religion Survey, Wave 3

This occurs when someone simply gives up pursuing her goals because she ceases to believe in her own agency. In fact, children can even learn helplessness from their parents, without actually understanding what constitutes social failure.[45]

People with lower incomes and less education are much more likely to feel alienated—no surprises there. In turn, these Americans are the ones most likely to be nervous, on edge, worried about life.[46] While clinging to the distant hope that anything is possible in the United States, poor people often feel that they have no control over their fate, fortunes, and failures. Their worthlessness is prescribed and becomes part of their self if not tempered by other, more positive assessments.

A person will feel that her public status defines herself to the extent that she believes in meritocracy. Michael Young coined the term in his 1958 book *The Rise of the Meritocracy, 1870–2033*, a fictional study of a merit-based society. In the future Young imagines, "merit is equated with intelligence-plus-effort, its possessors are identified at an early age and selected for appropriate intensive education, and there is an obsession with quantification, test-scoring, and qualifications."[47] This seems to be the perfect system; it only rewards those who deserve it. Raises, income, and wealth coldly quantify one's worth. Person A is understood to be $X better, more talented, more intelligent, and more useful than person B.

In singing the praises of meritocracy, Young reveals its pitfalls. One of those pitfalls is the quantification of self, which schoolchildren experience every day. They are taught to score high on tests, which will be decisive for their future. Their merit is quantified. When one's aptitude, intelligence, and work ethic are rendered in numbers, they become recorded fact. Low scores prove worthlessness.

Cruel assessments come in many forms. The worst actively seek to deprive individuals of their self-esteem and curtail them from believing in a greater purpose to their lives. Racism, sexism, homophobia, snobbery, and outright hatred can rob people of the feeling that they have meaningful lives.

The more subtle types of cruelty are those not intended to be outwardly degrading. Instead, they diminish a person's self by promoting impossible goals. Consumerism beguiles us with the promise that happiness and respect can be obtained by consuming the right goods. While this may get economies moving, it does little to make life deeply satisfying. The ideology of meritocracy also degrades us by identifying and extolling those few individuals who are deemed exceptional. It asserts that the financial icons of our society deserve their riches and the rest do not. Michael Young keenly understood how meritocracy slyly replaces overtly cruel assessments with coldly calculating ones. Within a merit-based culture, test scores, productivity evaluations, and year-end bonuses don't lie; they define a person's worth down to the penny and the percentile.

calculated assessments

Most people recognize that it is offensive to denigrate or discriminate against people based on race, income, religiosity, or sexuality. But that hasn't stopped us from classifying people based on these categories. The modern individual internalizes her demographic characteristics. She fills out forms constantly, fully understanding that the powers that be will catalog her based on that information. Each form is her, in summary. We understand that others see us as demographics, rankings, and test scores, and that is how we begin to see ourselves. These categories and assessments determine what schools we will attend, what careers are possible, what lovers are compatible, and what kinds of care we will receive.

Demographics and statistics, which supposedly provide us with objective and scientific evaluations of self, guide our paths in life.

Carl Jung championed the idea that we could systematically and scientifically sort people by distinct personalities. "Since the earliest of times," he wrote, "attempts have repeatedly been made to classify individuals according to types and thus bring to order into what was confusion."[48] This is how we come to understand others; we place them in groups. Social science provides new, modern, and precise ways to do it.

The theoretical premise of personality types, for instance, assumes that you have a core set of stable traits that guide and predict your behavior. Currently, the most widely used personality measure is the Big-Five, or OCEAN, which stands for the factors of Openness, Conscientiousness, Extroverted, Agreeable, and Neurotic. Social science provides wonderful tools to better understand individuals, groups, and societies. But social science can also shape the very things it tries to measure, as individuals use its techniques and findings to aid self-discovery. Today, most Americans will be familiar with these kinds of questions:

> Are you an extrovert or an introvert?
>
> Do you have a type A or a type B personality?[49]
>
> Are you inventive/curious or consistent/cautious?[50]
>
> What is your Myers-Briggs score? Are you ESTJ or INFP?[51]

The supposition is that knowing you have a INFP personality will give you some insight into your true self. But psychologist Bruce Hood argues that the idea that one has a measurable personality is flawed because "people are not necessarily consistent in all aspects of their lives. This is why you can live with someone who is fastidious at work when it comes to detail but hopelessly disorganized when it comes to the domestic situation." Consequently, personality types are calculated assessments of self that will always fall short of reality. Yet personality types may become self-fulfilling prophesies as individuals act out the ways they are *supposed* to behave according to their type.

Historian Sarah Igo traced the increasing importance of surveys in the twentieth century to show that Americans have become obsessed with knowing how they statistically compare to each other. She describes a shift in what statistics meant to people.

What was new was that consumers now paid for scientific expertise, not in the service of social knowledge but in the hope of individual, intimate transformation. In this sense, the late twentieth century saw the deepest penetration yet of social survey tools into everyday conversation and self-categorization. Corporate managers, popular experts, media figures, and ordinary citizens speak in a social scientific language that has become virtually indistinguishable from American culture at large.[52]

Today, magazines, television shows, and websites often give surveys that give us a score or a ranking or a type that purports to show us where we stand in relation to everyone else.[53] Many of these surveys are bogus, but their effect on us depends on how we interpret them. This is the way in which social science defines self. It tells us how we compare to the average score. It tells us our "type."

Men in the sexual dysfunction study I conducted were very interested in rankings and averages. They often asked: "How long does the typical erection last?"; "On average, how long does sex last?"; "How often does the average woman have an orgasm?"; and "How long is the average penis?" The reason these men were curious is obvious—they wanted to see if they were outliers. The less "average" they felt, the worse they felt about themselves. One man even described himself as a "freak," knowing that his sexuality had been shown to be statistically unusual or deviant.

When asked about their medical care, several men indicated that their doctors didn't really understand them; they felt treated like "a number." But by knowing *the numbers*—the research literature showing the probabilities that men of those ages, with those conditions, and with those BMIs could be cured—their doctors actually understood them better than they did themselves. These physicians understood the evidence-based medicine behind each diagnosis and therefore were in a better position to treat their patients. Of course, this didn't address how the men *felt* about themselves—an important part of their condition that went unnoticed when it came time to devise a treatment.

Positive psychology and quality-of-life research seek to fill this void by offering scientific ways to quantify and fine-tune a person's happiness, purpose, and life satisfaction. Barbara Fredrickson and Marcial Losada generated excitement by conducting a research project that purported to measure the ideal balance of positive to negative emotions that would lead to life of "flourishing." Their initial study, published in *American Psychologist* in 2005, stated:

> Participants (N = 188) completed an initial survey to identify flourishing mental health and then provided daily reports of experienced positive and negative emotions over 28 days. Results showed that the mean ratio of positive to negative affect was above 2.9 for individuals classified as flourishing and below that threshold for those not flourishing. Together with other evidence, these findings that a set of general mathematical principles may describe the relations between positive affect and human flourishing.[54]

Fredrickson later argued that "just as zero degrees Celsius is a special number in thermodynamics the 3-to-1 positivity ratio may well be a magic number in human psychology."[55] She asserts that the ratio can change your life and create an "upward spiral" of positivity. Sadly, the math proved to be inaccurate and the "flourishing ratio" remains a great mystery.[56]

While it must be true that more "positivity" in one's life is beneficial, the attempt to render this wisdom statistically reflects the modern desire to solve life's existential problems with science. As of yet, true self-discovery and all the meanings we attribute to existence defy quantification. And, ironically, quantifying the meaning of life, happiness, and human purpose simply adds another layer of meaning to them. Calculated assessments of self and life satisfaction give us a different kind of knowledge but not necessarily the kind that can cure our angst.

In fact, the calculated assessment of self can often be further disenchanting. A low LSAT score abruptly ends your dreams of being a great lawyer. A poor credit rating undermines any illusion that you are "responsible" and "steadfast." A Myers-Briggs score recommends that you *not* try to be the life of the party. A positivity ratio under 2.9 suggests that you aren't "flourishing." These numbers and assessments are deflating, and after a while we want to denounce their inadequacy—we are more than the sum total of our scores. But within a culture of quantification, our protests against standardized tests and scientific evaluations start to sound self-serving.

The tendency to systematically quantify and categorize everything is central to Max Weber's concept of *disenchantment*. It is the inevitable pull of modernity toward more efficiency, more predictability, more standardization, and more calculability. Why should the self be immune?

Gary Shteyngart imagines a future fully disenchanted by calculated assessments of self. In his novel *Super Sad True Love Story*, the protagonist, Lenny, checks his personal information device (an *äppärät*) to size up his chances at a singles bar:

> Streams of data were now fighting for time and space around us. The pretty girl I had just FACed was projecting my MALE HOTNESS as 120 out of 800, PERSONALITY 450, and something called SUSTAINABILIT¥ at 630. The other girls were sending me similar figures. "Damn," Noah said. "The prodigal Nee-gro Abramov is getting creamed here. Looks like the *chicas*, they no likey that big Hebraic snorkel our boy was born with. And those flabby Hadassah arms. Okay, rank him up, Vish."
>
> Vishnu worked my äppärät until some RANKINGS came up. He helped me navigate the data. "Out of the seven males in the Community," he said, gesturing around the bar, "Noah's the third hottest, I'm the fourth hottest, and Lenny's the seventh."
>
> "You mean I'm the ugliest guy here?" I ran my fingers through the remnants of my hair.
>
> "But you've got a decent personality," Vishnu comforted me, "and you're second in the whole bar in terms of SUSTAINABILIT¥."[57]

In Shteyngart's dystopia, social interaction is summarized in ratings and rankings. Lenny knows he is ugly not because his friend ridicules his "big Hebraic snorkel" but because his MALE HOTNESS score doesn't lie. And just as the soccer misfit Justin internalizes the criticisms of his team and the poor internalize the shame provoked by consumer culture, Lenny internalizes his RANKINGS. He is now objectively ugly, but at least he has good SUSTAINABILIT¥.

Our Facebook culture seems to be heading toward this imagined future. Dating websites have pioneered the science of mating with the promise that their compatibility surveys will scientifically narrow the field of suitors to pinpoint true love. How long will it be before we have iPhone apps that rank our attractiveness compared to everyone else in a bar? Or until a professor can, with 1-Click, check the intelligence-plus-effort scores of her students? Or until an employer no longer needs to get to know job candidates because their interpersonal skills have been pretabulated?

Leon Wieseltier argues that we may already be there.

> Quantification is the most overwhelming influence upon the contemporary American understanding of, well, everything. It is enabled by the almost unimaginable data-generating capabilities of the new technology. The distinction between knowledge and information is a thing of the past, and there is no greater disgrace than to be a thing of the past. Beyond its impact upon culture, the new technology penetrates even deeper levels of identity and experience, to cognition and consciousness.[58]

Consciousness is fully penetrated by the new technology, once we begin to believe that the meaning of life can be rendered in metrics. It is a faith that in assessing and quantifying things like brain structures, test scores, buying patterns, and match-making profiles, we will find the best, most efficient, and most efficacious ways to live. Life will no longer be mysterious but fully rational. Weber describes this modern possibility as akin to being trapped in a cage. He writes that calculated assessments "should only lie on the shoulders of the 'saint like a light cloak, which can be thrown aside at any moment.' But fate decreed that the cloak should become an iron cage."[59]

Still, modernity provides a way to break free of this iron cage fashioned from the plethora of cruel and calculated assessments that inevitably constrict us and thwart our purpose. Self-enchantment enables us to finally discard these oppressive weights, just as the saint throws off his light cloak and leaves his earthly affairs behind.

enchantment, take me away

Wittgenstein noted that "the solution of the problem of life is seen in the vanishing of the problem."[60] Self-enchantment is the modern way to solve life's problems; a new reality can silence the naysayers and bean counters. Plato's cave analogy is apt. You see shadows on the cave wall. They are images of self as evaluated and labeled. But you are not what you own. You are not what people call you. You are not how social science describes you. You are not a predicted probability. These are mere shadows. Walk out of the cave, into the light, and something different emerges: your personal power, your loving spirit, your ultimate Being—your *enchanted self.*

In the light of this new reality, you can awaken the giant within, save your soul, and discover pure consciousness. You can rise above the labels and stigmas and rankings of self by going *under* them. Under them all resides something more profound. It is a more authentic, a more magical, and most importantly, a more moral reality. The enchanted self is the "real me," which exists in a mystical realm beyond the narrow confines of science, society, and time.[61]

The most compelling aspect of self-enchantment strategies is that they are impossible to disprove. This is what the New Atheists and other individuals bent on "disproving" religious, spiritual, and New Age faiths cannot seem to comprehend. Faith creates a language, a logic, and a perception of the world and emotion—in sum, a reality all its own. This means that it *feels true* to the believer, regardless of what critics argue. As Durkheim realized, a nonbeliever trying to critique faith "is like a blind man trying to talk about color."[62]

The promise of self-enchantment simply feels true to many, which explains the wild popularity of religious and spiritual paths to self-discovery. The tactics, language, and metaphors can be vastly different, but the most alluring narratives of self-discovery are always hopeful and enthusiastic. As evidence, I will briefly discuss three highly popular articulations of modern self-enchantment.

Tony Robbins represents the seminar-style, results-driven aspect of self-help. Rick Warren epitomizes a contemporary Christian vision of salvation. And representing the enlightenment arm of self-discovery is Eckhart Tolle.

It is important to note that I am not disparaging or condemning these thinkers and their philosophies of life. Rather, I hope to indicate what unites and what divides them. Their unifying element is their shared attempt to define and locate an enchanted self. But they differ on *how* to do this.

Self, to Robbins, is an inner giant.[63] This seems appropriate because Robbins is larger than life, in body, in charisma, and in the self-help industry. He is an attractive and commanding figure who exudes warm enthusiasm and true empathy. He promises that we can find happiness and success—romantically, socially, and professionally—by simply following his strategy. It is a bold and unbelievable claim (which he readily admits). The process involves attending his seminars, meeting with his staff coaches, and utilizing his products (tapes, DVDs, books, etc.).

The key to Robbins's strategy is that change and results are dependent on *you*. No one can do this for you. You have to want it. Life needs to be on your terms. These are his mantras and they communicate a very definitive self, one that has all the power in the world at its disposal. The choice to use this power is ours!

Robbins writes, "We're all here to contribute something unique, that deep within each of us lies a special gift . . . Each of us has a talent, a gift, our own bit of genius waiting to be tapped."[64] His cheerful encouragement, interspersed with amazing stories and demonstrations of inner giants being let loose (like walking on hot coals), seek to help us tap our own genius. Robbins exhorts you to "focus on what *you* really want," and "find *your* own answer."

This is the elegance of the inner giant. The person you want to be and the life you want already within you. Robbins doesn't have to solve your life's problems, because only you can solve them. You need to be the giant. Once you become a giant, you can and will solve everything. The logic and psychology of this strategy appears sound. It is true that humans have agency. It is also true that people who feel empowered will be more likely to pursue their goals. Robbins's promise hinges on this basic premise—your self has power. Now, get up and use it!

But many people don't know how to use it. He suggests that they need to figure it out for themselves. While he cannot tell us specifically how to use our inner giant, he has endless stories of how others use theirs—presidents, movie stars, and business moguls. Consequently, failure to use your inner giant cannot be a function of his method (the rich and famous have already done it!); it must be your fault. This is the brilliance of Robbins's philosophy—if you don't believe in his message, it won't work. Faith is not an outcome of the process; it is a prerequisite for it, just like it is in most religious traditions.

Where Robbins is trying to release giants, Rick Warren is a giant-killer. Monotheisms greatly diminish the self, because the central character in the story of your life is not you, it's God. No little gods are allowed. Vanity, pride, opulence, and hedonism are offensive to him. Power, wealth, and status are bestowed by him. Consequently, the self is primarily a servant. And in the contemporary evangelicalism of Rick Warren, self is a servant only to God.

Consequently, Christian self-help helps you become a servant of God. Of course, the big question is "What does God want?" Monotheisms provide astoundingly detailed responses to this question. And the specifics are endless. But as to the self, they are all in agreement—the self is insignificant compared to God. And yet the self still matters. Why? Because God says it matters. Monotheism combines the feeling of mind-boggling insignificance with a sense of endless power because God loves *you*. The object of God's love is your enchanted self.

In *The Purpose Driven Life*, Warren describes our deepest selves: "Like God, we are spiritual beings—our spirits are immortal and will outlast our earthly bodies."[65] Your godlike spirit contains your purpose. As Warren explains, "you were created to become like Christ." Consequently, with deep self-awareness you will better understand God. Warren encourages readers to look into the self: "Don't just *read* this book. *Interact with it*. Underline it. Write your own thoughts in the margins. Make it *your* book. Personalize it!"[66] Warren's evangelicalism and that of millions of other American Protestants contain the central message that we can all have a deeply personal relationship with God—your true self is you in the eyes of God.[67]

This is how God becomes a believer's generalized other. In thinking deeply about self, the believer is trying to measure up to God's standards. Those standards, and not the cruel and calculated assessments of the world, will determine the most important things: salvation and eternal life. Mercifully, we are told that God is fair and loving. In fact, Warren is very upbeat about the whole relationship. There is no fire and brimstone in his theology. "The smile of God is the goal of your life," advises Warren.

Since pleasing God is the first purpose of your life, your most important task is to discover how to do that. The Bible says, "Figure out what will please Christ, and then do it." Fortunately, the Bible gives us a clear example of a life that gives pleasure to God. The man's name was Noah.[68]

Like Robbins, Warren relies on stories to illustrate the existence of the enchanted self. But these are not the stories of corporate, political, and entertainment luminaries. Rather, they are the ancient stories of the Bible. And around 60 million Americans think the Bible "should be taken literally, word-for-word, on all subjects."[69] An additional 100 million Americans believe that while the Bible must be interpreted, it is "perfectly true" if done properly. In sum, most Americans believe in a Christian self.

Still, the self-help industry races on. It is like the funeral business—steady in good times and bad. Even devout Christians need help in realizing their enchanted selves. And like the inner giant, the servant of God can be discovered by looking inward with a bit of encouragement and guidance.

Eckhart Tolle finds a wholly different enchanted self, one that is more palatable to individuals leery of the glitz of Robbins or weary of the traditional Christianity of Warren. Tolle's enchanted self is not a giant or God's servant; it is *Being* in the moment.

Like Eastern mystics, Tolle discovered his enchanted self through solitary examination. He describes his revelation:

> I couldn't live with myself any longer. And in this a question arose without an answer: who is the "I" that cannot live with the self? What is the self? I felt drawn into a void! I didn't know at the time that what really happened was the mind-made self, with its heaviness, its problems, that lives between the unsatisfying past and the fearful future, collapsed. It dissolved. The next morning I woke up and everything was so peaceful. The peace was there because there was no self. Just a sense of presence or "beingness," just observing and watching.[70]

The revelation of having no self fits with the findings of brain science and replicates the experiences of the Buddha, David Hume, and countless other deep meditators.

From Tolle's perspective, the loss of self inspires no lament. It brings him peace and, as he puts it, a state of deep bliss. This happy outcome is what makes Tolle's story appealing. He is not so much killing the self as he is awakening some deeper Being, a way of experiencing each moment with control and contentment.

He promises that "nonresistance is the key to the greatest power in the universe. Through it, consciousness (spirit) is freed from its imprisonment in form."[71] He further explains:

> The joy of Being, which is the only true happiness, cannot come to you through any form, possession, achievement, person, or event—through anything that happens. That joy cannot come to you—ever. It emanates from the formless dimension within you, from consciousness itself and thus is one with who you are.[72]

Like Robbins and Warren, Tolle asserts that the solutions to life's problems are already within you; you just need to look. He promises that if you look hard enough you will see that you are pure consciousness.

Where Tolle finds a timeless dimension of Being, Warren finds a spirit loved by God, and Robbins finds a customized genius. While very different in description, each of these enchanted selves suggest a better you—a happier, freer, more powerful, and more confident self. You are escaping the confines of a disenchanted society and shattering the bars of Weber's iron cage. Tolle, Warren, and Robbins are successful at articulating an intuitive and beguiling enchanted self.

The enchanted self is good by definition. There are no contemporary purveyors of purpose asserting that, at your very core, you are evil and despicable. Cold social science, harsh religions, and dark ideologies might sometimes offer a less-than-attractive picture of human nature, but self-help is upbeat by its very nature. The promises and strategies of this industry are premised on an unquestioned faith that an enchanted self exists.

In all cases, the enchanted self is thought to be found through deep introspection—in meditation, prayer, or seminar workshops. Religious groups, spiritual advisors, and personal gurus provide a framework from which we hope to lure out our enchanted self. People are attracted to transcendent metaphors like God, otherworldly genius, or transcendent Being. These visions, if we believe them, make our moral goodness feel absolute and eternal.

They make us self-enchanted, taking us to a place where the cruel and calculated assessments lose their sway, because we feel a grander significance. As moral egoists, it satisfies a deeply human instinct, our search for moral order.

The question becomes how one can come to believe in the enchanted self. We cannot trick ourselves into believing in Robbins's inner giant, or Warren's Christian soul, or Tolle's true happiness.

Faith, as all these writers assert, is *within* you. We are instinctually and reflexively drawn to narratives of moral order that reflect positively on us. But the metaphors and messages of successful purveyors of purpose are socially established and depend on communities and cultures to validate them. These social forces are what make certain articulations of purpose feel more real, and we cannot command them because they are imposed on us from without.

within you and without you

George Harrison, besides being a Beatle, was famous for his spirituality. His fascination with Hinduism coincided with a wave of Western interest in Eastern mysticism, and his music combined East and West in ways that mirrored his personal religiosity. His song "Within You Without You" is a prime example of this fusion, repeating that "the time will come when you see we're all one and life flows on within you and without you."

Harrison's song evokes a sense of mystical unity by unifying musical forms. The British have long had an interest in the East beyond mere colonization. Eastern mysticism is fascinating to a Western mind for many reasons; it is different, sensual, holistic, non-dogmatic (in its intellectual form), and highly logical. What is not to like?

It is also beautiful. The idea that one's Being bleeds into a harmonious Unity is pleasantly sublime. It is also true that the experience of this unity flows within you and without you. Our moral egoism is *within* our genes and gives us the capacity to feel moral emotions like goodness and love. *Without* us is a universe filled with metaphors and concepts that give names and directions to these feelings. Faith in Unity or God or even moral order is the product of our moral instinct as triggered by our language, metaphors, and community. Faith is produced within you and without you.

Jonathan Haidt explains that our moral instincts are like "taste buds."[73] We don't just logically deduce moral order but rather sense it. George Harrison's moral tastes were captivated by the Eastern concepts of universal love and cosmic unity. The concept of loving unity is a wonderful and vital expression of our moral instinct and can be found in countless religions, philosophies, and practices. In the best-case scenario, a person's social context triggers a benevolent and beautiful moral affinity toward compassion, forgiveness, and love.

But Haidt also understands "that human nature is not just intrinsically moral, it's also intrinsically moralistic, critical, and judgmental."[74] In fact, Haidt indicates that we have a deeply "righteous mind":

> We lie, cheat, and cut ethical corners quite often when we think we can get away with it, and then we use our moral thinking to manage our reputations and justify ourselves to others. We believe our own post-hoc reasoning so thoroughly that we end up self-righteously convinced of our own virtue.[75]

Our tendency toward righteousness, like our attraction to the feelings of universal love, is quite seductive because it validates the goodness of the self. Righteousness turns ugly when it motivates people to lash out in hatred and violence. These kinds of triggers lie deep within cultural and societal norms. In the worst-case scenario, righteousness is triggered by a culture steeped in ideologies of revenge.

In these situations, the goodness of self is validated by acts of moral vengeance and domination. Daniel Chirot and Clark McCauley describe the cultural source of this frightening phenomenon:

> Revenge can go well beyond any simple calculation of costs and benefits. For those who have internalized a code of honor that demands revenge, settling the demand becomes a leading goal. That is why so many violent conflicts, both between individuals and between groups, including some significant wars, seem to violate material self-interest. Anger at the thought of injured honor becomes a primary motive in itself.[76]

In such cases, individuals have acquired a taste for moral indignation, and it becomes the driving purpose of their lives. Groups united by nationalism, religious fundamentalism, or ideological extremism often instill strong feelings of righteousness.

Ironically, the universal desire to be good is what drives people to be bad. Righteous groups tell their members that they are *better* and *more moral* than anyone else; this satisfies a powerful moral hunger in us all. As Jonathan Turner points out, "pride provides a positive evaluation of self . . . Thus, pride focuses attention on the self and becomes a source of reinforcement that pushes individuals to do what is expected."[77] Consequently, the most righteous individuals also tend to be the most obedient to moral authorities.[78] Their sense of self is tied inextricably to the purpose of the group and in extreme cases may lead to terrible acts like suicide bombing.

Luckily, self-enchantment is not a one-way path to righteousness. It can also generate a healthy and touching love of self. And when a well-loved self is tied to something transcendent, like the Universe or God, that love can turn outward. Still, our innate capacity to condemn or be disgusted by others remains. Our taste for universal love and our taste for self-righteousness live side by side, enchanting us to very different ends. Communities and cultures determine where self-enchantment will lead and which one of these moral taste buds is most stimulated.

This makes self-enchantment a precarious process. The cruel and calculated assessments of others can easily derail our inner drive to feel good about ourselves. In fact, the modern world offers blaring wake-up calls that seek to rouse us from our happy delusions of self. We are told that we are nothing more than neural networks and predicted probabilities. While we see this to be true, people continue to pine for a deeper reality, one that can provide existential and moral solace to the soul.

Modern society responds to this longing with a therapeutic culture and the self-help industry, which asserts that a "soul" or some inner core self can be discovered, saved, or enlightened. Thus, modernity is not fully disenchanting. But we cannot take advantage of this opening by ourselves. The faith required to make self-enchantment a reality requires a community of support.

Only in an enclave of like-minded believers can we begin to feel that the good within us is actually, transcendently *True*.

5

truth and consequences

> The search for Truth . . . is the attempt to find
> a sense in one's existence by turning away
> from solidarity to objectivity.
>
> *Richard Rorty*

What is your purpose in life? Is it True?

In order to become self-enchanted you first have to believe that it is possible. You need the faith that things like personal power, salvation, and enlightenment are real and attainable. Without this, the benefits of self-enchantment will be frustratingly elusive.

Having faith is no easy task. We are rational beings who search for evidence to support our hunches. This tendency has served us well as a species and is the foundation of our vast and accumulated knowledge. We can build skyscrapers or fly to the moon because we collectively searched for truth, through experimentation and logical deduction. Faith requires us to suspend this incessant urge to examine and critique. Instead of looking for truth, we search for *Truth*.

Truth (with a capital "T") is different from scientific, logical, or mathematical truth—it refers to a transcendent reality that is beyond empirical observation. In fact, transcendent concepts like Truth describe a reality, as Wittgenstein put it, "*beyond* the world and that is to say beyond significant language."[1] For this reason, Truth can never be directly observed or proven by science, yet countless testimonials indicate that Truth can be *felt*. Believers *really* feel the Spirit moving within them; businessmen *really* feel their Inner Giant; Muslims *really* feel Allah in their bloodstreams; and expert meditators *really* feel a Universal Oneness all around them. You too can feel one of these Truths, provided that you believe in it.

The biblical tale of Doubting Thomas, the disciple who fails to believe the stories of Jesus's Resurrection, illuminates the rational dilemma of faith.

> But Thomas, one of the twelve, called Didymus, was not with them when Jesus came.
>
> The other disciples therefore said unto him, we have seen the LORD. But he said unto them, except I shall see in his hands the print of the nails, and put my finger into the print of the nails, and thrust my hand into his side, I will not believe. (John 20:24–25)

Thomas is smart. He is using his God-given reason to question the fantastical tale that Jesus has come back from the dead. Similarly, smart individuals question the claims that you can release your Inner Giant or that meditation can make you One with the universe or that Allah resides in your blood. Where is the proof of these fantastical tales?

Luckily for Thomas, Jesus gave him proof. He was allowed to touch Jesus's wounds and see for himself that the Resurrection was *real*. Yet Thomas's experience is unusual; we cannot touch Jesus's wounds ourselves and, in the end, the story of Doubting Thomas may be just another fable. Jesus understands the problem of having to prove Truth and says, "Thomas, because thou hast seen Me, thou hast believed: blessed are they that have not seen, and yet have believed" (John 20:29). Jesus alludes to something more profound than proof—*faith*.

Faith is the feeling that culturally specific images, metaphors, and narratives of transcendence describe, however imperfectly, an ultimate Truth. The other disciples accepted the story of Jesus's Resurrection because they felt that it was True in their hearts, even if it didn't seem true to their minds. Faith means that the Resurrection doesn't require proof, but even more interestingly, faith also makes the Resurrection immune to disproof. Counterevidence rarely shakes the faith of True believers.

Put simply, faith in a Truth can have more cognitive authority than observation or evidence. This fact is the reason why Truth is simultaneously liberating and confining. It liberates the believer from the messiness, meaninglessness, and bleakness of the material world, while also confining her to the obligations and strictures of the moral world. These are the consequences of Truth.

what is truth?

First and foremost, "Truth" is a word. Ludwig Wittgenstein explained that there are two common uses for the word "truth." The first use indicates a relative value and refers directly to facts about the world. The second use indicates an absolute value detached from any specific fact.[2] Following Wittgenstein, we can distinguish between "truth" and "Truth."

Relative truth refers to demonstrable facts.[3] These facts remain relative because they describe situations, circumstances, scenarios, and even ideas—all of which are temporal. Under this definition, the law of gravity would be a relative truth because, in theory, the circumstances of the universe could alter in such a way as to make the law false. While physicists don't expect this to happen in the near future, various theories about the end of time or perfect entropy indicate that physical laws depend on circumstance and perspective.

This sense of truth is what physicists Stephen Hawking and Leonard Mlodinow call "model-dependent realism." They write:

> It is pointless to ask whether a model is real, only whether it agrees with observation. If there are two models that both agree with observation . . . then one cannot say that one is more real than another. One can use whichever model is more convenient in the situation under consideration.[4]

In physics, some models of reality are more agreeable than others, but none is real. This is the nature of relative truth; it is expected to change with and according to our increasing knowledge and shifting perspective. Consequently, scientists talk mainly about relative truth. So does everyone, all the time.

But absolute Truth is a whole different matter. It is beyond temporality, beyond the world, and ultimately immutable.[5] God, moral law, and ultimate reality are all expressions of Truth.

Capital-T Truth is attractive because it gives people purpose. While many modern intellectuals have discarded the idea of Truth, blunt materialism—the idea that the world is composed *entirely* of matter and nothing else—is too much of a downer to be popular even among secularists. William James explains:

> A philosophy whose principle is so incommensurate with our most intimate feelings as to deny them all relevancy at one blow, will be even more unpopular than pessimism.[6]

Instead, we want our world and our life to be filled with meaning. We are naturally drawn to concepts that validate our feelings of moral goodness.

Transcendent Truth can set you free, liberating you from the cruel and calculated assessments of modern society. It makes self-enchantment possible within the context of modern life. Peter Berger notes that if "a charismatic Christian falls ill, he will spontaneously call a doctor; later on, or even at the same time, he may also ask a prayer group in his church to arrange a service of spiritual healing on his behalf." Here, the believer has faith in the truth of modern medicine *and* the Truth of divine grace with no sense of cognitive dissonance.[7] He can rely on science and God simultaneously.

Conceptual conflict occurs when specific metaphors and narratives of Truth directly refute what we know to be true. This is the case with creationism; a literal reading of Genesis and our current knowledge of biology, geology, and human history are simply irreconcilable.[8] Political ideologues are also quick to deny the truth of current events and public opinion when they contradict their political Truth. In cases such as these, Truth almost always beats truth.

George Orwell laments:

> The Catholic and the Communist are alike in assuming that an opponent cannot be both honest and intelligent. Each of them tacitly claims that "the truth" has already been revealed, and that the heretic, if he is not simply a fool, is secretly aware of "the truth" and merely resists it out of selfish motives.[9]

As Orwell notes, a person who thinks he knows the Truth can easily assume that nonbelievers are either stupid or evil. An exclusive claim to Truth, in turn, can motivate acts of revenge, shunning, and condemnation. As Orwell correctly observes, Truth is most unyielding in the religious and political spheres.

In the United States today, a person's religious affiliation and her political partisanship are the best predictors of whether she will believe in "ultimate Truth."[10] Specifically, Americans who are conservative—either theologically or politically or both—tend to think that everything has a final and objective meaning. In contrast, graduate school attendance is the strongest predictor of whether a person will believe truth to be relative.

Following these statistical relationships, I look at how religious groups, political ideologues, and academics conceptualize and experience Truth. In each instance, the idea of Truth (or lack of it) both liberates and confines an individual's sense of life's meaning. Those with Truth are liberated from pessimism and moral uncertainty but confined to the strictures of group authority. Those without Truth are liberated from intellectual dogmatism and xenophobia but confined to an endless riddle about the meaning of life. Some find this innocuous; others find it maddening.

Finally, it is important to note that there are many forms of Truth, and each has different consequences. Some can inspire terrible acts of violence while other types motivate altruistic, spiritual, and artistic passions. This paradox is illustrated starkly by the experience of Rodion Raskolnikov, the penniless ex-law student in Dostoevsky's *Crime and Punishment*. Russian graduate students in the nineteenth century predated the invention of postmodernism; they were still searching for the Truth. Raskolnikov finds it. Twice.

Like any socially conscious intellectual, Raskolnikov is concerned about stratification and injustice. He sees poverty first-hand and is disgusted at the way moneylenders take advantage of those in need. He wants to make moral sense of the suffering in the world and realizes that he must fight inequality by any means necessary. Convinced of his moral logic, he murders a pawnbroker and her sister and steals their meager riches with the intention of distributing their money to the poor. In his mind, a higher moral Truth justifies the crime.

Yet, after he commits murder, Raskolnikov falls into a haze of confusion and buries his treasure. He begins to agonize over his act of brutality and loses faith in his moral Truth; no longer can he fool himself with a philosophical justification that feels false. Then, he witnesses the quiet kindness of Sonia, a pious woman driven to prostitution in order to feed her family. Her moral example inspires him to confess his crime and, with her help, develop a faith in Christ. In his heart, a new moral Truth justifies his punishment and offers him salvation.

Acquiring faith is arduous, as Dostoevsky's narrative shows. Raskolnikov's tale depicts the importance of community to moral certitude. As Timur Kuran explains, "when a person's beliefs change this happens not through his own personal efforts but, rather, through a *social process* in which he is just one of many participants."[11] In despair over his terrible crime, Raskolnikov finds himself, an intellectual without any answers, spiritually drawn to another—a woman who embodies the kind of moral Truth he so desperately desires. Raskolnikov begins to see the world through Sonia's eyes and, in turn, begins to feel her Truth. His faith in Christ is a product of his love for Sonia. Faith is often tied to the love of others; passionate feelings of Truth reflect powerful social attachments. Ultimate Truth is always strongest when it is shared.

In fact, Truth's strength and durability depends on social solidarity. Raskolnikov only *feels* a moral Truth when he stops reasoning and falls in love. Through his relationship with Sonia he gains faith in something he formerly thought was illogical—God.

Religious faith demonstrates Truth's dependence on social solidarity. In a community of faith, believers start to *feel* the authority of Truth. This kind of moral certainty springs from and is maintained by group authority.

communities of truth

Three out of five Americans believe in "ultimate truth."[12] The meaning of this statistic is not immediately clear, but it becomes somewhat more so when we see that a believer in Truth is also likely to think that God has a plan for everyone and everything. Most Americans believe Truth comes from God (see Figure 5.1). In addition, most Americans feel that knowledge of Truth is exclusive to particular Christian groups. This is one of the important consequences of religious Truth; in the modern world, it tends to be restricted to particular communities.

Picture a young bald man wearing billowy orange robes and sandals walking down the street singing, "Hare Krishna Hare Krishna, Krishna Krishna Hare Hare . . ." Strolling toward him is a woman wearing a business suit, carrying a briefcase, and trying not to make eye contact. Who is more religious? Easy choice. The religious person stands out.

The Krishna devotee stands out because he is in "religious tension" with his surroundings. Rodney Stark and William Bainbridge were the first to define *tension* in this fashion.[13] They state that a religious group is in tension with its larger society to the extent that it promotes

1. different norms—like the Mormon eschewing caffeine;
2. feelings of antagonism—like the evangelical sense of secular embattlement;[14] and
3. separation from others—like the self-imposed isolation of the Amish.

This layered definition nicely summarizes what it means to be religiously "different." It can also be applied across a wide range of cultural types: you can have high- and low-tension Muslims in Iran, high- and low-tension Orthodox Christians in Russia, high- and low-tension Hindus in India. Still, the essence of religious tension is a little like pornography—it is difficult to define but you know it when you see it.[15]

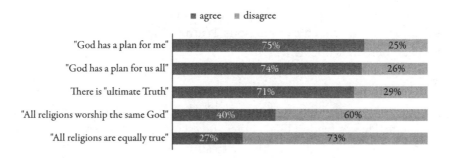

Figure 5.1 | Exclusive Truth
Source: Baylor Religion Survey, Wave 3; n = 1714

Upon seeing the Krishna disciple, you know instantly that this man is in high religious tension with those around him. He draws attention, usually negative, with his conspicuous dress and chanting. Conversely, the businesswoman walking with trepidation toward him is not identifiably religious in any way. She is in low religious tension with her surroundings.

But accurately gauging someone's purpose is tricky.[16] Who knows what lurks in the hearts of men?[17] Perhaps the man in the orange robe is an actor on his way to an audition; when not in character, he is a low-tension Presbyterian. Perhaps the woman in the business suit is a Jehovah's Witness; she spends every weekend knocking on doors, handing out *The Watchtower*. That's definitely higher tension than the Presbyterian's monthly Sunday brunch.

Appearance often defies reality, but knowledge of people's religious beliefs and behaviors provides a ready means to gauge their level of religious tension. Put simply, people seem *very* religious if their religious ideas and expressions stand out as either unusual or intense. These people are in higher religious tension because they are spiritually unconventional.[18] In turn, they are the ones whose faith in Truth will often be the strongest.[19]

This is logical and intuitive. Clearly, a person who is willing to look and behave differently, feels hostility from others due to these differences, and surrounds himself with like-minded individuals has a certain confidence in his purpose in life. He is content to be in tension with others because he knows that he has found the one True path. Why else would he suffer the strictures of a particular religious dogma if it were just one of many truth options? Moral clarity, confidence of purpose, and eternal salvation are the benefits of religious Truth.[20] The cost of religious Truth is that it demands obedience.

The Amish are a good example. They are the epitome of a group in tension with society. Picture the stereotypical Amish man dressed in a black suit and driving his horse-drawn buggy down the Pennsylvania interstate. He has made a bold choice; he eschews the conveniences of the modern world and dedicates his life to simplicity.

What makes the Amish man's rejection of modernity a conscious choice is that his traditions demand that religious Truth cannot be accepted out of ignorance.[21] While many conservative religious communities work hard to shield their children from undesirable influences, Amish believers are supposed to know about the outside world and all the lures of modernity *before* joining the church. Consequently, full membership occurs after a period of *rumspringa* or "running around." During this period of exploration, Amish teens see what it is like to drive cars, watch television, listen to modern music, and live outside the strictures of their communities. Some even use hard drugs, have sex, and generally behave as modern delinquents in their open quest for Truth.[22] Imagine the average evangelical church allowing its teenage members to "run around" like this.

Kids on rumspringa are pulled between their tightly bound community and the vastness of American culture. Will they ultimately commit to austere religious Truth or will they be lured away by American consumerism? The choice is a difficult one, but most Amish youths return to their humble existence. In the end, they favor keeping their connections to family and friends over making a solitary leap into an uncertain world.

Communities of Truth build confidence in their beliefs through emotional attachment rather than reasoned debate. For this reason, the power of Truth does not lie in a religion's doctrine or sacred text but rather in the dedication followers have to each other. Feelings of group love are fused with conceptions of religious Truth. In the case of the Amish, the goodness and righteousness of their lifestyle is *felt* in the loving bonds they have with one another. By rejecting Truth, the individual risks losing his loving community.

The interdependence of love and faith explains why public disputes over Truth are deeply emotional and often irreconcilable. In the United States today, approximately 26 percent of American Christians believe "the Bible means exactly what it says. It should be taken literally, word-for-word, on all subjects." While not as socially and culturally isolated as the Amish, biblical literalists foster an identity that separates them from what they see as "secular society."[23]

I told a self-proclaimed biblical literalist that non-literalists are not necessarily "secular." In fact, nearly one-third of American Christians believe that the Bible contains "human errors" or is composed of "legends" and therefore isn't "perfectly true." Upon hearing this, he winced, "How can someone call themselves a Christian and not believe in the Bible? I just don't understand that. It makes me sick."

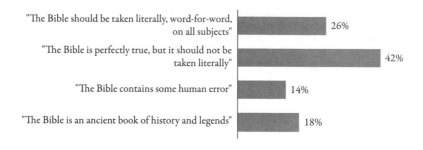

Figure 5.2 | The Truth of the Bible—According to American Christians.
Source: Baylor Religion Survey, Wave 3

I told a liberal Unitarian Universalist pastor about this encounter and he was not surprised. He explained that he was raised in a very conservative evangelical community and felt intimidated by the biblical literalism of his family and friends.[24] He came to see their faith as "ignorance" and in order to develop his own perspective he had to leave home and break ties with his family. This was extremely painful, but he now leads his own religious community and prides himself on blending ideas from Buddhism, Hinduism, New Ageism, Christianity, Judaism, and Islam into his sermons. What ultimately inspired him to completely change his life is unclear, but deep antagonisms between him and his family certainly played a role. Consequently, breaking bonds with his family helped him break his tie to biblical literalism; in fact, it may have instigated it.

The social bonds undergirding biblical literalism help to explain an initially bewildering reality, namely, the fact that more than one-third of Americans indicate that they don't believe in human evolution and think that the earth is less than 10,000 years old.[25] The popularity of creationism is so widespread that many of our highest-ranking political officials openly embrace it. When US senator Marco Rubio from Florida was asked about the age of the earth, he responded:

> At the end of the day, I think there are multiple theories out there on how the universe was created and I think this is a country where people should have the opportunity to teach them all . . . Whether the earth was created in 7 days, or 7 actual eras, I'm not sure we'll ever be able to answer that. It's one of the great mysteries.[26]

But the age of the earth is not a mystery at all. The earth is 4.54 billion years old.[27]

Yet Texas governor Rick Perry disagrees, saying, "I'm not sure anybody actually knows completely and absolutely how old the earth is."[28] Representative Paul Broun of Georgia more confidently asserts that the earth is "6,000 years old."[29] These influential leaders argue that American schools should, as President George W. Bush said, "teach the controversy." Here is the essence of the controversy:

> "The earth is 4.54 billion years old" is a statement of scientific truth.
>
> "The earth is 6,000 years old" is a statement of biblical Truth.[30]

Pretending that there is a legitimate scientific debate about the age of the earth upsets many scientists, some of whom have happily poked holes in creationism.[31]

For instance, Richard Dawkins hopes to end widespread ignorance about evolution by showing that only science can demonstrate what is "really true." In his book *The Magic of Reality*, Dawkins adroitly outlines the scientific evidence for evolution.[32] While the book is a necessary corrective to the misguided idea that public schools need to teach creationism in science classes, Dawkins doesn't address the central aspect of this debate, namely, that the Truth of creationism is premised on a reality far more enthralling than hard science. It is premised on the most urgent of human realities: social reality.

The science of evolution is no match for the emotional bonds among biblical literalists. Denying the claims of a faceless "science" is easy when you are enmeshed in a community of passionate believers. If anything less than biblical literalism can make a believer feel "sick," then an outright denial of the story of Genesis will be nothing less than nauseating. No argument, however well reasoned and empirically supported, can overcome that kind of emotional response. As Josef Stalin noted after years of trying to secularize Soviet citizens, "Religion is like a nail, the harder you hit it the deeper it goes."[33] Because faith in Truth is fostered by emotional bonds between believers, faith not only withstands attacks by authorities—scientific or otherwise—but may well be strengthened by them.[34]

Group loyalty also helps explain why believers are willing to pay the ultimate cost—martyrdom—for religious Truth. Marc Sageman analyzed the life stories of Westernized Islamic terrorists in hopes of uncovering a common cause for their radicalization. Why would a person who has numerous spiritual, political, and intellectual opportunities in a free modern society become a suicide bomber? Sageman argues that psychological disorders cannot explain the existence of these atypical people. Instead, he finds that

> social bonds are the critical element in this process and precede ideological commitment . . . As in all intimate relationships, this glue, this in-group love, is found inside the group. It may be more accurate to blame global Salafi terrorist activity on in-group love than out-group hate.[35]

The terrorist cell provides the individual with a sense of meaning, belonging, and love—all basic human needs. In return, the group demands total devotion, including the willingness to die for the group. In terrorist cells, the individual loses himself to the purpose of the group.[36]

If we can grasp this fact, then the logic of a suicide bomber becomes less bewildering. These individuals are not initially attracted to death or even to violence. Rather, they are attracted to moral certainty but have ended up in a group that channels those feelings into exaggerated self-righteousness. The suicide bomber discovers his True purpose by finding group love, but love demands total spiritual, political, and intellectual loyalty.

Overall, belief in Truth is strongest within high-tension religious communities. Believers tighten their emotional bonds as they grow more socially isolated and antagonistic toward popular norms and beliefs. We can express it as an equation:

$$\text{attachment to other believers} + \text{religious tension} = \text{dedication to religious Truth}$$

Religious Truth cannot be easily manipulated. It begins with community. Once socially embedded in a community of like-minded believers, a person begins to *feel* the shared faith in Truth. Communities in greater tension with society and blessed with tight emotional attachments will inspire the greatest faith.

This is why some religious seekers fail to find Truth. What they actually fail to find is a community where they feel loved and at home. Seekers can read books by Robbins, Warren, Tolle, and countless others. They can walk into churches, mosques, and temples. But hearing or reading Truth is a far cry from *feeling* Truth. The perpetual seeker has yet to find a community of like-minded believers with which she connects.

But if this Truth-seeker becomes a member of a Truth community, her confidence will grow and she will begin to feel their Truth. Religious groups, ideological collectives, and self-help gurus know this; it is the reason why communion, group prayer, ritual worship, cohabitation, and interactive seminars are essential to gaining followers and sustaining faith. Successful communities of Truth bring people together and foster emotional connections. Under these circumstances, the seeker finally becomes a True believer and receives what she so desperately desires—an unambiguous and self-affirming purpose.

truth in politics

Politics deals with the hard truths of life. To carry through a policy agenda, a politician requires popular support, yet the intricacies of policy tend to be highly detailed, complex, and—frankly—boring. A political leader needs to appeal to voters through rhetoric, metaphor, and narrative; he needs to get a crowd excited about social change. This aspect of politics has less to do with the truth of policy and everything to do with emotional resonance. In the best-case scenario, the politician finds a deeply held Truth and links it to his platform, making the messiness of politics appear simple and the purpose of government clear.[37]

Politics is emotional because it directly affects people's lives; it determines who gets what opportunities and what behaviors get rewarded. The emotions of politics stem not only from how policies impact our individual lives but also from our attachment to specific visions of a just and good society. For this reason, political rhetoric draws on what people find meaningful in life; it taps into popular conceptions of moral Truth. In turn, political rhetoric can shape how individuals understand their position in society and the purpose of the nation.

President Obama won his first presidential bid on a vision of "hope." Hope is an emotional state, the opposite of despair, but it is not a policy platform or even a political ideology. Obama explained his vision this way:

> I'm not talking about blind optimism, the kind of hope that just ignores the enormity of the tasks ahead or the road blocks that stand in our path. I'm not talking about the wishful idealism that allows us to just sit on the sidelines or shirk from a fight. I have always believed that hope is that stubborn thing inside us that insists, despite all the evidence to the contrary, that something better awaits us so long as we have the courage to keep reaching, to keep working, to keep fighting.[38]

For Obama, hope is not "wishful idealism" but rather an informed rejection of fatalism. It is the hope of a pragmatist as opposed to a dreamer.

This alters a particular stereotype of what it means to be a liberal. Namely, the liberal is supposed to be the bleeding-heart idealist who wistfully dreams about an equal and just society, while the conservative is supposedly the hard-nosed pragmatist concerned with class and party loyalty. President Bill Clinton summarized this stereotype when he said that "Democrats want to fall in love; Republicans want to fall in line."[39] While many Democrats fell in love with Obama, the president's style and rhetoric leans toward pragmatism over romanticism.

President Obama's pragmatism reflects different liberal and conservative stereotypes. From this perspective, the liberal is the nerdy academic more interested in spreadsheets than lofty ideals, while the conservative has deep moral and social values that guide his decision-making. William F. Buckley summarized this perspective, saying, "Conservatism aims to maintain in working order the loyalties of the community to perceived truths ... which in their judgment have earned universal recognition."[40]

While stereotypes of liberals and conservatives will always fall short of reality, Americans who self-identify as conservative are much more likely to believe in an ultimate Truth (see Figure 5.3). Researchers have longer theorized about the fundamental differences in liberal and conservative moral perspectives, but these data suggest that conservatives tend to view their moral beliefs as worthy of "universal recognition," as Buckley has said.[41] In other words, both liberals and conservatives have strong values, but conservatives are more likely to feel that their values reflect an ultimate Truth.

This finding might simply reflect the fact that conservatives are, on average, more religious. For instance, high-tension religious people are more likely to vote Republican *and* believe in Truth. But even after controlling for religious tradition, level of religiosity, and education, conservatives are *still* more likely to believe in Truth.[42] This means that there is something about conservative culture and ideology that is more closely aligned with absolute moral Truth.

The Left has also been criticized for moral absolutism. The communist, as critiqued by George Orwell, was the epitome of moral certitude and blind ideology. Liberals certainly are more invested in Truth when they strongly identify with the Democratic Party (see Figure 5.4).[43] Yet in the United States today, Truth appears to be mainly the domain of the GOP.

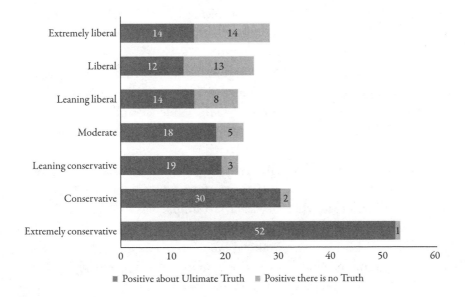

Figure 5.3 | Political Ideology and Truth
Source: Baylor Religion Survey, Wave 3

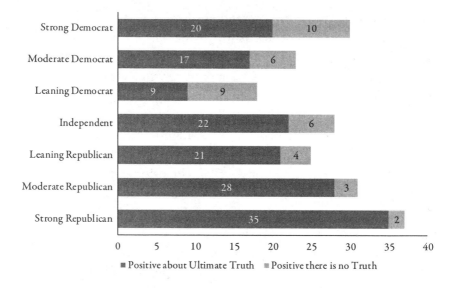

Figure 5.4 | Political Party and Truth

Source: Baylor Religion Survey, Wave 3

After spending decades studying ideological trends in American politics, Thomas Mann of the Brookings Institution and Norman Ornstein of the American Enterprise Institute concluded:

> The GOP has become an insurgent outlier in American politics. It is ideologically extreme; scornful of compromise; unmoved by conventional understanding of facts, evidence and science; and dismissive of the legitimacy of its political opposition.[44]

Of course, Mann and Ornstein are denounced as partisans themselves. But their reputations as honest analysts of American politics indicate that there is much more to what they say than simple bias.

Conservative Truth reflects the deep cultural underpinnings of American political identity. Political labels have become cultural identifiers passed from generation to generation just like ethnic pride and reverence for family tradition.[45] In fact, policy preferences may actually be secondary to political identity.[46] Our political identity is reflected in how we dress, what we eat, and what kinds of television shows we watch.[47]

James Hunter's use of the phrase "culture war" is apt. Political divisions reflect not just policy preferences but entire lifestyles.

A predilection for Truth attracts many conservatives to what Jeffrey Berry and Sarah Sobieraj call "the outrage industry." Celebrity political pundits have created media empires based almost entirely on the expression of political rage. Berry and Sobieraj explain:

> Outrage discourse involves efforts to provoke emotional responses (e.g. anger, fear, moral indignation) from the audience through the use of overgeneralizations, sensationalism, misleading or patently inaccurate information, ad hominem attacks, and belittling ridicule of opponents.[48]

Sound familiar? Cable television and talk radio are overrun with outrage discourse. It is emotionally and morally satisfying for listeners to share in the righteous indignation of their pundit of choice. Righteousness confirms the goodness of self; it affirms that our choices and preferences are morally superior to everyone else's. In fact, neuroscientists find that feelings of rage can stimulate the brain in ways similar to feelings of romantic love.[49] Outrage excites, focuses, and gives us direction.

In the end, outrage discourse provides an emotional charge to one's moral identity. While there is a vast and ever-expanding outrage industry, no one embodies the essence of this phenomenon like Rush Limbaugh. He didn't invent outrage discourse, but he is one of its most talented practitioners.

Limbaugh listeners are a near-homogeneous demographic group. They are middle-aged and middle-income white men who believe in Truth.[50] They collectively feel the sting of a historical paradox—they have been taught to be proud and commanding men, yet lack the political and economic power they think they deserve.[51] Theirs is a frustrated, entitled masculinity, and Limbaugh is their moral beacon.

Limbaugh rarely offers a coherent argument, but he does offer Truth. After the Supreme Court voted to uphold the Affordable Care Act, Limbaugh asserted that the uninsured are mainly rich college kids who don't want insurance anyway. He claims that Justice Ginsburg prefers European rule of law over the American Constitution, and he blames this debacle on "academics" "who all wear Che Guevara t-shirts." No part of this rant is rooted in logical truth. Instead, it boldly asserts a moral Truth.

At root, Limbaugh's Truth is the faith that his rage and frustration, and that of his followers, emerge from a sacred moral purpose—the duty to defend an imagined "perfect America." The idea that personal emotions mirror a larger moral struggle is one of the most common forms of Truth. Limbaugh's True emotions define how a True American *should* feel—he should feel like a "Dittohead."

That's right, Limbaugh listeners proudly refer to themselves as Dittoheads. Critics of Limbaugh's show wondered how Limbaugh's listeners could passively accept his ranting at face value. Weren't they just mindless rubes? In typical fashion, Limbaugh thumbed his nose at his critics and proudly invented the "Dittohead Nation." What the critics saw as ignorance, Limbaugh reframed as loyalty, patriotism, and emotional solidarity. You can even purchase Dittohead T-shirts and bumper stickers on Limbaugh's website.

In this way, the Dittohead Nation resembles biblical literalism. High-tension religious groups instill Truth by forging close emotional bonds. These attachments enhance the confidence that one's emotions reflect a grander Truth. The outrage industry creates similar bonds, but these attachments are not as personal. Rather, they rely on cultural compatibility. Limbaugh's persona, style, and language feel familiar to his listeners; this familiarity bonds his nation of Dittoheads together. As a virtual nation, Limbaugh's audience will never be as dedicated as members in a tight-knit religious group, but the Dittohead Nation still offers a sense of moral belonging and meaning. Limbaugh's Truth was never premised on facts but rather the strong feeling his listeners have that they are *like* him—united by their shared outrage.

The outrage industry is also premised on identifying moral outsiders. This requires pundits to promote broad stereotypes that clearly distinguish good guys from bad. Limbaugh's monologue is a ritual refrain of these stories and identities, solidifying in the minds of his listeners that they wear the white hats and have much to fear from their scheming enemies. Limbaugh consoles his listeners with the idea that their frustration is warranted and their anger should be directed at the perpetrators of America's decline. They are easy to recognize—they are "terrorists," "liberals," "elites," "femi-nazis," "socialists," "intellectuals," "Democrats," and "people who don't want to work for a living." For Limbaugh, these people are guided by impure thoughts—impure because they question his emotional Truth and that of his listeners.[52]

Still, Truth in politics does not necessarily lead to outrage. Deep emotional connections to ideals of freedom, justice, and equality can motivate individuals to selflessly work to help others. How Truth is framed and from what emotional tendencies it draws determine its political consequences.

But in America today, politically inspired rage is a potent emotional intoxicant and can become a guiding Truth. It is our natural tendency as moral egoists to find comfort in ideologies and faiths that express our moral superiority. Currently, a vibrant outrage industry gives conservatives steady doses of self-righteousness. But this kind of Truth can be just as alluring to progressives.

academic truth

Stories of political correctness are common on college campuses. The academic community is vigilant about inclusiveness and civility. We pride ourselves on not wanting to offend or misrepresent others. While this is a noble purpose, it can sometimes spiral out of control when we become blindly intolerant of any hint of intolerance.

In his novel *The Human Stain*, Philip Roth skewers the politically correct culture of academia. His protagonist, Coleman Silk, is a respected professor who makes a casual remark in class with disastrous consequences.

> The class consisted of fourteen students. Coleman had taken attendance at the beginning of the first several lectures so as to learn their names. As there were still two names that failed to elicit a response by the fifth week into the semester, Coleman, in the sixth week, opened the session by asking, "Does anyone know these people? Do they exist or are they spooks?"
>
> Later that day he was astonished to be called in by his successor, the new dean of faculty, to address the charge of racism brought against him by the two missing students, who turned

out to be black, and who, though absent, had quickly learned of the locution in which he'd publicly raised the question of their absence. Coleman told the dean, "I was referring to their possibly ectoplasmic character. Isn't that obvious?"

It wasn't obvious to the dean, and Silk was labeled a racist and summarily attacked by his colleagues. Roth's story credibly evokes the ugly righteousness that can emerge in our halls of higher education. In this case, the word "spooks" is understood, without second thought, as a racial slur. The assumption that "spooks" could have no other meaning suggests that Silk's critics were less concerned with the truth of the matter and more excited to uncover a racist in their midst. In this way, political correctness becomes a powerful moral Truth in which the world is starkly divided into oppressors and the oppressed. Like other moral Truths, political correctness can lead individuals to ignore day-to-day truths in service of their moral egoism.

Racism, sexism, and other forms of ideological hatred of specific groups are real and dangerous threats in our society. The outrage industry feeds off of these kinds of "us vs. them" dichotomies. The irony of political correctness is that in attempting to combat racism and sexism it can produce its own form of oppression. Back in 1995, Timur Kuran noted:

> Hundreds of colleges have instituted speech codes that make it a potentially punishable offense to say or do things upsetting to designated "minorities"—women, homosexuals, and ethnic groups deemed oppressed. The University of Connecticut has gone so far as to prohibit "inappropriately directed laughter." Colleges are also putting their students through "sensitivity" sessions where they learn, in addition to unobjectionable rules not to challenge, what vocabulary to avoid, and what euphemisms to use.[53]

While speech codes still exist at many universities, the consequences of these regulations have often been ironic. For instance, Kuran indicates that restraints on speech can make students and faculty "more reluctant to speak freely on race-related issues, ever more afraid of using a word or uttering a thought that might be construed as a sign of bigotry."[54]

Conservative commentators are still quick to point out the moral superiority and snobbery of the "politically correct police." For instance, Karl Rove is convinced that conservatism is routinely criticized in colleges and universities because the academy feels that conservatives are politically incorrect. He declared, "As people do better, they start voting like Republicans . . . unless they have too much education and vote Democratic, which proves there can be too much of a good thing."[55] For Rove, higher education instills a decidedly liberal Truth, which discounts conservative values and ideals out of hand.

While Americans with more education are more likely to vote Democratic, as Rove claims, higher education does not instill an allegiance to any stated liberal Truth. Regardless of cases of political correctness gone awry, academia actually tends to diminish a person's sense that she has any grasp of some ultimate moral Truth. In fact, graduate school usually undermines a person's faith that Truth is even possible.

In the *Journal of Philosophical Logic*, Hannes Leitgeb explains the latest thinking on the idea of Truth:

> We introduce a theory of dependence according to which a sentence ϕ is said to depend on a set Φ of sentences if the truth value of ϕ supervenes on the presence or absence of the sentences of Φ in/from the extension of the truth predicate.[56]

Got that? This is how academics talk. They speak to one another in a language that requires insane amounts of highly specified knowledge to interpret and critique.[57] Do academics believe in Truth? No, they don't.[58] Is this postmodernism? Not really.

Christopher Hitchens describes the intellectual's wariness of Truth:

> Objective truth . . . is another term that has lost some of it shapeliness lately. There is a tendency, in our "postmodern" discourse, to inquire first about *whose* truth and *which* power stands to gain, and only then to take an interest in things like verification.[59]

Hitchens critiques a sentiment that has been popular in the social sciences for centuries. It is the idea that Truth is ideology. As such, Truth is a social construct passed down within groups.

This perspective gets complicated quickly.[60] No longer can academics consider our findings part of some grander understanding of reality. Social structures cannot be observed objectively—we can only look through the prism of our position within society. The economist Robert H. Nelson even argues that "to the extent that any system of economic ideas offers an alternative vision of the 'ultimate values,' or 'ultimate reality,' that actually shapes the workings of history, economics is offering yet another grand prophesy in the biblical tradition."[61] For Nelson, faith in economic theory is like a religion, because it is a faith in a decisive yet unproven Truth.

While some economists might be accused of being True believers in a particular economic theory, few of the highly educated retain a faith in Truth. Sociologist Elaine Howard Ecklund found that elite scientists are far less religious than the American public.[62] While there remain a few leading scientists with traditional religious beliefs, Ecklund shows that they tend to practice a "closeted faith." And she identifies another group as "spiritual atheists," scientists "who practice a new kind of individual spirituality—one that has no need for God or a god—that flows from and leads into science."[63]

Spiritual atheism seems a far cry from the Truth of traditional religion. Perhaps the academy assaults scholars with so many complexities, both in theory and in methods, that an ultimate Truth seems impossible.[64] In the swirling and endless sources of knowledge provided by higher education, where could Truth possibly find its home? The foundations of truth change too quickly for any Truth to take root.

Does this make the academy liberal? It is true that the academy can be hostile to conservatism and traditionalism because it teaches individuals to tirelessly question common assumptions.[65] And groups asserting a shared sense of Truth don't want to be constantly questioned. Consequently, the academy becomes their enemy even when not questioning them directly. Karl Rove disdains higher education because it doesn't legitimate his political Truth. But academics won't grant anyone Truth—not even each other. That's not a political bias; it's a well-honed instinct to critique and undermine any system of thought.[66] It may be frustrating, but it is not ideological.

What's one left to do? Give up. And that is what most academics have done. This is not a failure but a different kind of solution to the problem of Truth. If you can't find Truth after great searching, stop looking. Or at least stop trying to put it into words. Academics have stopped speaking about ultimate Truth for this very reason. Many are outright atheists, some are spiritual atheists, and a few are traditional believers. But they don't talk about Truth, at least not at work. They work in a community where the problem of Truth has ceased to be a problem, because it has simply vanished.

This means that academia does not define the moral order in the same way that religious or political culture does. Communities of Truth express the prevailing notion that a person must be guided by some ultimate and unifying sense of moral purpose. High-tension religious groups tend to promote the idea that one should be first and always a "servant to God," while the outrage industry tends to promote the idea that one should be first and always an "American patriot." Truth provides a sense that life *must* have a singular purpose stemming from an absolute moral core.

Life purposes in academia still have moral and existential components, but they tend to be expressed in terms of discovering truths and increasing knowledge. For instance, Richard Dawkins describes his connection to science as "magical." He explains that "magical simply means deeply moving, exhilarating: something that gives us goose bumps, something that makes us feel more fully alive . . . the facts of the real world as understood through the methods of science [are] magical in . . . the poetic sense, the good-to-be-alive sense."[67] Dawkins's description of the magic of inquiry has an emotional and moral component—for him, scientific study *feels* good and is life affirming.

Many academics feel the same way about their disciplines and find a purpose in life through the expansion and dissemination of knowledge. This purpose is antithetical to having faith in a distinct Truth. As Neil deGrasse Tyson put it, "My view is that if your philosophy is not unsettled daily then you are blind to all the universe has to offer."[68] Tyson, like many academics, feels that Truth is too confining and favors the idea that knowledge is ever-expanding and never absolute. Without Truth, people still find purpose in life, but it tends to be more flexible, undulating, and diverse. Academia has no central Truth other than an overarching faith that hunting for truth is innately good and life-affirming.

the purpose of truth

Richard Rorty explains that when considering the meaning of life we must make a choice.

> There are two principal ways in which reflective human beings try, by placing their lives in a larger context, to give sense to those lives. The first is by telling the story of their contribution to a community . . . The second way is to describe themselves as standing in immediate relation to a nonhuman reality.[69]

We all tell the first story. It describes our relation to those around us and roots the meaning of our lives in what Rorty calls local "solidarity." Our jobs, families, friends, and passions offer immediate ways to "contribute" to something greater than ourselves. We find multiple purposes through all of those social commitments. The second way is an attempt to turn these contributions into a unified purpose. This story traces the many changing purposes of our life back to a common source—a "nonhuman reality." Rorty calls this Truth.

This kind of Truth provides people with a singular purpose. Truth is the idea that reality has a logical, objective, and moral structure. We can never perceive this Truth completely or directly. For this reason, it remains an article of faith rather than an object of science.

Religions, political ideologies, and moral philosophies offer visions of an objective moral reality that purports to exist outside our selves. These systems of meaning provide concepts, metaphors, and narratives that describe an ultimate Truth. God, Justice, and the Good are things that supposedly transcend place, culture, and individual perspective. With regard to such concepts, Wittgenstein concluded, "There are, indeed, things that cannot be put into words. They make themselves manifest. They are what is mystical."[70] Believers feel the reality of a Truth and seek to put into words a feeling that lies beyond language.[71] Faith is the conviction that certain words, concepts, and stories describe, however insufficiently, a manifest Truth.

With Truth, of course, come consequences.

The first is that Truth provides a singular moral focus. If Truth is deeply felt, it makes your life's purpose unambiguous and your moral obligations unequivocal.

One of difficulties in feeling Truth is that you have to have faith *first*. In other words, you will never feel the Truth of a mystical or moral reality if you don't already believe that Truth exists. This suggests an endless paradox. How are we to build confidence in something that cannot be shown, is imperfectly described, and is not directly felt? Social solidarity is what turns feelings of love, outrage, or ecstasy into Truth.

Communities of Truth, such as religious groups, generate strong feelings of attachment between members. A person who is lovingly connected to a community of Truth will begin to associate her feelings for the others in the group with the concepts, metaphors, and narratives the group shares. This is the process which Emile Durkheim thought produced our deep sense of "sacred" and "profane"—the good and bad poles of any moral system. Durkheim understood that we cannot feel moral reality by ourselves. "The individual alone is not a sufficient end for his activity," Durkheim wrote. "He is too little. He is not only hemmed in spatially; he is also strictly limited temporally."[72] Transcendence arises from shared experience.

A second consequence of Truth is that it sometimes requires believers to ignore or discard contradictory truths. The Truth of biblical literalism leads believers to dispute the truths of modern science. Dittoheads have to ignore facts that contradict the emotional Truth Rush Limbaugh propagates. In the cost-benefit analysis of Truth, moral certainty is weighed against empirical reality. If a Truth community is sufficiently bonded, moral certainty will always win.

Andy Warhol titled a painting "50,000,000 Elvis Fans Can't Be Wrong," a title that gets at the notion that confidence in something that is immeasurable is bolstered by consensus—not science, deduction, or even aesthetic expertise.[73] Consequently, sixty million biblical literalists (in the United States alone) can't be wrong, because their confidence in biblical Truth is sustained by their solidarity. Similarly, fourteen million Rush Limbaugh listeners can't be wrong, because the Dittohead Nation is united in its outrage at liberals.[74] Social support and confirmation enhance each believer's faith in their chosen Truth.[75] It will be a rare and daunting collection of truths that can successfully challenge the emotional, moral, and spiritual solidarity of True believers. While those without Truth are free to follow empirical reality wherever it leads, they risk finding some very ugly and unwelcome truths.[76] For believers, Truth provides necessary respite from the ugly truths of life.

I met a man named Eli whose life was marked by a long series of ugly truths. His addiction to alcohol and crack cocaine turned him into an uncaring and brutal monster; Eli stole from his friends, beat his wife, and abandoned his children. And then he found Jesus. Eli fits the cultural stereotype of a recovering addict. He was battered but resilient, and ultimately saved by Jesus.

In his church, I saw the power of Jesus first-hand. Eli was jumping and sobbing and writhing, all at once. He was in the throes of religious ecstasy—he had a full-on emotional catharsis. Jesus does save. The therapeutic utility of God is clear in church and beyond. Alcoholics Anonymous effectively use God in their twelve-step program. The idea that there exists a loving Power greater than any individual seems to help the helpless. This was certainly apparent in Eli's church, which pulsated with ecstatic worshippers. If anyone was conspicuous, it was me. I stood motionless, untouched. But Eli was filled with the Spirit and it inspired him to take control of his life, stop drinking, get to work, and reconcile with his family. It gave him a singular moral purpose.

Maintaining that focus is an ongoing battle. Religious Truth has changed Eli's life, but can he sustain it? Will he take a drink tomorrow? Will Jesus be there for him in times of dire need? On this particular Sunday, everything was in sync; the congregation harmoniously swayed to the Truth of the Spirit. But the feeling was momentary. After a few hours we all shook hands and went our separate ways.

Feelings of Truth can be disappointingly fleeting. In order to sustain faith, we need a steady emotional connection to Truth. Church services supply a weekly routine by which members can recharge their sense of religious Truth. Likewise, the outrage industry offers daily opportunities to recharge viewers' sense of political Truth. Left alone and without social confirmation, feelings of Truth can wither and die. Time is the enemy of Truth. This is why communities of Truth stick together; in solidarity they can weather moments of doubt and cognitive dissonance.

Some life purposes are geared toward the next life, while others are determinedly focused on the here and now. What both of these approaches share is the problem of time. Will the believer sustain her True faith? Will the nonbeliever have enough time to live according to his plan?

Eli might one day use drugs, but right now he knows a greater Truth. This Truth gives him a completely a new rhythm to life. And life, after all, is mainly about timing.

6

about time

The time of our feelings is not the same as the time of the clocks.

Salman Rushdie

What is your purpose in life? Or is now not a good time to ask?

Some people cannot be bothered to ponder the meaning of life. They don't find it useful. They experience life as a streaming series of challenges—you win or you lose, and you move on to the next one. Any attempt to discern an overall purpose to these rolling tasks and goals is a fool's errand. Better to just focus on the next item on the list instead of assessing what it all means.

Approximately 20 percent of Americans indicate that it is "useless" to spend time searching for life's grander purpose.[1] They flip Socrates's famous adage that "the unexamined life is not worth living" on its head. Examination could very well be a waste of time, because in today's world, time is in short supply. We simply have too many other things to do.

Yet in doing things we are implicitly deciding how best to live life. Even if there are no ultimate Truths or philosophical principles guiding us, life can still feel purpose driven. Its purpose is felt in the "story" we tell ourselves about our daily struggles and triumphs. People quite naturally talk about life as a sequence of critical events that are leading somewhere; we imagine life as having a kind of narrative arc. As such, living feels like a play with dramatic flourishes, love interests, and tragic twists.

Those who seek a heavenly afterlife, a timeless Oneness, or immortal renown are guided by a singular life goal. But constructing a personal narrative requires no cathartic denouement. Life stories unfold through our daily struggles. We know our purpose from moment to moment and that provides us with all the necessary plot points to construct a meaningful story—even if it has no overarching message.

Just as the True believer and spiritual seeker are guided by popular cosmologies, nonbelievers and non-seekers draw from prevalent narratives to better understand themselves and their life objectives. While these narratives are not as all-encompassing as, say, religious faith, they are no less moral. We are the protagonists of our personal narratives.[2] From this perspective, our accomplishments are seen as vindications and our failures become tragic.

Timing is a major factor in whether we end up a well-deserved winner or an ill-fated loser in our life story. While True believers assert faith in eternity, our personal saga is always constrained by time. We focus on events and schedules, not some mystical realm where time is infinite. Our rigidly scheduled time is fraught with meaning; we fall behind deadlines and miss fleeting opportunities. Or we luck out by running into the right person at just the right moment. Time can feel like it is on your side, but it more often feels like it's working against you.

How time feels is a function of our environment. We live in *social time*, which sets the pace of the story of our lives and has at least two components: tempo and rhythm.

Cultural tempos are variations in the speed of social interaction and societal change. This is an ugly truth about modern living—the pace of life is simply faster now than ever before. Society sets the speed and we can either run along with it or fall behind.

Yet within cultural tempos people develop different *rhythms*. These rhythms reflect how someone schedules her time, which in turn indicates which facets of life she deems most important. Rhythms of life reveal which times we seek to maximize or minimize; they expose the implicit purpose of our daily living. Sometimes a person's priorities are tragically out of sync with her cultural tempo. But if she's lucky, rhythm and tempo align to produce a lovely harmony and her day-to-day story remains upbeat. Good times prevail.

Still, every life story is presaged by the looming specter of a closing curtain. As Franz Kafka is believed to have said, "the meaning of life is that it ends." So before getting into the specifics of cultural tempos and rhythms of life, let's begin at the end. We must first look death in the face, before wisely and quickly moving on to better times.

the end is near

More than 2,000 years ago, the philosopher Seneca pondered the shortness of life. Widespread fear of death, he wrote, has even "caused kings to bewail their power" as they are "terrified by the thought of its inevitable end."[3] About 500 years before Seneca, the Buddha noted that *annica* (impermanence) was an essential and undeniable truth—nothing is constant and there is nothing we can do about it. Success, luck, a rewarding occupation, a loving spouse, a vibrant faith, healthy children, even a powerful kingdom are all merely momentary. The Buddha traced the source of human suffering to our inability to accept this fact.

Impermanence continues to weigh heavily on the modern mind. Psychologist Ernest Becker believed that "the idea of death, the fear of it, haunts the human animal like nothing else; it is a mainspring of human activity."[4] And modernity only makes our impermanence more acute. We now grasp the vastness of human history, not to mention cosmic history, and can see more clearly than ever before how infinitesimal and fleeting our own existence is in comparison. We also have better means to calculate our life expectancy and the life expectancies of our loved ones, the entire planet, the solar system, and even our galaxy. Our modern knowledge renders an ever more precise countdown to non-existence, happily unknown to the Buddha and Seneca.

Yet many modern people deal with the specter of impermanence in surprisingly premodern ways. Becker argued that humans have always attempted to "deny" the reality of death by constructing hero myths, both secular and religious, that offer a sense of moral permanence through the passage of time.[5] Or as Hannah Arendt put it, heroic and saintly deeds give us "a purpose that extends beyond the grave."[6]

The idea of moral permanence is a deeply embedded Truth in Western faith traditions, allowing people to escape death, at least emotionally, through faith in the existence of eternal goodness. The afterlife is its most concrete form, a safe place where we can continue to exist in moral glory even after our bodies decay and die.[7]

The idea of the afterlife is so ingrained in Western Christian culture that even secular individuals have trouble shaking it. A former evangelical Christian who, after much soul searching, became an atheist, sincerely asked me what would become of him in the afterlife. I did not have the heart to tell him that if he was truly an atheist, there was no afterlife. His belief in moral eternity and final retribution persisted even after his faith in God had died. He simply wanted the self to live on.

Seneca and the Buddha had different answers for the problem of impermanence, and both of their solutions remain popular today. For the Buddha, accepting the reality of *annica* was the only logical path. Eckhart Tolle explains that you must "realize deeply that the present moment is all you have. Make the now the primary focus of your life."[8] The ability to focus on the now requires the acceptance of *annica*. According to Tolle, "there is no greater spiritual practice than this."[9] Contemporary meditators, yoga practitioners, and others refer to this as a sense of "presence" or "mindfulness." They deal with non-existence by accepting the now rather than imagining an afterlife or falling into complete despair. Those who claim to live in the now, like Tolle, express a sense of earthly serenity similar to those who believe in an afterlife.

This is no easy task. Being present can sometimes have the opposite effect. The writer Colum McCann notes the dangers of paying too much attention to the now; he warns of a dread lying deep in our consciousness: "Just stand still for an instant and there it is, this fear, covering our faces and tongues. If we stopped to take account of it, we'd just fall into despair. But we can't stop. We've got to keep going."[10] Like belief in eternity and attempts to be present in the now, constant activity is another popular means to "deny" our rapidly approaching non-existence. We've just got to keep moving.

Seneca suggests that diversions, alternatingly serious and amusing, are the best way to keep one's mind off death. And modern living certainly offers us a lot of diversions. We can easily occupy our minds with climbing a career ladder, buying new things, seeking new entertainments, and just keeping our momentum moving "forward" (without too much thought as to where forward is ultimately leading). Our frantic modern existence may come with a nice side effect—it might prevent us from brooding over the more ugly truths about life.

Death is denied in these ways. It can be reconceptualized as a doorway to a greater existence, it can be reimagined by focusing on the now, or it can be actively ignored in the daily commotion of life. These various strategies reflect our different experiences and perceptions of time.

time changes

> A woman sees her neighbor in the front yard
>> holding a pig over his head. The pig is biting
>> apples off a tree branch and splitting them on the
>> lawn. The woman asks, "What are you doing?"
> "My pig and I are picking apples," the neighbor
>> replies.
> "Wouldn't it save time to put the pig on the ground
>> and pick them yourself?" she presses.
> The neighbor thinks to himself, "but what's time to
>> a pig?"

What *is* time to a pig? Nothing.

The pig lives in the present. Humans, on the other hand, ponder time all the time. We ordinarily contemplate a threefold division of time—past, present, and future—and our grammatical tenses reflect this. But there are other ways to divide time, such as into now and not-now. Werner Bergmann explains that the former suggests that time is "ordered in a linear way" with "duration."[11] As in:

If I put the pig down and start picking apples, maybe I can get to my next project more quickly.

The latter is "not experienced as duration, but as contrast."[12] As in:

It was better when I was on the ground.

The number of ways in which we conceptualize time isn't entirely clear.[13] What is clear is that the pig does not experience the *social time* of humans.[14] Emile Durkheim first posited the concept of social time.

> The concrete duration that I feel passing within and with me could never give me the idea of time as a whole. The first expresses only the rhythm of my individual life; the second must correspond to the rhythm of a life that is not that of any particular individual, but one in which all participate.[15]

Social time is the tempo and rhythm of social participation. We feel in sync (or sadly out of sync) with the pace of society. Because life is easier when we are in sync with others, we naturally seek a shared sense of time. The "schedule" is a self-conscious attempt to establish social time, invented to put us in sync. It is a great equalizer because everyone, even the most powerful, is slave to the schedule. While societal elites have lots of advantages, they also tend to have lots and lots of appointments.

The increasing precision of schedules is a function of modernization.[16] Along with it comes a corresponding change in tempo. How long do you wait before returning an email? Certainly less time than it would take to return a letter. Cultural tempos are getting faster. It is a common and obvious observation that modernization speeds up and intensifies social time.[17] Pitirim Sorokin explains:

> One year of existence of a modern social group is packed with more numerous and greater changes than are fifty years of existence of some isolated primitive tribe. The rhythm of events—through which and by which we judge the flow of time—is different, like a symphony with a slow movement and with a fast scherzo, each of which is felt directly and not with the help of a watch.[18]

If we are lucky, the tempo is pleasing and we find our daily rhythm easily. If we are less fortunate, the tempo is off-putting and we engage in a clumsy struggle to keep pace with the norms of society. Rhythm implies that even a fast scherzo will have its slower moments, and modern culture retains its holidays, vacations, and downtimes to provide contrast to the breakneck pace of daily life. The beat is faster but it remains rhythmic.

Yet some social scientists fear that we have no respite and are falling headlong into a state of "cultural arrhythmia."[19] This occurs when social time no longer ebbs and flows but simply races on, providing no sense of variation. A person becomes disoriented and his life has no rhythm.[20] Zygmunt Bauman called this the problem of "liquid modernity," in which the perpetual motion of modern living provides no foundation or certitude in life.[21] We are at sea with no predictable current.

For the modern business person, this is a familiar feeling. Imagine that, at this very instant, flying above the United States is a woman glued to her laptop, responding to emails and meeting deadlines from a height of 30,000 feet. She is in sync with the times. Consumer and technological culture flow through her and make her heart race. "Once I reformat this spreadsheet and email it to accounting, I can order those engraved sterling vases before I land and drive to the Marriott to shower quickly enough to make the 7:10 meeting which I think is across the street—I should make a note now before I forget," she says to herself, working and purchasing and traveling and planning at the speed of thought. She has no moment of dread because there simply isn't time. Still, she *feels* overwhelmed.[22]

How does she feel about her upwardly mobile, fast-paced existence? Is she grooving to the rhythm of her professional schedule? Or is she drowning in liquid modernity—terrified of falling behind? Perhaps she is doing both simultaneously, or at least alternating between them. In one moment, she is uplifted by a compliment at work or a tender email from her partner. In the next moment, she is overwhelmed by a tense meeting or a domestic squabble.

Her story is a common one and reflects the frantic pace of modern living. She doesn't have time to ponder her larger purpose, so for *now* she keeps the faith that good moments will come and provide a satisfying respite, which will ultimately justify her frantic schedule. She must keep moving and assume that the meaning of it all will be revealed in time.

The pig doesn't care about any of this. What is time to a pig? He has all the time in the world; he is in the permanent now.

high times

How do you feel right now? I hope you are having a good time reading this. Good times come in infinite varieties. The ones we seek over and over again determine the course of our lives. We often sanctify good times with photos and videos, recording these moments for eternity. We don't keep a record of the dreary meetings, the commutes home, or the lonely nights. These memories are deemed profane—times we would sooner forget.

Remember Eli, the recovering drug addict I met in church? He used to chase the euphoria of chemical highs, but now he chases the highs of religious euphoria. What's the difference? They are both good times, but if they are pursued again and again they produce very different narrative arcs. When he got high on crack, Eli achieved a momentary pleasure that quickly faded, leading him to seek yet another momentary pleasure. It created an unhealthy and unproductive cycle. Eli lost his job, his family, and all sense of self-respect.

Eli's narrative shifted when he found Jesus. I witnessed him in a state of religious catharsis that, at least from the outside, resembled the intensity and euphoria of a crack high. He wailed and jumped and writhed on the floor. He does this every week with dozens of people.[23] Eli's church provides a means to a very different kind of high—it is the high of *collective effervescence*.

Collective effervescence is a time better felt than defined. One of the reasons is that we have to be part of the experience *and* the community to understand it.[24] We can witness collective effervescence but fail to understand the experience of it.[25] Still, if we go to a faith healing, a political march, or a music festival, we will *feel* the crowd. There is an emotional energy that is palpable if you give yourself over to it.

Because it is about feeling *others*, collective effervescence cannot be reproduced in solitude. Meditation, prayer, memory, pharmacology, an excellent sound system, or even awesome special effects cannot do it justice. It is a function of togetherness—the visceral dimension of social interaction. Social time is its conduit and its frame.

We have all been to events where the energy of the crowd either ignites or fizzles. Randall Collins breaks down the elements of each. He theorizes that successful "interaction rituals" require

1. *bodily co-presence*—face to face is the best;
2. *barriers to outsiders*—a clique or clan is the best;
3. *mutual focus of attention*—a beloved topic or goal is the best;
4. *and shared mood*—excitement is the best.[26]

Collins further explains that rhythm is what glues rituals together. It is shared social time— you are in sync with another, in focus and mood, at *exactly* the same moment.

Good rhythm is crucial to the success of all rituals. Congregations rise in joyous anticipation and then pause right before the inevitable eruption of frenzied religious ecstasy. This kind of rhythm is difficult to fake. Unfortunately, we more often find ourselves at flaccid gatherings that lack all sense of rhythm—think of a dreary office gathering. But at a boisterous party where the rhythm feels right, you feel in sync—even if only for a brief moment—with others in mood and focus. It is a moment of collective effervescence.

Everyone is dancing to the same beat and then your eye catches the stare of a stranger and it feels like you might be making a love connection. This is another one of those high times in life; the moment of love's bloom. It is a primal energy on par with collective effervescence and the subject of countless romantic narratives.

Ann Swidler investigates how we talk about love. One of the stories we tell is modeled on the love idealized in fiction. Swidler calls this "true love," in which passion becomes "a clear, all-or-nothing choice."[27] Anna Karenina finds true love and dives head first into one of the most passionate relationships in the history of literature.

Count Vronsky first sees Anna Karenina at the train station. The two exchange furtive glances:

> In that brief look Vronsky had time to notice the suppressed eagerness which played over her face, and flitted between the brilliant eyes and the faint smile that curved her red lips. It was as though her nature were so brimming over with something that against her will it showed itself now in the flash of her eyes, and now in her smile. Deliberately she shrouded the light in her eyes, but it shone against her will in the faintly perceptible smile.[28]

Is it getting hot in here? Anna and the Count are generating a collective effervescence all their own. Just like the build-up of an ebullient church service, an exciting sporting event, or an intense political protest, love at first sight is the beginning of a shared rhythm.

Anna and the Count are drawn to each other despite their reservations. The immediate and long-term consequences of their affair are devastating (more on this later), but for a blissful period they experience a universally sought-after high—a moment of true love.

Of course, there are other kinds of good times, not all of them premised on being in sync with others. Sometimes you experience a period of bliss in which you are so engaged with something that you forget about the clock, forget about nagging problems, and even forget to be self-conscious. You look up and an hour has passed—it seemed like minutes. You feel elated and accomplished. Mihaly Csikszentmihalyi calls this *flow*.

Flow requires a solitary focus on a pleasing activity. But like collective effervescence and true love, flow offers people an uplifting experience around which they structure their lives. To do this consistently and efficiently, one needs a plan. Csikszentmihalyi explains, "As long as enjoyment follows piecemeal from activities not linked to one another in a meaningful way, one is still vulnerable to the vagaries of chaos."[29]

So, we invent narratives to validate and maximize our good times.

Times of collective effervescence, true love, and flow gain moral relevance and social support through narratives of faith, real love, and professional calling, respectively. These narratives not only give meaning to our good times but also provide the means to revisit them again and again. They turn moments of bliss into lives of purpose.

rhythms of life

In church, Eli experiences eternity—but only momentarily. In a moment of collective effervescence, he sees God and feels the timeless power of the universe. After that transcendent high, Eli takes a long bus ride back to his dilapidated and desolate apartment. At home, boredom and loneliness creep back into his life and replace his feeling of otherworldly bliss with the harsh *now* of his everyday struggles.

How does Eli keep the faith? Surely, in sad and solitary moments, he must be tempted to again seek out chemical highs. For now, though, Eli has found a new rhythm to life centered on weekly church attendance. At regular intervals, it boosts his spirits and increases his confidence that the bad times serve a larger purpose. While his collective effervescence lasts only as long as the worship service, the memory of it burns brightly until the following week.[30] Eli now carries Jesus with him wherever he goes. He speaks to Jesus when he is alone, but grueling realities can begin to weaken the divine signal. Jesus needs to be recharged at least once a week.[31]

Eli returns to church to recharge Jesus *and* to reunite with his fellow believers. In fact, these two things are synonymous. The social solidarity Eli feels during worship is one and the same as his feelings of transcendent reality.[32] He feels Jesus by communing with others.

The symbols, concepts, and metaphors that help give meaning to moments of collective effervescence become embedded in the minds of participants.[33] One need only mention Jesus and Eli's eyes light up. The word evokes what is best about Eli's life, and with the support of his church and the rhythm of weekly attendance, Eli's faith will remain strong. The narrative of faith embodied by a community of believers has become the story of his life. The cross he wears and the picture of Jesus above his door remind him that bad moments will not last forever. He knows that, if he just keeps up his current rhythm, his story will end in eternal bliss.

Like Eli, Anna Karenina's good times are short-lived. She experiences the intensity and passion of true love—but only momentarily. Her connection with Vronsky fades as societal pressures force them apart. A moment of true love results in shame and regret. Her story does not end in eternal bliss but rather (spoiler alert) with Anna hurling herself under a moving train.

Anna's passion was too hot to handle, and she got burned. But does true love have to end in pain? Can't we make it last forever? Ann Swidler notes that true love is supposed to occur "in defiance of social forces" and will forever fix one's ultimate "destiny."[34] The story of Anna Karenina is made significant by its social context. It is a love that defies public norms (she is married) and determines destinies (she commits suicide). It represents the truest kind of love because the circumstances have forced Anna to risk everything on it.

Not surprisingly, Swidler finds that long-term couples tend to scoff at such theatrical versions of true love. These practiced lovers smile patronizingly at the naïveté of youth. Think you will have a love like Anna Karenina? Well, get ready for disappointment to hit you like a train. The experienced couple lays claim to a "real love," which flips true love on its head. Real love "does not require a dramatic choice"; there is "no one true love"; real love is based on "compatibility" and "does not necessarily last forever."[35] It is an everyday love.

These different love myths appear to map onto different time horizons. True love is ardent but transitory, whereas real love is restrained yet durable. Love in the moment (true love) becomes the reverse of the love of a lifetime (real love). Interestingly, those who have long-term love still tend to get doe-eyed. Swidler explains:

> Images of romantic love continually resurface even among people who consciously disavow them . . . Two cultures of love persist, neither driving out the other, because people employ their understandings of love in two very different contexts.[36]

Real love is the narrative that couples reference in their day-to-day routines and struggles. Steadfastness and shared preferences (we love the same movies!) are proof of real love. Pragmatism and compatibility provide a love that can last. Yet, true love occasionally winks.[37] Long-term couples can still have Vronsky-Karenina moments, in which true love "shows itself now in the flash of her eyes, and now in her smile."

Successful couples link such moments of "true love" to the "real love" of daily life. Unromantic moments are balanced by flashes of true love.

A husband wears a ring to symbolize that, in good times and in bad, loyalty will endure. Similarly, Eli wears his cross to remind himself and others that, even in times of temptation, his faith will endure. These are symbols constructed by the community that remind believers of their commitment to a long-term life purpose.

Flow is also the subject of narratives. Career counselors work to find a person's professional "passion" and "calling." The idea of a calling needs no cosmic or spiritual framework because it can draw on moments of flow for motivation. In these moments, the individual feels timeless and elated in ways that resemble spiritual fulfillment. One's calling justifies all the arduous, unpleasant, and tedious moments between experiences of flow. In fact, our selves often come to be primarily defined by our professions, as in "I am a plumber," "I am a teacher," or "I am unemployed."

The modern world can provide a satisfying and all-consuming purpose in the form of a professional calling, especially for educated and affluent people. Mihaly Csikszentmihalyi sought to discover which professions offer good flow by tracking the experiences of one hundred people eight times a day for one week. He found that everyone was more likely to experience flow at work than at leisure. This comes as quite a shock. Shouldn't leisure be more engaging and satisfying than work? Csikszentmihalyi notes:

> Our subjects usually report that they have had some their most positive experiences while on the job. From this response it would follow that they would wish to be working . . . Instead, even when they feel good, people generally say that they would prefer not to be working . . . The converse is also true: when supposedly enjoying their hard-earned leisure, people generally report surprisingly low moods; yet they keep wishing for more leisure.[38]

Csikszentmihalyi's study suggests that our moment-to-moment experience of work belies the cliché that we are just working for the weekend. Perhaps leisure cannot provide the meaning and satisfaction that we gain from work.

Those of us lucky enough to be living in wealthy countries work fewer hours than we would have in the past and have more free time and more time with our families than those in poorer countries.[39] Still, many modern workers have responded ironically to the historic trend in decreased work time—they have become workaholics.

While clinical definitions differ, a workaholic is someone who feels guilt when not working, thinks about work obsessively, and mixes work with personal life.[40] Sound familiar? Many workaholics seek status and professional success as well as the satisfaction that comes from moments of flow. These types of workaholics are sometimes called "happy workaholics" because they labor willingly and find deep value and meaning in their work.[41]

The happy workaholic has found her calling in life. She is doing meaningful work, moving up the professional ladder, and is respected and maybe even envied by her peers. Her purpose and life are in sync, speeding along with no time to contemplate the passage of time. In fact, busyness is an important plot point in the narrative of professional calling.

In modern times, important people are busy people. The languid and opulent eighteenth-century aristocrat is replaced by the overscheduled twenty-first-century billionaire seeking to become an overscheduled gazillionaire. Marcel Proust, one of the strongest advocates of slowing down and paying attention to time, disdained this new creature. He wrote of "the self-satisfaction felt by 'busy' men—however idiotic their business—at 'not having time' to do what you are doing."[42] Proust believed that the busyness of business people wasn't valiant; it was escapist. Their work ethic was really a way for them to avoid pondering the meaning of their existence and the moral significance of their lives. This kind of pondering requires time, something they had in short supply.[43]

Still, the "happy workaholic" can achieve life satisfaction through her career while avoiding dreadful existential and moral issues. Some modern careerists have found an exciting, distracting, and socially sanctioned rhythm to life. For them, it feels *good* to be busy, and their professions provide them the means to be busy all the time. This explains the paradox of workaholics who don't actually *have to* work that much. A professional calling gives us more status and more flow. And to top it off, leisure time might actually be overrated.

Consistently reliving good moments, like flow, requires a framework of meaning—a purpose to justify the many dull and onerous moments between the good times. Csikszentmihalyi indicates that a person who can successfully create this framework will achieve "inner harmony."[44] A satisfying faith, a satisfying marriage, and a satisfying profession help us achieve this. These goals help us understand who we are, what we want, and how to get it. A successful life is one in which we consistently turn good times into lasting feelings of inner harmony. Such a person has found perfect rhythm.

Yet a perfect rhythm is dependent on circumstances beyond our control—we can only achieve it if we are in sync with a larger community. Anna Karenina sought true love but was ostracized and humiliated; she was a victim of her time. The tempo and rhythm of society always favors some people over others. While we all seek to feel good about the self by turning good moments into larger purposes, this is much harder for some than others.

time victimization

Most people in the history of the world have been victims of their times. They lived in eras that imposed political, economic, and social constraints that caused them terrible pain and anguish. We are never fully autonomous in determining our purpose, but some times are more oppressive than others. Who is most likely to have lots of bad times? Today, it is people who live in industrial and preindustrial societies.

Even in postindustrial democratic countries, many people suffer from time victimization—but of a different kind. They live in relatively happy times, historically speaking, but still experience fewer good times than the rest of their cohort. They are victims of time, because their circumstances have made life difficult. Some, of course, are too stressed out to experience any sense of calm. Others are lulled into apathy and depression because nothing ever happens. Time can kill you with stress or with boredom.

Cultural tempos determine our levels of stress and boredom. But within any culture, people who are guided by faith, love, and calling are the lucky ones. The unlucky ones experience few, if any, moments of collective effervescence, true love, and flow. Without those moments, what will become of their life stories?

Faith requires that you *feel* the Truth of a community of believers. But some sit in church and feel nothing. How can they embrace a life of faith when it feels empty? Those who don't feel Truth but still live among believers feel perpetually "lost." This simple statement communicates two important points.

1. The person feels morally confused.
2. The person believes she can be saved.

The idea of being lost requires the possibility of being found. The lost seeker constantly searches for Truth but falls short.

In fact, the most miserable Americans are those who believe that Truth exists yet cannot find it.[45] They search out moments of enlightenment and divine inspiration without success and begin to feel morally lost. They lack purpose.

Similarly, some single people pine hopelessly for love. They search for companionship, explore matchmaking sites, and go on dates, but never experience a true connection. Popular narratives of true love in movies and novels add insult to their injury by vividly depicting unbridled passion and emotional connection these people have never felt. In harsh juxtaposition to such love stories, they live constantly alone. All their moments of failed intimacy become part of a sad life story.

People who feel loveless and lost need better times. The bad moments vastly outnumber the good.

The sources of time inequality are many. For instance, a person may feel "lost" simply because he has yet to encounter the religious or spiritual group that would make him feel whole. He is living within a religious market that doesn't offer the right products. Perhaps in a different community or culture, he would begin to experience moments of collective effervescence and feel Truth. Similarly, unequal sex ratios can misalign marriage markets. For instance, one could be living in a community in which there are simply fewer available partners. As a result, one is less likely to feel a moment of true love leading to a life of real love.

Lack of access and opportunity limit our ability to find purpose. Yet rich people can certainly feel lost and loveless, and even desperately poor people will have transcendent moments. A weary migrant laborer gazes up at a sunset and, for a brief moment, beholds unfathomable beauty; a prison inmate hugs her child during a rare visit and feels true love; an unemployed Pentecostal Christian speaks in tongues and is filled with the Holy Spirit; and a street thug shoots heroin and his dark and vicious existence is briefly supplanted by peaceful euphoria. No oppression or inequality (physical, economic, or ideological) can ever fully extinguish such transcendent moments. They provide a glimpse of a brighter reality even when life feels meaningless.[46]

Still, these disadvantages tend to map directly onto wealth and status inequalities. This is most obvious when we look at flow. Csikszentmihalyi found that workers who are paid more experience more flow (see Figure 6.1). People who have the "good" jobs are not only rewarded with

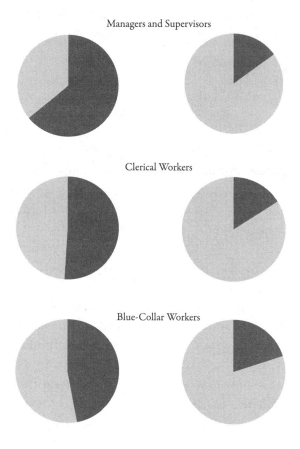

Figure 6.1 | Percent of Time Spent in Flow (dark gray areas)

Source: Csikszentmihalyi 1990

money and prestige but also tend to have more satisfying work lives. This should come as no shock.

Blue-collar workers experienced slightly more flow at leisure than at work. Perhaps this provides some cosmic solace for manual laborers—they can have a bit more fun on their days off. At least in comparison to their non-flow work time, blue-collar leisure time feels a little less dreary. We cannot know whether these findings apply to a larger swath of Americans, but they follow an intuitive logic.

With the right amount of status, good pay, and lots of flow, a modern professional can potentially become a "happy" workaholic. But what about all the workaholics in low status, low pay, and low-flow jobs?[47] Are they happy? I spoke with a forklift driver about his workaholic coworker, Gary. He said:

> I don't get why Gary takes all the overtime. He never spends [his pay] on anything. He works every holiday. I know that he doesn't like unloading trucks. It makes no sense.

Is Gary experiencing flow as he zooms around the warehouse floors in a hypnotic quest for palette A43 in dock F? No, Gary doesn't find driving a forklift intrinsically enjoyable.[48] Nor is he working in order to save for a timeshare, get a promotion, or keep pace with his coworkers. Gary is having no fun and has no professional calling. Consequently, his tireless work ethic is a little confusing.

Yet Gary's behavior makes some sense given his circumstances. Gary does not attend church or any community functions. He has little or no exposure to collective effervescence. Gary doesn't have a close family or a romantic relationship. He says that he has given up on finding true love. Gary feels *lost, loveless*, and lacking a *calling*. Sadly, it appears that Gary is a workaholic because he has nothing else to do.[49]

While he lives in a fast-paced culture, Gary's experience of time is much slower; his work plods on day after day with no modification (he even works holidays). David Foster Wallace warns that if you "pay close attention to the most tedious thing you can find (Tax Returns, Televised Golf) and, in waves, a boredom like you've never known will wash over you and just about kill you."[50] Gary understands this feeling well; he is slowly being bored to death by working incessantly.

Gary's life more closely resembles that of a worker in an industrial or preindustrial country than that of most Americans. Specifically, workers in poorer countries are much more likely to feel that they are wasting their lives at work (see Table 6.1). It is a lousy feeling. They are at work with nothing interesting to do and without liberty to leave. The 190 minutes left until quitting time feel like an eternity—the clock has stopped!

Workers in poorer countries feel this way often. The economic and institutional health of a country powerfully predicts how much time a citizen will waste on the job. People in poorer countries are also much less likely to have free time or spend quality time with their families.

Table 6.1 Correlations between Measures of Modernity and Measures of How Time Was Experienced

	AVERAGE NUMBER OF HOURS YESTERDAY SPENT		
	WASTED AT WORK	WITH FREE TIME	WITH FAMILY
Per-capita GDP	−.31	.50	.32
Community Basics Index	−.39	.26	.21
Citizen Engagement Index	−.44	.21	
Suffering Index	.32	−.19	

SOURCE: *Gallup World Poll (n = 141 countries); all listed correlations are significant.*

At the end of each day, these workers come home from boring jobs that have kept them away from friends and loved ones for long periods of time.

They are victims of their circumstances. They live in societies in which they must spend many of their waking hours bored and uninspired at work. This is the essence of alienation, as described by Karl Marx.[51] The worker sees no purpose in his labor yet is forced to complete routinized tasks over and over. In contrast, the postindustrial worker tends to be less bored; she has too much to do, many places to travel, countless distractions at her fingertips (Angry Birds), and televised golf. Within this fast-paced professional world, the upwardly mobile workaholic avoids the abyss of alienation but is nevertheless pushed to the breaking point by her frenzied schedule. She lives within a cultural tempo that leaves her in a constant state of exhaustion and hypertension.[52]

This is how cultural tempos victimize us; they prescribe a pace of life we are powerless to escape. In fact, tempos determine the purpose and meaning of entire cultures.[53]

cultural tempos

Bálint Balla lamented that "the deficit between the time necessary to realize your goals . . . and the actual available time is constant."[54] Actually, it isn't; the deficit is constantly increasing, at least in the postindustrial world. Many people complain about not having "enough time." This complaint is less about the shortness of a lifespan than about the need for more minutes within each hour. We are assaulted by too many things to do and too many places to be with too little time. We can never get to it all. The feeling of being perpetually overwhelmed is a product of modernity or, more specifically, the increasing cultural tempo of modernity. One of the clearest outcomes of this is the heightened state of anxiety in which many people live. Forty-six percent of Americans said that they experience "a lot" of stress.

People in wealthier countries are more likely to say they experience a lot of stress.[55] Yet, in a poorer country, people are much more likely to face premature death, weather-related emergencies, environmental degradation, government corruption, extreme violence, acts of terrorism, and political and economic instability.[56] That sounds really stressful. Yet the people who lead secure and comfortable lives in wealthier nations report more stress.

While stress is based on objective conditions, it is also based on how someone perceives his circumstances.[57] Psychologists John Carr and Peter Vitaliano explain:

> The degree to which an event or condition is stressful is "in the eye of the beholder." As such, one person's severe "stressor" may be only another person's moderate challenge. Thus, the impact of a stressor is determined in part by the individual's appraisal, or judgment of significance and meaning.[58]

A person's expectations and his circumstances determine stress. Individuals in poor nations certainly experience greater uncertainty and harsher tribulations, but they also expect these things. Their survival depends on seeing life's many hardships as challenges to be accepted and, hopefully, overcome. This helps to explain the head-scratching finding that people in war-torn, drought-stricken, and economically depressed countries report less stress. If they were as stressed as their circumstances seem to demand, they would be immobilized—they have to resolutely face tragedy or else give up.

The ordeals, deadlines, and strains of rapid cultural tempos produce more stress because of constant multitasking. While the stakes are not life-or-death, the intensity of a fast-paced life makes them seem that way. The workaholic has a 30-minute PowerPoint and a four-site conference call to prepare for this evening and a 20-page report to write tomorrow morning before picking the kids up from after-preschool. Down-to-the-minute planning helps this workaholic hold her career and family together. One tiny misstep and her day or week could unravel into chaos. She is *really* stressed, though no one's life is at stake.

Close to half of working Americans say that they are overworked, and the feeling is common across the industrialized world.[59] In Japan, *karoshi*—death from overwork—is on the rise. Nearly 10,000 Japanese die from *karoshi* annually and the Japanese government fears that over 1 million Japanese professionals are at risk because they work more than 80 hours a week.[60] *Karoshi* is an unusual and extreme manifestation of workaholism. Other, more common outcomes include poor health, stress, anxiety, depression, marital estrangement, and mistrust of others.[61]

The cultural tempo of modernity has made the workaholic frantic. It gets much harder to be a good worker, compete with peers, and buy up-to-date gizmos when social time keeps speeding up.[62] Technology is supposed to make life simpler and more efficient. But for the modern workaholic, technology and globalization make work time move at the speed of light.

As time races onward, people try to keep up, and some inevitably fall victim to the breakneck pace. *Karoshi* is the direct result of a cultural tempo gone berserk. The same thing can happen when tempos get too slow.

Figure 6.2 depicts the percentage of people in a nation who say they are either stressed or bored *a lot*. Black circles represent countries with higher per-capita GDP and white circles represent countries with lower per-capita GDP. Two trends emerge. The first is that higher GDP tends to reduce boredom and increase stress. It makes sense that people in wealthier countries would be less bored—they have more distractions. For instance, Americans are only moderately bored compared to others, but they are one of the most stressed out groups.

A second, more surprising trend is that, within countries, boredom and stress are related. This seems counterintuitive. If people are stressed, they shouldn't be bored—they have their stress to occupy them. But it is very possible to be bored and stressed, and in the United States, the two are significantly correlated. While really bored and really stressed people tend to be distinct, 15 percent of Americans report being stressed and bored "a lot" on the same day.[63] As psychologist John Carr explains, people

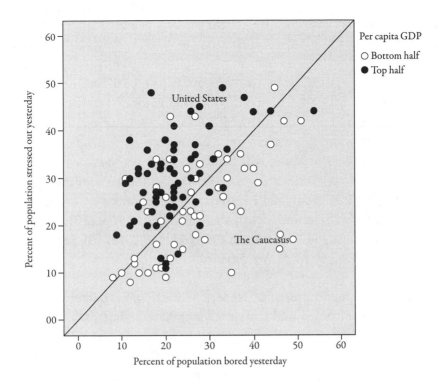

Figure 6.2 | Bored and Stressed Averages by Country (GDP identified)
Source: Gallup World Poll

"are bored wishing for something to happen" and "stressed because it is not happening." Gary, the forklift driver, fits this profile.

The Caucasus—composed of Georgia, Armenia, and Azerbaijan—is an entire region mired in cultural ennui. These nations were once part of the Soviet Union but fell into economic and political chaos following its collapse. By 2000, nearly 50 percent of people in the Caucasus said that they were bored often. Compare that to places like the Netherlands, where only 9 percent of the population is bored, or the international average—around 24 percent.

How did Georgians, Armenians, and Azerbaijanis get so bored? Poverty and social inertia certainly play a role. But to understand their exceptional boredom in comparison to similar nations, we must return to the idea that feelings are also perceptions. Just as one person's stress is another's challenge, one person's boredom is another's peace. The history of the Caucasus has primed its citizenry to expect a very different tempo than they currently experience. Thomas De Waal explains:

> Many things that people [of the Caucasus] take for granted are a product of the Soviet Union. They include urban lifestyles, mass literacy, and strong secularism. All three countries still live with an authoritarian political culture in which most people expect that the boss or leader will make decisions on their behalf and that civic activism will have no effect. The media is stronger on polemic than fact-based argument. The economies are based on patron-client networks that formed in Soviet times. Nostalgia for the more innocent time of the 1960s and 1970s still pervades films, books, and Internet debates.[64]

Memories of relative prosperity, secure political and economic cultures, and promises of steady and certain growth have collided with the reality of interminable economic and political inertia. With energy resources and a skilled and educated population, people of the Caucasus had good reason to expect a clear path to democratic self-rule and economic modernization. But ethnic conflicts and residual Soviet corruption subverted this dream. The result is a culture mired in inaction and impotence. It is felt most powerfully by the young.

The International Monetary Fund estimates that about 15 percent of Azerbaijani young adults and up to 35 or 40 percent of the youth in Georgia and Armenia are unemployed. The Caucasus Barometer, a 2009 survey of the region, found that an overwhelming 60 percent of the population report that they "miss having people around," a measure of loneliness. Lacking work and feeling isolated, the people of the Caucasus live in a culture where time drags on. They languish in a sluggish tempo that is not of their making.

In his ethnography of Georgian youth, Martin Demant Frederiksen finds a "tension between subjective and societal time" that "create[s] experiences of marginality."[65] Fredericksen argues that young Georgian men live within a subjective time reflecting the vigor of youth but also within a societal time reflecting the lethargy of age. They are out of rhythm with their history and their punishment is crushing boredom. A culture that can never achieve the future it thinks it deserves falls into this kind of cultural ennui. The Caucasus is caught in these doldrums, wearily hoping for the historical winds of change to bring some relief.

Gary hopes for some change too. But he is stuck in a rut; he needs to find a purpose that will give him the motivation and focus to make a change. Sadly, he has few good experiences to spark such a shift. He doesn't know how to capture these good moments, and there is no one around to help him. He is unlikely to find inner harmony because he lives in social disharmony.

time's up!

Pencils down. Why is time so important to purpose?

Cultures and communities create the tempos and rhythms of our lives. These social forces determine how we experience the passage of time from moment to moment and year to year. In the novel *Luka and the Fire of Life*, Salman Rushdie writes about a father explaining the importance of this to his child:

> The time of our feelings is not the same as the time of the clocks. We know that when we are excited by what we are doing, Time speeds up, and when we are bored, it slows down. We know that at moments of great excitement or anticipation, at wonderful moments, Time can stand still.
>
> There are places in the world where nothing ever happens, and Time stops moving altogether . . . We know that when we fall in love, Time ceases to exist, and we also know that Time can repeat itself, so that you can be stuck in one day for the whole of your life.[66]

The time of our feelings is not the same as the time of the clocks. Clocks count out units of time, consistently and continually. The time of our feelings is social time, which can speed up or slow down. There are places, like the Caucasus, where time feels like it has stopped. In other places, like the United States and Japan, it races forward. Time can freeze in moments of transcendence—collective effervescence or true love or flow. With luck, these moments will repeat themselves to form a rhythmically pleasing life.[67]

But many fall victim to time. The tragic Anna Karenina experienced a bewitching moment of true love but was denied the possibility of a life guided by real love because of the era in which she lived. Gary, the blue-collar workaholic, is also trapped; he is stuck in endless days of dreary work. He has no flow and feels lost, lonely, and without a calling.

Eli, the recovering drug addict, has found his rhythm. After encountering Jesus in a moment of sublime revelation, he constructed a brand new purpose. Formerly driven by drugs, Eli is now guided by faith, which is reaffirmed every Sunday at ten o'clock. Against all odds, Eli has found inner harmony and purpose. He became part of a community, and his feelings, thoughts, and actions fell into sync with other people.

Social harmony occurs when collective feelings, thoughts, and actions are in congruence. Eli found himself in a moment of perfect social harmony and it changed him. Gary has receded from social interaction altogether, so his chances of striking a chord with others have become slim. Anna got into sync with Count Vronsky, but she was tragically out of sync with her times. The unlucky ones like her are undone by social disharmony.

Like inner harmony, social harmony is rare. Social time and personal rhythm can easily become misaligned. Tempos speed up, robbing us of crucial moments to rest and contemplate. Or they slow down to create cultural ennui, a time devoid of excitement and promise. When the rhythm you seek is out of step with your cultural tempo, time is not on your side. You feel stressed or bored or something much worse. When we are not aligned with social time, purpose can be elusive.

I met an imposing man named Saul who has sailed the world on naval ships and has seen his share of disharmony. A tattoo of a human vanquishing a demon covers his back. When I asked Saul about it, he replied, "You've got to keep the devil in the hole." Saul understands that evil lurks in the human heart—we must actively fight our inner demons in order for our better self to prevail. Saul's tattoo is permanent, which suggests that the struggle is enduring. Keeping the devil in the hole requires constant vigilance.

Saul is absolutely correct—we are continually at *cross purposes* with our selves and our societies.

7

cross purposes

The only truth which I have ever found
out for myself is, I think, this one: of the
unavoidability of conflicting ends.

Isaiah Berlin[1]

What is your purpose in life? Are you confused?

You should be. The self is a bundle of contradictions. Similarly, our relationships, communities, and cultures are endlessly complicated. Life sometimes feels like a struggle to make sense of an endless stream of internal and external information. Human beings are hard to pin down. Niccolo Machiavelli thought he had them figured out. He asserted the still popular notion that people are, at heart, "ungrateful, fickle, dissembling, anxious to flee danger, and covetous of gain."[2] That sounds about right.

But human achievements seem to belie Machiavelli's assertion. To build a society requires coordination and cooperation, which, in turn, require us to be reliable, dedicated, and honorable citizens. Mahatma Gandhi noted that humans, overall, are basically decent. "Humanity is an ocean," he said, "if a few drops of the ocean are dirty, the ocean does not become dirty."[3]

Machiavelli and Gandhi offer us two opposing notions of human nature. In one we are fundamentally selfish and in the other we are inherently compassionate. On the one hand is the corporate shark willing to do whatever it takes to win. She reads Ayn Rand for inspiration. On the other is the social worker, willing to take less pay and work long hours in service to the poor. He reads Martin Luther King, Jr., for inspiration.

But perhaps the corporate exec feels some compassion for her employees, so she doesn't cut costs to the bone, even if it would increase profits. And maybe the social worker has grown cynical and ridicules his clients behind their backs. For each, a deeper nature rumbles beneath the surface. Friedrich Hayek thought, "Although man never existed without laws that he obeyed, he did, of course, exist for hundreds of thousands of years without laws he 'knew' in the sense that he was able to articulate them."[4]

In theory, if we can articulate these laws, we can predict human behavior. We can put Machiavelli and Gandhi to the test. Are we more likely to be selfish or compassionate? If most of us are compassionate, then Gandhi wins—the ocean is not dirty.

Fyodor Dostoevsky challenged the idea that there was any point in trying to answer this question. His antihero, the Underground Man, pondered whether

> science itself will teach man (though to my mind it's a super-fluous luxury) that he never has really had any caprice or will of his own, and that he himself is something of the nature of a piano-key or the stop of an organ, and that there are, besides, things called the laws of nature; so that everything he does is not done by his willing it, but is done of itself, by the laws of nature.[5]

According to the latest in evolutionary theory, Underground Man is correct: the laws of human nature are a fiction. Biologist Paul Ehrlich explains that "human nature as a singular concept embodies the erroneous notion that people possess a common set of rigid, genetically specified behavioral predilections that are unlikely to be altered by circumstances."[6] So we are not predominantly selfish or compassionate but rather a jumble of contradictions.[7]

Biologists may say that human nature is imaginary, but we can't help imagining it. We come up with ideas about human nature all by ourselves. And we search ceaselessly for further inspiration. Through a better understanding of ourselves and others we hope to achieve a modicum of inner and social harmony. We want to have purpose.

Life would be so much easier, I think, if people (myself included) would be more rational and coherent. But then I realize that I also want things to be unpredictable. As Dostoevsky's Underground Man asserts, "the whole work of man really seems to consist in nothing but proving to himself every minute that he is a man and not a piano-key!"[8]

The Underground Man's assertion puts him at cross purposes with the world around him; he *wants* to subvert norms. It also puts him at cross purposes with himself. His urge to be enigmatic makes self-knowledge much more difficult—he is, in contemporary parlance, an antisocial head case. Still, he successfully resists becoming a piano key.

Each of us possesses something that ensures that our true nature will never be defined and that none of us is, at heart, a piano key. It is our *imagination*.

imagination

You don't get to choose your purpose in life. It depends on systems of meaning ascribed to you by your social and historical circumstances, which determine your belief in Truth, your sense of self, and your experience of time. Together these define your purpose. Isn't that uplifting?

No, it is downright stultifying. Now I am just a piano key, played upon by my circumstances. My history, my Truth, my self, and my time are dictated to me. Talk about disenchanting. But something softens this oversocialized portrait of the human: our ability to imagine. Using that, we can bend the forces of socialization to surprising ends.

Imagination is the ability to create images in the mind's eye.[9] While imagination is a product of evolution and its parameters are culturally defined, the images before your mind's eye are never exact replicas of anyone else's. Psychologist Otto Rank claimed that we have an "instinctive urge to abstraction."[10] We find it satisfying and even thrilling to concoct new concepts and fantastical ideas. We waltz on whimsical waves of magical splendor to weave webs of . . . Sorry, I am letting my imagination get away from me.

But imagination is not without limits. While your brain might feel like a runaway train, it is still guided by norms. Rank was interested in the wonders of abstraction but realized that we are all subject to rules of expression that are determined by our cultures; he called these rules "collective style laws." Norms of beauty, goodness, and the transcendent guide our creativity. Often, we fantasize in clichés. The fantasy lover is a porn star. The fantasy accolade is an Academy Award. The fantasy God is a bearded white man. These predictable fantasies employ prepackaged images.

Two hundred years ago, the poet Samuel Taylor Coleridge argued that imagination needs to be exercised, not just for one's "fancy," but to become a fully developed person.[11] Tapping one's imaginative faculties means questioning dominant narratives and subverting expectations. Coleridge lamented that this potential, which we all have, often lies dormant. He rebelled against what he saw as the staid complacency of his era. Of course, he ended up creating a style law of his own. Coleridge and other imaginative thinkers of his time gave birth to a different cliché—the Romantic artist. Now we are under pressure to be fantastically imaginative, on top of everything else.

The Romantic artist is at odds with society; the bourgeois sensibilities of her peers attempt to stifle her creative genius. But this myth has become its own bourgeois norm. Victoria Alexander describes its development as a response to structural changes in the production of art, which

> was transformed [from the eighteenth century onward] from patronage and academic systems, in which artistic expression was closely controlled by individuals or institutions well integrated into society, to market systems where artists were free to pursue their unique vision. The market system, however, left artists vulnerable to poverty. The philosophy of "*l'art pour l'art*" (art for art's sake) offered an important compensation to starving artists—creating great art may not pay, but is a higher calling than more mundane pursuits.[12]

Once the myth of the starving artist became popular, becoming a starving artist was no longer original. It was predictable. Black-clad artistic types have simply become piano keys. Their imaginations blindly follow cultural norms.

Still, the artistic poser, as well as his cultural foe, the bourgeois conformist, cannot help but be imaginative. Living requires it. Zygmunt Bauman correctly maintains:

Life can't *not be* a work of art if this is a *human* life—the life of a being endowed with will and freedom of choice. Will and choice leave their imprint on the shape of life, in spite of all and any attempts to deny their presence and/or hide their power by ascribing the causal role to the overwhelming pressure of external forces.[13]

The most unimaginative and socially repressed among us are still endowed with will and freedom of choice. The *idea* that we can choose our purpose is a modern invention. Yet, the universal ability to choose is as old as Homo sapiens, if not older.[14]

Archeologist Steven Mithen presents a theory of how imagination developed over human history. He argues that we have developed, over thousands of years, four types of imagination, each one a major step in the human drive toward abstraction:

1. Choice—which requires the ability to imagine different possible outcomes
2. Empathy—which requires the ability to imagine the thoughts and feelings of others
3. Narrative—which requires the ability to invent stories
4. Fantasy—which requires the ability to imagine transcendent worlds[15]

Mithen argues that choice was the first of our imaginative abilities; our ancestors were urgently sifting through their options when facing saber-toothed tigers. Cognitive scientists have maintained that empathy was the basis for imagining the first gods; we were contemplating what deities were thinking while we were still in caves. Narrative then began to express social and political ideals—robust and appealing stories of "the good society" or tales of your saber-toothed tiger-fighting exploits that made you look strong and reliable in the eyes of your brethren. And fantasy brought them all together in amazingly inventive worldviews, religions, and philosophies.

When we tell the stories of our lives we may be confined to culturally defined menus of images and inherited philosophical/religious fantasies, but we still must choose from among them. And our choices make us individuals instead of piano keys. We may copy others and fantasize in clichés, but no matter how boring or contrived our choices appear, they remain our own. Our capacity to choose, empathize, narrate, and fantasize makes every life a work of imagination. Purpose is its intellectual product, the meaning of life we imagine for ourselves. As such, each individual purpose is unique.

Imagination also creates social order. We imagine and articulate ideas about collective purpose and what makes a good society. If others share this purpose, or we can persuade them of its value, we can work together to try to create it. Utopias, social ideals, and systems of morality are imaginative products that guide collective action. The social outcomes may not be exactly what we imagined, but imagination is required to begin with.

Imagination also destroys social order. It inspires us to subvert collective purpose. Michael Hechter writes about an inherent "conflict of interest between the individual and the group."[16] He and Christine Horne explain:

> The problem arises because human beings are both individual and social. If we were each living alone on a private planet, we could do whatever we wanted and would never have to worry about anyone else. Or, if each of us were attached to one group mind, we would have no individual impulses and urges.[17]

Our ability to imagine a collective purpose softens our urge to be antisocial. But our ability to imagine selfish alternatives prevents us from being attached to "one group mind." Social order would be so much more efficient and tidy if there were one universal purpose, but our imaginative lives muddy the social order with diverse human preferences.

Still, modern humans imagine new sacred canopies that seek to unite humanity in a shared purpose. Here are three such fantasies:

1. *One cause*—a shared vision of the good society
2. *One God*—a shared sense of the sacred
3. *One reality*—a shared perception of truth

Ideologues, evangelists, and intellectuals promote these modern sacred canopies, which can unite millions of party loyalists, True believers, and rational materialists.

But humans have never agreed on the purpose of life. The diversity of experiences and varieties of imagination make such agreement impossible. Richard Rorty explains the maddening result of thousands of years of philosophy: "The point is always the same—to perform the social function which Dewey called 'breaking the crust of convention,' preventing man from deluding himself with the notion that he knows himself, or anything else."[18]

Imagination twists and adapts all prescribed meanings, breaking the crusts of convention. We are driven to it out of sheer curiosity.

one cause

"There are invisible rulers who control the destinies of millions," wrote Edward Bernays in his 1928 book *Propaganda*.[19] The study and science of propaganda became popular after the rise of oppressive, ideologically driven fascist and communist regimes. The Soviet Union, a primary example, was a massive attempt to create one common cause—global communism. Soviet officials obsessively and incessantly produced propaganda.[20]

While Bernays was opposed to communism, he was not opposed to propaganda. In fact, he argued that "the conscious and intelligent manipulation of the organized habits and opinions of the masses is an important element in democratic society."[21] He warned the leaders of such societies that "intelligent men must realize that propaganda is a modern instrument by which they can fight for productive ends and help bring order out of chaos."[22]

While Bernays thought propaganda could be used for good, many feared that his tactics would be applied for evil ends. But whether for good or evil, propaganda done right supposedly wields tremendous power, enough to undermine people's ability to think for themselves. George Orwell warned that "political language is designed to make lies sound truthful and murder respectable, and to give an appearance of solidity to pure wind."[23] Even our most basic sensibilities seemed to be at risk under the perverse sway of propaganda.

The spread of communism appeared to prove the point. Weren't Cubans blinded by Castro's charisma? Weren't Russian children brainwashed by the rhetorical wizardry of Marxist-Leninism? With the proper techniques, propagandists could indoctrinate an entire population. Once the values of official ideology were properly disseminated, people would simply respond to directives like piano keys.

This supposition was based on the premise that the individual is compulsively compliant, bending easily to authority and social norms. Bernays explains:

> A man buying a suit of clothes imagines that he is choosing, according to his taste and personality, the kind of garment which he prefers. In reality, he may be obeying the orders of an anonymous gentleman tailor in London ... The fashionable men in New York, Chicago, Boston, and Philadelphia wear him. And the Topeka man, recognizing this leadership, does the same.[24]

Like fashion trends, ideology and meaning were thought to spread by suggestion. Authorities disseminate ideas about the good society and the meaning of life; in turn, the individual absorbs these values—they become his new sacred canopy. For Bernays, the ultimate goal of propaganda was to make individual interests and public interests one and the same.

In theory, a society could unite everyone around one cause.

We internalize meaning, values, and ideology through repeated exposure—this is the essential truth of socialization. Therefore, Bernays and the Soviets theorized that the state, given proper control, could manipulate us into sharing a universal collective purpose. While communists assaulted citizens with slogans and ideological tenets, Western capitalists played with the subconscious. By the 1970s, American researchers had reportedly found that subliminal images were intentionally placed in ads for the express purpose of manipulating viewers.[25] While the myth of subliminal messaging remains popular, scholars Garth Jowett and Victoria O'Donnell have shown that these studies have been debunked:

> These concerns about the manipulative nature of advertising, suggesting that the public was just a "pathetic lump of clay" readily molded to suit the advertiser's needs, were, in fact, just another variation of the outdated "magic bullet" or "hypodermic syringe" model of communications from the turn of the century. It took

more sophisticated research in the next three decades to establish that advertising did not work in such a simple manner.[26]

While we are not pathetic lumps of clay, humans are certainly susceptible to suggestion, especially when it is highly controlled.

Jowett and O'Donnell stress that "wherever a dominant definition of the situation is accompanied by a consistent, repetitious, and unchallenged message, the influence of the message is greater."[27] For instance, studies of public opinion in the Soviet Union and Eastern Bloc countries indicated that a vast majority of citizens really did believe in socialist ideals.[28] This was the case even after decades of unfulfilled promises and transparently dishonest propaganda.

Still, voices of opposition to communist rule tended to remain committed to socialism as a theory. Problems with the Soviet system were assumed to be operational and not ideological. Chinese communists today still depict social problems in this manner; setbacks are presented as the result of local corruption and not some larger systemic flaw. A few dirty drops have not muddied the ocean of communism.

The greatest irony of Soviet propaganda is that it lost legitimacy among most committed believers in social democracy; in fact, many socialists began to use communist rhetoric against the propagandists. As Steven Pfaff shows in his analysis of the collapse of East Germany, "By 1989 official socialist ideology, along with its clear articulation of the nature of injustice, had become a threat to the system it was meant to legitimate."[29] Massive uprisings against Soviet rule (Hungary in 1956, Czechoslovakia in 1968, and East Germany in 1989) were not motivated by a desire for free-market capitalism but rather by a desire for a purer form of socialism.[30]

Here lies the unpredictability of propaganda. Propagandists might be able to spread their messages through consistent and unchallenged repetition, but they cannot control how the messages will be interpreted.[31] Soviet leaders hailed Marxism as the legitimating ideology of their rule. But in the end, citizens critiqued their rulers through the lens of Marxism, casting a disapproving eye on the rigid stratification and open corruption of Soviet society. Soviet propagandists were unsuccessful because they assumed that individuals were completely malleable. Instead, communist ideology was attractive only to the extent that its *meaning* was malleable.

Individual imagination allows propaganda to appeal to millions for a million different reasons. Each individual fits the meaning to her life.

Ann Swidler explains how a worldview can survive the unpredictable complexities of actually living.

> Because life is uncertain, people keep multiple cultural meanings on tap. In this sense, what appears as cultural incoherence is also adaptability, flexibility, keeping options open. And this is as much a cognitive as a relational activity. A worldview that could be shattered by a single setback or contradiction would be a very fragile one.

The communist worldview was not a fragile one, because it faced many contradictions and still endured. Its tenets and language were flexible enough to adopt multiple social and individual meanings, which (ironically) was never the propagandists' intent.

The top-down imposition of Soviet propaganda stands in direct contrast to the gentler process of political persuasion in American politics. "Persuasion is interactive and attempts to satisfy the needs of both persuader and persuadee."[32] Candidates in democratic societies don't pretend to lecture the masses but rather seek to charm their would-be followers. While their goal is the same as the propagandists'—to achieve political legitimacy and public support—their methods are indulgent rather than overbearing.

Soviet rulers dreamed of a society of ideological clones, guided by the one cause of Marxist-Leninism. American leaders see a different kind a citizenry, one that is bored by political details and has to be coddled and entertained. The less ideological a citizen is the more compliant he is. In fact, the latest thinking on political persuasion is unconcerned with the logic of political philosophy or the details of theology or morality. Psychologist Drew Westen explains that "a central aspect of the art of political persuasion is creating, solidifying, and activating networks that create primarily positive feelings toward your candidate or party and negative feelings toward the opposition."[33] Positive emotions, not great ideas or universal values, are what persuade voters.

The sciences of propaganda and persuasion posit different types of human nature. The propagandist assumes a malleable individual and straightforwardly tries to instill clearly defined values and purpose. The persuader assumes that the individual already has sacred values and cultural preferences; he coyly seeks to finesse each individual worldview to fit his political agenda.

The political persuader is successful to the extent that he makes his listener *feel* good about him. To do this, he plays to the cultural norms of his audience, associating himself with various sacred symbols (like wearing a flag pin and a cross), and using key words with cultural resonance (like "freedom"). This greatly oversimplifies the real-world theatrics of political persuasion, but the underlying theory is the same.

Of course, the persuader will always fail to win over some, but if his cultural radar is on target he can develop a dedicated following.[34] Consequently, the art of political persuasion seeks to exploit the embedded scripts, key words, and images that "just feel right" to the individual.[35] Americans may pride themselves on seeing through all this political theater, but most play along nonetheless. Why? Because it feels right.

Both propaganda and political persuasion seek shared meaning; they are attempts to instill a collective purpose. Both techniques are relatively successful at legitimating political authority. Propaganda's effectiveness is related to its ubiquity, flexibility, and longevity. As Jowett and O'Donnell find, "the greater the monopoly of the communication source . . . the greater the effect."[36] Still, propaganda cannot completely repress individual imagination. Revolutionary comrades will still envision utopia differently.

Political persuasion works to the extent that it "is in line with relevance, existing opinions, beliefs, and dispositions of the receivers."[37] But the ideological diversity of modern and democratic societies ensures that no single persuader will appeal to all.[38]

No political ideology has ever united a population around one cause. Religions have come closer to uniting populations in one faith. Just like political leaders, religious groups employ tactics of propaganda and persuasion. The rise of Christianity and spread of Islam attest to the power of religious concepts to unite billions in a single faith.

one god

God has captured the imagination of humans like nothing else in history. As Rodney Stark describes it:

> Many scholars have noted the tendency for religion to evolve in the direction of monotheism. The fundamental principle is this: As societies become older, larger, and more cosmopolitan they will tend to worship fewer Gods of greater scope.[39]

While societal growth fosters ideological and cultural diversity, it coalesces around the concept of one God. Stark notes the religious rationale for why belief in the supernatural naturally tends toward monotheism—one God is simply more rational, responsive, and dependable than many gods.[40] In addition, one God is a beautifully simple and exceedingly pliable concept.[41]

Capitalists, socialists, fascists, nationalists, anarchists, rationalists, Democrats, and Republicans can all be equally fervent monotheists. There is no necessary contradiction in believing in God and believing in a vast array of conceptions of the good society. In each believer's mind, God shares her values.

For this reason, the popularity of monotheism does not lead to a universal purpose or meaning. In fact, belief in one God is compatible with the broadest range of purposes.

Steven Prothero explains:

> It is comforting to pretend that the great religions make up one big, happy family. But this sentiment, however well-intentioned, is neither accurate nor ethically responsible. God is not one. Faith in the unity of religions is just that—faith (perhaps even a kind of fundamentalism). And the leap that gets us here is an act of the hyperactive imagination.[42]

Prothero warns against the naïve notion that the world's religious traditions are simply cultural variations on a common theme. Quite the contrary, religions "diverge sharply on doctrine, ritual, mythology, experience, and law. These differences may not matter to mystics or philosophers of religion, but they matter to ordinary religious people."[43] Stark also emphasizes this fact. While he notes the growing popularity of one God, he stresses "the extraordinary capacity of monotheism to *unite* and to *divide*."[44] In sum, people can agree that there is one God but on very little else.

Americans largely agree that the United States is "one nation under God"—this basic sentiment suggests that one God can bond a citizenry to a single national purpose. The reality is much different. In fact, within the United States, which is predominantly Christian, God has become a receptacle for a vast array of political, moral, and scientific attitudes. God can justify war *and* condemn it. God can be pro-choice *and* pro-life. And God can advance the theory of evolution *and* belief in Creationism. Belief in one God explains little; the kind of God the believer imagines explains much.

Christopher Bader and I set out to better understand Americans' belief in God and found some very deep divisions.[45] While around 90 percent of Americans believe in God, the kind of God Americans describe varies on multiple dimensions. One of the most critical dimensions is the extent to which a believer thinks that God is *engaged* in the world. Some Americans believe in a God who can alter the outcome of football games, produce hurricanes and tornados, and cure your aunt's arthritis—this is an extremely engaged God. On the other end of this continuum are believers who imagine God to be a remote cosmic force, something akin to the laws of nature or the Big Bang—this is a distant and unengaged God.

In turn, the way an American understands God's level of engagement reflects something deep about his entire worldview. What a person thinks about God determines what she thinks about morality, politics, science, economics, and more.[46]

Believers in a less engaged God tend to be secular in their attitudes toward politics and science. They understand politics as the negotiated pursuit of distinct goals. They tend not to challenge the opinions and findings of professional scientists. In sum, their God is fully compatible with a rational modern worldview.

Believers in a more engaged God see the world differently. For them, God is an active player in both politics and science. And they tend to experience God directly. Forty percent of Americans believe that God has "called them to do something." And around 15 percent of Americans claim to have heard the "voice of God." This is as engaged as God gets.

T. M. Luhrmann closely studied Americans with a very engaged God. She was interested in how these believers talk to God. In one study, Luhrmann investigated the effectiveness of scriptural daydreaming in eliciting the voice of God. She found that her participants

> entered the project with a broad, generic desire to hear God speak or perhaps just to get their prayer life moving again; they spent thirty minutes a day imaginatively immersed in the scriptures; and then they had unplanned, idiosyncratic experiences that they saw with their eyes and heard with their ears.[47]

Speaking to God is an imaginative act that results in "unplanned" and "idiosyncratic" experiences.

Conversations between believers and God follow no script. The interaction is unpredictable because the believer has given herself over to the flow of her imagination. This flow may circle around traditional conceptions of the supernatural, but the intricacies of each believer's thought patterns yield an entirely personal God. No two will ever be identical.

A believer's image of God reflects her imaginative powers. A believer *chooses* what scriptures are significant to her; she *empathizes* with her God; she *narrates* the story of their relationship; and finally, she *fantasizes* about what God is telling her. This is not to say that monotheism is a mere fantasy, but rather that it is in an endless state of re-creation. And this is what makes the idea of God so durable and so useful.

Secularization theorists suggest that the concept of God has lost its power in the modern age. They cite drops in religious identification and participation levels as proof.[48] While the spread and progress of globalization, technology, and science could spell trouble for religious organizations and traditional doctrines that resist the cultural changes of modernity, it has done little to diminish faith in one God. In fact, levels of belief in God are essentially the same across the preindustrial, industrial, and postindustrial worlds.[49]

Modernization may kill the vitality and significance of anachronistic religions but it won't kill God. Instead, modernization changes the kind of God people imagine. Figure 7.1 depicts the relationship between a

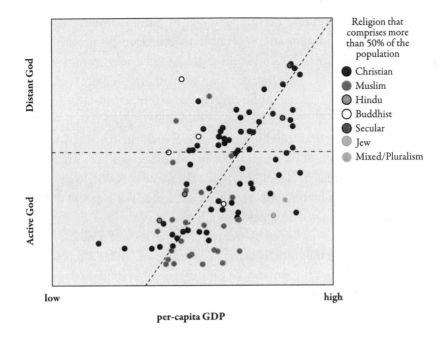

Figure 7.1 | God around the World (correlated with per-capita GDP)
Source: Gallup World Poll 2008

nation's per-capita GDP (a simple indicator of a society's level of modernization) and the extent to which the population imagines an engaged God. Very clearly, people in poorer countries tend to believe in a *more* engaged God. These believers feel that God is an active participant in world events and their personal lives. Citizens in more modern countries still believe in God, but a more distant one. This God doesn't favor particular nations, overturn the latest science, or help you win the lottery.

The modern believer imagines God in that moment before the Big Bang. No science can touch God there. And the modern believer conjures God with her imagination. No psychology can dislodge God from there. As science explains more of our universe and our inner states, God simply goes deeper. A less engaged God—one who is not believed to win wars or cure cancer— is beyond the realm of science. Accordingly, it makes sense that God becomes less engaged as a society modernizes.

This is all to say that God is one of the most universal concepts in the world today. In fact, belief in one God is actually growing. Vast populations who historically favored polytheism or syncretic folk religions have become more monotheistic. Scholars of Hinduism have noted the tendency among contemporary Hindus to "collapse Hinduism's many gods into one Brahman."[50] And studies of China's underground religious markets indicate the growing popularity of monotheistic traditions.[51] Monotheism is not in danger of dying out any time soon.

Still, secularization theorists can take heart. Traditional religious doctrines and practices might yet be in jeopardy in the postindustrial world. And the kind of God imagined in these "secular" countries is not the God of our forefathers. Yet, this is not the same as saying that belief in the supernatural is incompatible with modern life. The concept of God is too broad to be defeated so quickly or simply.

The modern world might threaten the specifics of a religion, but it doesn't undermine the human capacity to imagine God. God is so much more than any one religion. While church memberships rates, shifting religious identities, and fluctuating spiritual practices should matter to social scientists, political leaders, and clerics, they are tangential to an individual's experience of God. This aspect of religion—the spiritual imagination—is ubiquitous and limitless. A person's spiritual imagination is certainly influenced by the cultural norms and religious doctrines of her era, but she nevertheless personalizes even the most dogmatic religion. This is because the concept of one God requires our greatest imaginative powers.

Seeking to unite a population around one cause requires suppressing our imaginative powers. The idea of God is less oppressive simply because the concept lends itself to creative input—God can have a billion different faces. A universal political or social ideology fractures under the strain of diversity, but diversity and imagination are not God's enemies but rather His life's blood. God lives on because God can take any form we can imagine.

While billions can share the idea of one God, the God who is imagined by each is different. Consequently, one God may unite billions but will never create one cause.

Globalization undermines the notion that the world could be united around one cause—be it democracy, equality, or human rights—that is a dream of the past. The notion of one God, by contrast, shifts with the times. The idea of God, like water, can fill any available space. Yet many think that modernity has taken up all of God's space. They advance a vision of one reality in which God is cast out of existence, leaving room only for science.

one reality

In 2013, President Obama launched the $100 million BRAIN (Brain Research through Advancing Innovative Neurotechnologies) Initiative, a scientific project to map the human brain. Francis Collins, director of the National Institutes of Health, remarked that

> the brain is the most complicated organ in the universe. We have learned a lot about other human organs. We know how the heart pumps and how the kidney does what it does . . . we have read the letters of the human genome. But the brain has 100 billion neurons. Each one of those has about 10,000 connections. So that means there's something like 1,000 trillion connections inside your brain . . . right now.[52]

Inner space appears just as deep and mysterious as outer space. As in space exploration, any advancement in brain science is naturally followed by a desire for more. For some, neuroscience will not only help to map the 100 trillion connections in your brain, it will also resolve philosophical arguments about truth, morality, and aesthetics. Colin McGinn calls these exaggerated expectations a product of "neuromania."[53]

While neuromania is far from a widespread affliction, it has affected some of the best contemporary minds. They lust for a solution to all human questions within the vast recesses of neural networks. And if their brains are big enough, these neuromaniacs hope to one day discover the source and structure of morality and meaning.

Sam Harris thinks this will happen. He believes that neuroscience along with the systematic study of what policies and behaviors lead to better "well-being" can produce a "science of morality." He asserts that

> questions about values—about meaning, morality, and life's larger purpose—are really about the well-being of conscious creatures. Values, therefore, translate into facts that can be scientifically

understood … The more we understand ourselves at the level of the brain, the more we will see that there are right and wrong answers to questions of human values.[54]

For Harris, cultural and social norms will cease to be the main determinants of how we *should* act. Science will render these norms transparent and consequently irrelevant. Harris explains that brain science has conclusively shown that "each of us is a phenomenological glockenspiel played by an unseen hand. From the perspective of your conscious mind, you are no more responsible for the next thing you think (and therefore do) than you are for the fact you were born into this world."[55]

Once Harris and other neuroscientists have scientifically identified this formerly "unseen hand" of human motivation, they can plot which triggers lead to good individual and social outcomes. The science of Harris's imagination would wipe away thousands of years of moral conflict. Harris believes he has found the means to discover not only neurological truth but also moral Truth.[56]

This is the Underground Man's greatest fear. Harris insists that the Underground Man is deluded if he thinks he can resist being a piano key, a "phenomenological glockenspiel." The Underground Man's antisocial impulses are nothing more than electrical pulses in the brain, which, in Harris's view, could be mapped and rendered predictable. Perhaps with the proper pill or cognitive training the Underground Man could be cured; he would no longer be the iconic antihero of modern literature but an endearing protagonist. Neuroscience could find a way to ensure that any future Dostoevsky can come to terms with his subversive impulses and never again create a creature such as the Underground Man. Instead, we could scientifically approve only the writings which serve human "well-being" by stimulating the morally appropriate neural connections.

Jean-Pierre Changeux similarly views ethics (along with philosophy and art) as a matter of neurobiology. The history of ideas is, for him, a history of material phenomena—amounting to nothing more than neurons firing in mechanistic fashion. As such, Changeux promises to "place the Good, the True, and the Beautiful within the characteristic features of the human brain's neuronal organization."[57]

Colin McGinn argues that Changeux has confused "the subject matter of the mental state, such as a belief, with the mental state itself."[58] Ideas about the Good, or Beauty, or Truth may be linked to specific neurological processes, but these correlations do not mean that the brain's activity and the meaning it produces are one and the same. In other words, knowing that a feeling of righteousness or a sense of Truth is tied to a neurological state does not tell us whether that feeling is morally justifiable or that idea is logically coherent.

The problem is that brain functions generate feelings and concepts that mean different things to different people. Changeux wants to say that Truth is x—a specific type of neuronal organization. Harris wants to say morality is y—a systematic and rational pursuit of well-being. They want to treat human meaning as a concrete and static object of scientific study. But as McGinn points out, "Changeux can only hope to establish his materialistic metaphysics by going beyond science. What he doesn't seem to realize is that he holds a *philosophical* position."[59] Similarly, Harris's concept of "well-being" is not a neurological state or a social outcome; it is philosophical position. One man's well-being is another man's misery—just ask the Underground Man.

Wittgenstein explains why the quest to find scientific answers to philosophical questions will always be fruitless. People discussing transcendent and moral questions can never and will never specify the concepts they utilize to the degree that scientific discourse demands. Indeed, the very spirit of such discussions centers on the fact that these topics can never be fully or precisely defined; the meaning of transcendent concepts is precisely what these discussions are about.

Consequently, imposing one's own meaning on the ideas of morality or human purpose or God is not scientific; it is simply boorish. To respectfully and productively engage in these discussions, you have to go with the creative and imaginative flow. Wittgenstein explains:

> I see now that these nonsensical expressions were not nonsensical because I had not yet found the correct expressions, but that their nonsensicality was their very essence. For all I wanted to do with them was just *to go beyond* the world and that is to say beyond significant language.[60]

For Wittgenstein, discourse concerning "reality" or "God" or "Truth" or the "Good" is scientific nonsense, not because these conversations don't elicit deep meaning, but because they cannot possibly have a shared meaning.

We cannot point to an object or phenomenon and say *that* is "reality" or "morality" or "Beauty." And if we can, then we have made the term relative to a situation or object and it therefore loses its initial intent. Words like "God" and "reality" and "good" seek to express something greater—so great as to be beyond language. We cannot talk scientifically about universal morality or Truth because we cannot define these terms universally. Neuromaniacs want to reduce these meanings to neural processes, but as Richard Rorty keenly observes, "to suggest that the mind is the brain is to suggest that we secrete theorems and symphonies as our spleen secretes dark humors."[61] We don't secrete meaning; we create it with our imaginations.

Without a doubt, neuroscience will greatly enhance our understanding of brain function and human cognition. But it will never yield what the neuromaniacs seek: a scientific understanding of art, morality, and transcendence. These are interpretive activities that exist in a never-ending state of imaginative flux.

We never fully grasp the meaning of reality because meaning keeps falling apart.

meaning falls apart

Things Fall Apart, a novel by Chinua Achebe, depicts the negative effects of globalization on a fictional Nigerian village. Set in the 1890s, Achebe's tale describes the failed efforts of local tribesmen to combat their changing culture. One villager sums up the result:

> The white man is very clever. He came quietly and peaceably with his religion. We were amused at his foolishness and allowed him to stay. Now he has won our brothers, and our clan can no longer act like one. He has put a knife on the things that held us together and we have fallen apart.

Christianity and British colonialism shattered the village's traditional morals, beliefs, and hierarchies. The very meaning of this world had fallen apart.

Modernity tends to get a bad rap. It fragments meaning and dis-enchants shared purpose. The history of globalization contains brutal instances of colonization and exploitation of poor populations. But the forces of British rule and Christian mission were not expressly intended to destroy communities. Some missionaries and colonists genuinely sought to unite the modern and premodern worlds. Seeking to create one cause, one God, or one reality is not necessarily an oppressive act.

Politicians want to unite humanity around one cause, so that we can stop bickering and work together toward a shared vision of the good society. Proselytizers want to unite humanity under one God, so that we come together in shared worship of the sacred. Neuromaniacs want to unite humanity with one reality, so that we can temper our flights of fancy with systematic efforts to discover truth.

These are noble pursuits. But as Achebe tragically illustrates, attempts to unite also tend to destroy. Modernity has diversified human purpose. Sacred canopies have been shredded. Ultimate reality comes down to individual perspective. Life's meaning continually splinters, fall-ing apart, only to be momentarily repackaged to the specifications of each age and each individual.

The modern ethos of individuality has come to dominate the con-struction of life's meaning. Robert Wuthnow explains:

> Individuality focuses on the moral responsibility of the individual toward his or her own self . . . The result . . . is a tendency to become preoccupied with relations purely within the self and therefore to become withdrawn from public roles (i.e., from moral relation-ships with other individuals).[62]

Individuality makes purpose a personal choice. Purpose was always a choice, but the idea that life's meaning is consciously invented came with modernity. Now the onus of finding a purpose is on our shoulders.[63]

One does not need the permission of the state or the church, or even the authority of science to discover a purpose. All that is required is the freedom and the will to self-explore. If self-exploration goes as planned, seekers will find a good within themselves and be rewarded with an enchanted self. Our ability to create meaning and self-enchantment will not be drowned out by the drone of ideological repression, the cacophony of religious pluralism, or even the buzz of neurobiology. Our instinct to choose, empathize, narrate, and fantasize impels us to continually imagine new meanings and purposes.

Are humans really all that creative? Doesn't the modern postindustrial man just return from work, suppress his existential angst, and turn on the television? In his predictably humdrum behavior, he resembles a drone, a sheep, a piano key. But even while watching mindless television, the proverbial couch potato is reflexively inventing life's meaning, in sleepy daydreams and lazy fantasies. He is gently exercising his involuntary urge to break the crusts of convention. He may be a non-achiever lacking any guiding purpose or creative flare, but he is not a piano key. Sitting on his ugly sofa, drinking his flat beer, and watching his monotonous program, he can still imagine.

This is what makes the future of human purpose unknowable. Who can predict what I or you or the couch potato or Achebe's villagers will think or do next? Not the politician, nor the priest, nor the scientist. Some think they can, but as Wittgenstein noted:

> When we think about the future of the world, we always have in mind its being at the place where it would be if it continued to move as we see it moving now. We do not realize that it moves not in a straight line, but in a curve, and that its direction constantly changes.[64]

Human imagination curves the future in unimaginable directions. Meanings continually fall apart. While this can be destructive and produce conflict, it also provides space for new causes, new Gods, and new realities.

We need not despair at the fragility of life's meaning, because we will always imagine new purposes.

the art of purpose

Imagination makes inner and social harmony possible but implausible. We imagine shared ideals, which become the basis for collective achievement. But imagination also subverts convention, becoming a source of conflict in both society and the self. Imagination builds and destroys life's meaning with equal fervor.

Richard Rorty describes these competing tendencies as the driving force in the history of ideas. He notes consistent and undulating shifts between building and destroying philosophies:

> Great systematic philosophers, like great scientists, build for eternity. Great edifying philosophers destroy for the sake of their own generation. Systematic philosophers want to put their subject on the secure path of a science. Edifying philosophers want to keep space open for the sense of wonder which poets can sometimes cause—wonder that there is something new under the sun.[65]

The history of ideas is the continuing saga of builders versus destroyers. Both require imagination but seek different purposes. Both tendencies lie deep within each of us.

Still, individuals favor one tendency over the other. Many people yearn for clear moral order. They hope to systematize their sense of purpose with traditional modes of thinking, established moral codes, and popular narratives. They become True believers, because they have found a time-honored religion or philosophy in which to have faith.

Rorty notes that "when we have justified true belief about everything we want to know, we may have no more than conformity to the norms of the day."[66] This is one of the consequences of Truth. It requires moral conformity; there can be no breaking of conventional crusts once the True purpose of life is found. Ideological conviction, religious faith, and moral certitude all restrict one's imagination to a singular form of Truth. This does not make a True believer any less imaginative or creative, but it limits her to distinct vocabularies, theological structures, and moral concepts. But within the confines of Truth, the believer can more easily imagine the possibility of one cause, one God, or one reality. By living according to a systematic philosophy, believers in Truth are building for eternity.

Others reject the moral restrictions of Truth and seek to establish their own moral meanings. They are leery of traditional modes of thinking, established moral codes, and popular narratives. Instead, they *feel* drawn to rebellion, art, and deviance, and they destroy systematic meanings in pursuit of something new. Their imagination is turned loose in ways that are taboo to believers in Truth. Yet those seeking a new philosophy of life must pay a price for their nonconformity. Swimming against the social currents places their inner and social harmony in constant peril. Without Truth, it is hard to gain sight of and confidence in life's purpose.

Because we are all builders *and* destroyers to some extent, the True believer and the nihilist both live in tension with themselves and their society. The believer will sometimes doubt Truth, ensuring that no cause, God, or reality is immune to suspicion. And the nihilist will sometimes feel the reality of goodness, ensuring that moral order persists in even the most desolate of philosophical landscapes. Each possesses the imaginative capacity of the other, and for that reason the meaning of their lives will never be one-dimensional. They will invent images of moral transcendence alongside images of moral emptiness.

In order to make life tolerable (as Durkheim put it), you have to keep the devil down in the hole (as Saul put it). The devil is meaninglessness. Without meaning, there is no morality and no purpose to life. Thankfully, we create meaning without breaking a sweat. Humans have evolved this most impressive talent—we can imagine a meaningful self, a meaningful life, and a meaningful universe. The imaginative process that creates this meaning is no different from the artistic process that creates great literature.

Literature requires the imagining of a complete fictional world. Michael Chabon explains that as writers

> the most we can hope to accomplish with our handful of salvaged bits—the bittersweet harvest of observation and experience—is to build a little world of our own. A scale model of that mysterious original, unbroken and half-remembered . . . We call these scale models "works of art."[67]

In imagining a meaning of life, we are harvesting bits of observation and experience to build a little world of our own. It is the process by which everybody builds a model of what they want their life to be; the model draws on the salvaged bits of what's available (the images of God, the philosophical concepts, the moral codes, and the popular narratives). While we may copy others, follow collective style laws, obey cultural cues, voice moral platitudes, and never question Truth, our life's meaning remains a singular, personal, and artistic creation. It is a work of art because it is wholly imagined.

We imagine it within certain guidelines—we are guided by the popularity of certain Truths, the sway of cultural rhythms, and basic norms of self. While no one can ever escape these social forces, each person bends them in her own way to imagine an entirely unique life purpose.

8

the moral

Salvation is a matter of social planning.

Will Self[1]

Now that you have reached the end (of this book, not your life), you probably want something to tie it all together.[2] I still can't tell you the meaning of life, but I can tell you about the meaning of this book.

Stated simply, your purpose is whatever you believe it to be. Every person has the power to imagine a unique life purpose. The possibilities are limitless—in theory. But, in practice, we are limited by material realities. We don't enjoy the same opportunities. Our economic inequalities lead to inequalities of purpose—the more money you have, the more options you have. We are also dependent on our friends and family; they tell us who we should be and what we should do. That tension—between seemingly unlimited internal possibilities and carefully constrained external realities—is at the heart of the way people find their purpose in life, and thus at the heart of this book.

For some, that tension evaporates and the result is wondrous; they easily imagine a purpose-filled life because they are embedded within a community and culture that makes them feel significant. Others are not so fortunate; they find themselves in situations where they are unable to feel significant, and their existence begins to seem directionless and meaningless.

In *The Quantity Theory of Insanity*, Will Self describes a fictional psychologist who discovers that "salvation is a matter of social planning."

The doctor realizes that mental disturbance is a finite quantity distributed across populations. As such, mental health becomes a function of geographically balancing the ratios of healthy to disturbed people. To stabilize low levels of psychic distress, the health department needs only to keep the proper ratios in each location—it is a matter of social planning.

This may sound absurd, but it rings morally true to me. Salvation *is* a matter of social planning. Salvation, in general, is finding one's moral significance and avoiding the abyss of meaninglessness; the specifics depend on your social context. Whether our moral imaginations can achieve salvation is inextricably tied to our place in history, our position in a community, our cultural tempo, and the cruel and calculated assessments others ascribe to our sense of self.[3]

Because we can never fully control these social forces, we cannot plan our own salvation. Instead, salvation appears to be the product of social planning or—if no hidden hand or omnipotent health department is guiding us—salvation is simply a matter of luck. You find yourself in a social context that saves you from meaninglessness and despair—your existential fortune is determined by a roll of the dice.

Fate smiles upon some, offering an abundance of self-esteem and achievable goals. It sneers at others, yielding only heartbreak and disappointment. While social forces can crush the strongest of spirits, they never fully define us. We always retain the ability to create meaning in the world—even when the fates are at their cruelest.

Maya Angelou grew up in a time and a place where to be an African American female was to be considered less than human. She suffered sexual abuse. Eventually, she stopped speaking—muteness seemed an appropriate response to the cruelty she was forced to endure. But she ventured back into dialogue with others and discovered a grander purpose to her life in literature and art. The title of her autobiography, *I Know Why the Caged Bird Sings*, comes from a poem by Paul Laurence Dunbar, which reads in part:

> *I know why the caged bird sings, ah me,*
>
> *When his wing is bruised and his bosom sore,—*
>
> *When he beats his bars and he would be free;*
>
> *It is not a carol of joy or glee,*

But a prayer that he sends from his heart's deep core,

But a plea, that upward to Heaven he flings—

I know why the caged bird sings![4]

Deep in our heart's core is the ability to create something—a vision, a prayer, a song. Maya Angelou was a caged bird who created a meaningful life by speaking, writing, and singing; she found a purpose that helped her to transcend her many trials.

While we don't all have Angelou's genius, we do have the ability to create meaning amid the trials of life. It is in our nature to attribute meaning to our every experience in the world. We imbue mundane, everyday situations with a momentary purpose and routinely invest considerable time and effort in pursuit of long-term purposes. Most remarkably, we create meaning out of abstractions, like love, Truth, beauty, God, and life. To do so is uniquely human.

Life is a big concept; to grasp it, you must imagine the scope of your existence, posit your death, and weave your many selves into a single moral narrative. A seahorse can't do that. Consequently, the seahorse does not perceive her life as meaningful. Perhaps the singing bird does, because she creates a pattern of communication—the very essence of meaning. But humans directly articulate the meaning of life *itself,* in rich and diverse ways that reveal an imaginative genius dwelling within each of us. Think of the creative virtuosity we require to not only give life meaning, but also give purpose to the seahorse, the bird, the ocean, even the universe. And it all comes quite naturally to us.

We envision a meaningful universe as naturally as the flower blooms. And like a seed, our imagination blossoms or wilts depending on the ground in which it grows. History, culture, community, and language provide the soil from which our minds cultivate meaning. This book explores these soils and their various properties. I hope I have demonstrated how society is like a plot of soil in which we try to grow meaningful lives; it nourishes some and deprives others. Luckily, even in the most desolate grounds, our imagination retains its ability to create meaning, allowing the human spirit to flourish.

This, I imagine, is the moral of this story.

Acknowledgments

Was there ever a time you thought—I am

doing this on purpose, I am fucking up and

I don't know why.

A. M. Homes, from May We Be Forgiven

There were countless times while writing this book that I thought, I am doing this on purpose, I am committing years to a futile project and I don't know why. Historian Edward Blum consoled me with the idea that perhaps we *all* need to try and "fail bigger."

My sincerest thanks to:

Theo Calderara: *You were way too hard on me . . . and I really appreciate it.*

Jeff Streber: *You were my steadfast audience . . . and also came up with the idea of a chapter about time. Nice.*

Chris Pieper: *You prevented me from losing confidence . . . in my text and self.*

Roque Ruggero: *You offered me a new perspective . . . and good times.*

Menno and Margaret Froese, and Jack Carr: *You happily read . . . my miserable drafts.*

Rodney Stark, Daniel Chirot, Steven Pfaff, John Mohan, F. Carson Mencken, Charlie Tolbert, James Davidson Hunter, Byron Johnson, and Daniil Kharms: *You helped make this book possible; I owe you much . . . but I am a little light on cash right now.*

Notes

Chapter 1

1. Durkheim, Emile. 1951. *Suicide: A Study in Sociology*. Translated by John A. Spaulding and George Simpson. New York: Free Press, 37.
2. Baylor Religion Survey, Wave 3. See http://www.thearda.com for codebooks and data.
3. Bracke, Piet, Kevin Bruynooghe, and Mieke Verhaeghe. 2006. "Boredom During Day Activity Programs in Rehabilitation Centers." *Sociological Perspectives* 49 (2): 191–215.
4. Barrett, William. 1975. "Liebnitz's Garden: Some Philosophical Observations on Boredom." *Social Research* 42 (3): 551–555.
5. O'Keeffe, Georgia. 1977. *Georgia O'Keeffe*. New York: Penguin Books, 47.
6. Damon explains, "A purpose is the reason behind the immediate goals and motives that drive most of our daily behavior." Damon, William. 2008. *The Path to Purpose: Helping Our Children Find Their Calling in Life*. New York: Free Press, 33.
7. Ibid., 34.
8. Seligman, Martin. 2011. *Flourish*. New York: Free Press, 12.
9. Taylor, Charles. 2007. *A Secular Age*. London: Belknap Press of Harvard University Press.
10. Baylor Religion Survey, Wave 4.
11. Baylor Religion Survey, Wave 3.
12. Happy people are more likely to say they know their purpose. But the causal direction of this relationship is unclear—does purpose make you happy or do happy people more easily imagine a purposeful life? I take up the confounding relationship between happiness and purpose in the next chapter.

    Also, parents and married couples are all more likely to say they know their purpose. Love is a deep emotional attachment to something bigger than oneself. Many people express their life's purpose as a love of God, community, family, friends, and humanity.

Stephen Hawking, one of the most famous living scientists and a man dedicated to advancing human knowledge, has a lot to live for and a lot to give. But when asked directly about his life, he simply stated, "Falling in love gave me something to live for." Intimate and positive relationships can give life meaning like nothing else. Is love all you need?

13. Fankl called this the "will to meaning," arguing that the quest for a moral purpose was the "primary motivation in life." Frankl, Victor. 1959. *Man's Search for Meaning*. Boston: Beacon Press.

14. De Botton, Alain. 2012. *Religion for Atheists*. New York: Random House.

15. Religious confidence can be personally fulfilling, but it can also breed social intolerance and conflict. Having a commitment of faith requires eschewing other options.

16. Baylor Religion Survey estimates from Waves 1, 2, and 3.

17. See Zuckerman, Phil. 2014. *Living the Secular Life: New Answers to Old Questions*. New York: Penguin Press.

18. Jackson, Phil. 2013. *Eleven Rings: The Soul of Success*. New York: Penguin, 12.

19. Spence, Roy M. 2009. *It's Not What You Sell, It's What You Stand For: Why Extraordinary Business Is Driven by Purpose*. New York: Portfolio, 9–10.

20. Einstein, Albert. 2013 [1949]. *The World As I See It*. New York: Important Books.

21. Stephen Vaisey argues that our gut reaction moral sensibilities reflect our moral ideology, even if we cannot clearly articulate our worldview. See Vaisey, Stephen. 2009. "Motivation and Justification: A Dual-Process Model of Culture in Action." *American Journal of Sociology* 114 (6): 1675–1715. This suggests that one's moral culture is deeply embedded in how we perceive the world. People might not be able to precisely define "good" or "evil," but they know it when they see it.

22. Oprah Winfrey sees her media empire as "an offering" to the public; she explains that "if you want to be more fully present and live your life with a wide-open heart, this [the Oprah Winfrey Network] is the place to come. I'm trying to raise consciousness in snackable bites." "Walter Scott's Personality Parade." *The Austin-American Statesman*. May 11, 2014.

23. Warren, Rick. 2002. *The Purpose-Driven Life: What on Earth Am I Here For?* Grand Rapids, MI: Zondervan, 9.

24. Ibid., 10.

25. Smith, Christian. 1998. *American Evangelicalism: Embattled and Thriving.* Chicago, IL: University of Chicago Press

26. Robbins, Anthony. 1992. *Awaken the Giant Within.* New York: Free Press, 22.

27. Ibid.

28. Covey, Stephen R. 2004. *The 7 Habits of Highly Effective People: Powerful Lessons in Personal Change.* New York: Free Press, 42.

29. See Reker, Gary T. 1997. "Personal Meaning, Optimism, and Choice: Existential Predictors of Depression in Community and Institutional Elderly." *The Gerontologist* 37: 709–16; Krause, N. 2003. "Religious Meaning and Subjective Well-Being in Late Life." *The Journals of Gerontology: Series B* 58: S160; Mascaro, Nathan, and David H. Rosen. 2006. "The Role of Existential Meaning as a Buffer Against Stress." *Journal of Humanistic Psychology* 46: 168–190; Steger, Michael F., and Patricia Frazier. 2005. "Meaning in Life: One Link in the Chain from Religiousness to Well-Being." *Journal of Counseling Psychology* 52: 574–582; Krause, N. 2004. "Stressors Arising in Highly Valued Roles, Meaning in Life, and the Physical Health Status of Older Adults." *The Journals of Gerontology Series B: Psychological Sciences and Social Sciences* 59: S287; Park, Crystal L., Marc R. Malone, D. P. Suresh, D. Bliss, and Rivkah I. Rosen. 2007. "Coping, Meaning in Life, and Quality of Life in Congestive Heart Failure Patients." *Quality of Life Research* 17: 21–26; Smith, Bruce W., and Alex J. Zautra. 2004. "The Role of Purpose in Life in Recovery from Knee Surgery." *International Journal of Behavioral Medicine* 11: 197–202; Reker, Gary T. 2000. *Exploring Existential Meaning: Optimizing Human Development across the Life Span.* Pp. 39–55. Thousand Oaks, CA: Sage Publications.

30. In one extensive study, Crystal L. Park shows that individuals without purpose will be more likely to engage in self-destructive behavior. See Park, Crystal L. 2007. "Religiousness/Spirituality and Health: A Meaning Systems Perspective." Journal of Behavioral Medicine 30: 319–328.

31. For instance, Salovey, Detweiler, and Steward (2000) demonstrate that a sense of purpose indicates better immune system functioning.

See Peter Salovey, Alexander J. Rothman, Jerusha B. Detweiler, and Wayne T. Steward. 2000. "Emotional States and Physical Health." *American Psychologist* 55:110–121.

32. http://www.stevepavlina.com/blog/

33. It is impossible to get a representative sample with such a small number, but I attempted to diversify my sample by race, gender, and religious type. Ten of the respondents were men, and 15 were women. Thirteen respondents were white, 6 were Hispanic, 5 were African-American, and 1 was Asian-American. Fifteen respondents were Christian, 5 were spiritual but not religious, and 5 were not religious or spiritual.

34. Simmel, Georg. 1997. "Contributions to Epistemology of Religion." In *Essays on Religion*. Edited by Hosrt Jurgen Helle and Ludwig Nieder. New Haven, CT: Yale University Press, 131.

35. There are stories of spontaneous epiphanies. For instance, Brian Nichols, escaped from police custody by killing 3 people. He took refuge in a local home and kept the resident, Ashley Smith, hostage. During her time with Nichols, Ms. Smith read to him Warren's *Purpose Driven Life*. The book resonated with Nichols and he eventually gave himself peacefully over to authorities. I wouldn't deny the validity or power of this story but merely point out that it is a highly unusual case and doesn't represent the norm.

36. Mitchell, David. 2004. *Cloud Atlas*. New York: Random House.

37. Lofland, John, and Rodney Stark. 1965. "Becoming a World-Saver: A Theory of Conversion to a Deviant Perspective." *American Sociological Review* 30: 862–875.

38. Lindhout, Amanda, and Sara Corbett. 2013. *A House in the Sky*. New York: Scribner, 291.

39. Mourkogiannis, Nikos. 2006. *Purpose: The Starting Point of Great Companies*. New York: Palgrave MacMillan, 6.

40. What is interesting about Mourkogiannis's perspective is that it begins with the assumption that "wealth creation and success" are universally accepted values. It also assumes that the market will naturally reward businesses that behave morally, that is, with a purpose. Mourkogiannis never questions the morality of capitalism but rather overlays it with an ethic about how individual businesses *should* treat each other and give back to society. Individuals who

think that capitalism is inherently corrupt simply inhabit a different moral universe than Mourkogiannis. For them, his words are mere sounds and inscriptions.

41. Weber, Max. 1946. "The Social Psychology of the World Religions." In *From Max Weber: Essays in Sociology*. Translated by H. H. Gerth and C. Wright Mills. New York: Oxford University Press.

Chapter 2

1. Krause, N. 2003. "Religious Meaning and Subjective Well-being in Late Life." *The Journals of Gerontology: Series B* 58:S160.
   Krause, N. 2004. "Stressors Arising in Highly Valued Roles, Meaning in Life, and the Physical Health Status of Older Adults." *The Journals of Gerontology Series B: Psychological Sciences and Social Sciences* 59:S287.
   Mascaro, Nathan, and David H. Rosen. 2006. "The Role of Existential Meaning as a Buffer Against Stress." *Journal of Humanistic Psychology* 46:168–190.
   Park, Crystal L. 2007. "Religiousness/Spirituality and Health: A Meaning Systems Perspective." *Journal of Behavioral Medicine* 30:319–328.
   Park, Crystal L., Marc R. Malone, D. P. Suresh, D. Bliss, and Rivkah I. Rosen. 2007. "Coping, Meaning in Life, and Quality of Life in Congestive Heart Failure Patients." *Quality of Life Research* 17:21–26.
   Reker, Gary T. 1997. "Personal Meaning, Optimism, and Choice: Existential Predictors of Depression in Community and Institutional Elderly." *The Gerontologist* 37:709–716.
   Reker, Gary T. 2000. "Theoretical Perspective, Dimensions, and Measurement of Existential Meaning." In *Exploring Existential Meaning: Optimizing Human Development across the Life Span*. Thousand Oaks, CA: Sage Publications
   Salovey, Peter, Alexander J. Rothman, Jerusha B. Detweiler, and Wayne T. Steward. 2000. "Emotional States and Physical Health." *American Psychologist* 55:110–121.
   Smith, Bruce W., and Alex J. Zautra. 2004. "The Role of Purpose in Life in Recovery from Knee Surgery." *International Journal of Behavioral Medicine* 11:197–202.

Steger, Michael F., and Patricia Frazier. 2005. "Meaning in Life: One Link in the Chain From Religiousness to Well-Being." *Journal of Counseling Psychology* 52:574–582.

2. According to the Baylor Religion Survey, Wave 4, Americans who say that they are "searching for purpose" are significantly less happy than other Americans regardless of their income, education, gender, race, political party, or religious affiliation.

3. Gilbert, Daniel. 2006. *Stumbling on Happiness.* New York: Knopf.

4. In fact, this quote alone is ubiquitous on spiritual and humanistic websites.

5. http://www.aceswebworld.com/classics_dostoyevsky.html

6. Smith, Christian. 2003. *Moral, Believing Animals: Human Personhood and Culture.* New York: Oxford University Press.

7. Max Weber provides the most inclusive micro-foundations of sociology, indicating the humans are a) rational egoists, b) value rational, c) emotional, and d) habitual in their behaviors. For Weber, all four tendencies are at work in every action, but one of these ideal types of action plays a larger role depending on the circumstance.

8. The moral and emotional importance of family, friends, and community is universal. What becomes sociologically interesting is how these personal relationships guide and influence the myriad ways that individuals articulate specific life objectives.

9. Contemporary psychological research appears to support this claim, in so much as it links mental health to purposefulness. The growing field of positive psychology reveals that optimism and contentment are obtainable goals that depend on a clear sense of purpose. In turn, the concept of "depressive realism" proposes that people with more realistic perceptions of their relationships, their abilities, and life's possibilities tend to be clinically depressed.

10. Salinger, J. D. 1955. *Franny and Zooey.* Boston: Little, Brown, and Company, 29.

11. Economists built complex mathematical models based on Smith's suggestion of a universal tendency toward egoism. This basic assumption has been refined and developed into what is called rational choice theory, and applied successfully to the study of far-reaching topics from the purchasing of cars to the selection of churches.

12. Smith, Adam. 1976. *The Wealth of Nations.* In *The Glasgow Edition of the Works and Correspondence of Adam Smith.* Edited by R. H. Campbell and A. S. Skinner. vol. 2a, 456.

13. Mill, John Stuart. "On the Definition of Political Economy, and On the Method of Investigation Proper to It." *London and Westminster Review.* October 1836. *Essays on Some Unsettled Questions of Political Economy,* 2nd ed. London: Longmans, Green, Reader and Dyer, 1874.

14. Along with technologies used to create comfort, we also tend to create technologies that can impose incredible suffering. For instance, Daniel Chirot and Clark McCauley (2006) argue that the motivations for mass killing and genocide are ancient, but it is the tools of modernity which have allowed them to occur on scales never before imagined.

15. Wilkinson, Richard, and Kate Pickett. 2009. *The Spirit Level: Why Greater Equality Makes Societies Stronger.* New York: Bloomsbury Press, 8.

16. De Botton, Alain. 2004. *Status Anxiety.* New York: Vintage Books, 25–26.

17. Relative deprivation refers to the feeling of being less well-off in comparison to our immediate acquaintances. Consequently, an objectively wealthy man can *feel* poor if his neighbors and friends have more wealth. See Walker, Iain, and Heather J. Smith. 2001. *Relative Deprivation: Specification, Development, and Integration.* New York: Cambridge University Press.

18. See Whitters, W. L., and P. Jones-Whitter. 1980. *Human Sexuality—A Biological Perspective.* New York: Van Nostrand.

19. Thankfully, humans have never been subjected to the pleasure center experiment performed on rats. But in the movie *Sleeper,* Woody Allen envisions a future with machines that can provide users with orgasms—they are called "orgasmatrons." Mr. Allen emerges from the orgasmatron clearly exhausted, yet alive.

20. Mill, John Stuart. 2002. *Utilitarianism.* Edited by George Sher. New York: Hackett Publishing.

21. Collins, Randall. 2004. *Interaction Ritual Chains.* Princeton, NJ: Princeton University Press, 109.

22. Davidson, Adam. "Are the Rich Worth a Damn?" *The New York Times Magazine.* May 6, 2012, 38.

23. Smith, Christian. 2003. *Moral, Believing Animals: Human Personhood and Culture.* New York: Oxford University Press, 120.

24. McCoid, Catherine, and LeRoy McDermott. 1996. "Self-Representation in Upper Paleolithic Female Figurines." *Current Anthropology* 37(2): 227–275.

25. The *Oxford Dictionary of Philosophy* explains that "a topic of question is transcendental if its resolution is not purely a matter of logic or mathematics, and also lies beyond the scope both of sense experience and of the proper use of theory answerable to sense experience" (380). Within the context of sociological theory, both Durkheim's sense of "the sacred" and Randall Collins's concept of "macroreality" are ways to describe how humans naturally invent a transcendent realm. In the case of macroreality, it is how we imagine a larger social realm which cannot ever be perceived or measured directly.

26. Shryock, Andrew, and Daniel Lord Smail. 2011. *Deep History: The Architecture of Past and Present*. Berkeley: University of California Press, 47.

27. Quoted in Wiley, Norbert. 1994. *The Semiotic Self*. Chicago: University of Chicago Press, 113.

28. Tremlin, Todd. 2006. *Minds and Gods: The Cognitive Foundations of Religion*. New York: Oxford University Press, 75. Tremlin explains that "the two most important of these mental tools are the Agency Detection Devices (ADD), which recognizes the presence and activities of other beings around us, and the Theory of Mind Mechanism (ToMM), which ascribes sentience to agents and tries to interpret their intentions" and indicates that "attention to cognition accounts both for the striking *similarities* of gods found around the world and why these kinds of gods are so easily—so *naturally*—rendered by the types of minds that all humans possess."

29. This speaks to a side-bar issue of whether science proves atheism. The "new atheists" of the twenty-first century have updated this intellectual tradition but want to get rid of the term altogether. Their arguments rely less on untangling the logic of theology and more on the findings of contemporary science combined with a social theory positing "religion" as the source of most social ills. It is what philosopher A. C. Grayling has called the "triumph of physics over metaphysics." So what does physics tell us about the meaning of life? In *A Universe from Nothing* and other writings, physicist Lawrence Krauss attempts to demonstrate that scientifically valid descriptions of the creation of the universe do not require a "creator." In the book's afterword, evolutionary biologist Richard Dawkins forewarns that Krauss's "title means exactly what it says. And what it says is devastating." Presumably for Dawkins, it devastates the foundations all religious belief systems.

Stephen Hawking agrees. In his most recent book *The Grand Design,* which is intended to explicate the current state of theoretical physics for a popular audience, Hawking asserts that questions about the existence of the universe can be sufficiently answered "without invoking any divine beings." Statements such of this by prominent scientists have refueled the age-old fear that science kills off religion.

So maybe science will replace God as a source of meaning.

Sam Harris, author of *The Moral Landscape: How Science Can Determine Human Values,* thinks so and posits that the scientific method is capable of not only uncovering the mysteries of the universe but also constructing the moral systems which guide and inform our lives. For Harris, relinquishing religious faith is a necessary step in coming to realize a better morality, one based in science.

Sam Harris outlines the basic argument for a "science of morality" in *Moral Landscape: How Science Can Determine Human Values.* Harris asserts that "the moment we admit that we know anything about human well-being scientifically, we must admit that certain individuals or cultures can be absolutely wrong about it." While Harris's argument is not philosophically new, his achievement in book sales and, by inference, his influence is.

So there we have it. Prominent scientists in physics and biology assure us that their theories do not require gods. And cognitive scientists tell us that we are all evolutionarily predisposed to believe in gods. While these two claims are logically compatible, they create a dilemma for those few scientists convinced that we need move past religion. You can argue with theologians and moral philosophers but you cannot argue with genetics.

In fact, given what the cognitive scientists say, those who have given up conventional concepts of gods are simply prone to replace them with something equally faith-based—whether they call it "God" or "Science" or some other such transcendent abstraction.

30. A documentary by Werner Herzog, titled *Cave of Forgotten Dreams,* provides access to some of these paintings. The fact that many were painted in areas of the cave with no natural light and attempt to re-create motion in their affects suggests that early people sought out imaginative experiences which not only re-created their daily lives but enhanced and exaggerated them to produce heightened feeling

of terror or excitement or respect. This has led some to assume that these painting were used in ritual activities of worship.

31. Bellah, Robert. 2011. *Religion in Human Evolution: From the Paleolithic to the Axial Age.* Cambridge, MA: Harvard University Press, xiv.

32. Ernest Becker, author of *The Denial of Death*, argues that Freud and his followers noted the importance of the "death instinct" but became too focused on the psychological centrality of sexual repression. Becker thought that it was really our attempts to avoid thinking about death, mortality, and meaninglessness which drove our daily routines and machinations. While sexual frustration and fantasy are certainly fascinating topics, they are just one more way to divert attention from the horror that looms over us all. Becker believed that "those who speculate that a full apprehension of man's condition would drive him insane are right, quite literally right."

33. Sapolsky, David. 2004. *Why Zebras Don't Get Ulcers.* New York: St. Martin's Press, 6.

34. Campbell, Joseph. 1988. *The Power of Myth.* New York: Doubleday.

35. Examples are everywhere. Isaiah 26:4 declares, "Trust in the Lord forever, for the Lord God is an everlasting rock" (Isaiah 26:4). The Quran (2:255) proclaims, "There is no god but [Allah], the Living, the self-subsisting, the eternal." Religious doctrine is the definitive *higher purpose* because it seeks to explain not just your purpose but everyone's and everything's for all eternity. This is mainly done through the idea that existence and morality have a singular transcendent source—an eternal and transcendent force which thinks and judges—in other words, "God." Monotheists of all ilks assert that God *is* and *will be* regardless of circumstance; this is as transcendent as it gets. They tell us what we *should* do, what *everybody* should do. Higher purposes often contain an assertion of moral universality. *All* mothers should be like this. *All* Muslims should worship Allah this way. This is not just *my* purpose; it should be everyone's.

36. Stark, Rodney. 2007. *Discovering God: The Origins of the Great Religions and the Evolution of Belief.* New York: Harper One, 10–11.

37. Ibid.

38. Stark, Rodney. 2001. *One True God: Historical Consequences of Monotheism.* Princeton: Princeton University Press.

39. Nietzsche, Friedrich. 1974. *The Gay Science.* Translated by Walter Kaufmann. New York: Vintage, 328.

40. Ibid., 283.

41. Wilson, James Q. 1993. *The Moral Sense.* New York: Free Press, 225.

42. For instance, Enlightenment philosophers and thinkers tended to be fond of secularized versions of absolutes. John Locke spoke of the "laws of nature" as the substance of cosmic structure which not only defined the effects of gravity but also moral and social ideals. He argued, "We should not obey a king just out of fear . . . but because the law of nature decrees that princes and a lawmaker, or a superior by whatever name you call him, should be obeyed." (John Locke 1663–64, 120). One hundred and fifty years later, Thomas Jefferson wrote, "I believe . . . that [justice] is instinct and innate, that the moral sense is as much a part of our constitution as that of feeling, seeing, or hearing."—Thomas Jefferson to John Adams, 1816. While Locke and Jefferson still talk about God, their descriptions of transcendence rely much more heavily on logical argumentation and secular language than the revelations of scripture. This indicates that transcendence doesn't necessarily need to tie itself to the supernatural to assert absolutist ideas about individual morality, political justice, and social order.

43. See Turner, James. 1986. *Without God, Without Creed: The Origins of Unbelief in America.* Baltimore: Johns Hopkins University Press. Also see Baker, Joseph, and Buster Smith. Forthcoming. *American Secularism.* New York: New York University Press.

44. Sam Harris, a neuroscientist and a leading voice in the "New Atheism" movement asserts that *only* secular modern science can establish moral law. Harris is offended that religious traditions assert codes of morality while claiming to be beyond empirical critique. Harris makes a good point about how religions tend to impose their sacred on everyone else, but he mimics the philosophical absolutism of religion in his demand for no religion. Scientific atheism is a term used by the Soviets to describe their philosophy of religion, and I am not calling Harris a communist. But if you do read the main writings of Soviet-accepted thinkers on the topic of morality and religion, they sound strikingly similar to Harris. Again, this has absolutely no implications concerning the possibility that their science of morality could one day be real science. But it is undeniably a bold claim.

45. Weber, Max. 1946. "The Social Psychology of the World Religions." In *From Max Weber: Essays in Sociology.* Translated by H. H. Gerth and C. Wright Mills. New York: Oxford University Press.

46. Bragg, Billy. 2013. "No One Knows Nothing Anymore." *Tooth & Nail.* Sony/ATV Music.

47. Blackburn, Simon. 1994. *The Oxford Dictionary of Philosophy.* Oxford: Oxford University Press, 235.

48. Lederman, Leon, and Dick Teresi. 2006. *The God Particle: If the Universe Is the Answer What Is the Question?* New York: Mariner Books, 22.

49. The word "God" explodes with meaning, the kind of meaning which reaches deep into our creative reserves and challenges our imagination to picture transcendence. It evokes feelings of awe for many, disgust in a few, and indifference from a few more.

50. It also blessed them with a Nobel Prize.

51. Berger, Peter. 2014. *The Many Altars of Modernity: Religion and Secularity in a Pluralist Age.* New York: De Gruyter Mouton.

52. Scorsese, Martin. 2013. "The Persisting Vision: Reading the Language of Cinema." *The New York Review of Books.* 15.

Chapter 3

1. Turgenev, Ivan. 1959. *Fathers and Sons.* New York: Bantam, 98.

2. Ibid., "Introduction" by Alexandra Tolstoy. New York: Bantam, vii.

3. May, Rollo. 1953. *Man's Search for Himself.* New York: W. W. Norton, 4.

4. Michalski, Krzysztof. 2012. *The Flame of Eternity: An Interpretation of Nietzsche's Thought.* Princeton, New Jersey: Princeton University Press, 3.

5. Durkheim, Emile. 1897 [1951]. *Suicide: A Study in Sociology.* Glencoe, IL: Free Press.

6. If people say their life has no meaning it suggests that society no longer provides the values, the sacred obligations, and the social bonds which give life its purpose.

7. Haybron, Daniel. 2008. *The Pursuit of Unhappiness: The Elusive Psychology of Well-Being.* New York: Oxford University Press, 34.

8. Wallace, David Foster. 2009. *This is Water: Some Thoughts, Delivered on a Significant Occasion, about Living a Compassionate Life.* New York: Little, Brown, and Company, 3–4.

9. Berger utilizes the phrase "taken for granted" to great effect in his brilliant work *The Sacred Canopy*; while the phrase is certainly

cumbersome it evokes the meaning of the concept perfectly. Which is, something is taken-for-granted when it so seamlessly blends with its surrounds that its impression is ignored utterly by consciousness. This describes the extent to which Berger argues that religion was and is "taken for granted" in some cultures; if you questioned the faith, people would just look at you quizzically as if you randomly said, "7 render pre."

10. Boswell, James. 1986. *The Life of Samuel Johnson*. Edited by Christopher Hibbert. New York: Penguin Classics.

11. Berger, Peter. 1967. *The Sacred Canopy: Elements of a Sociological Theory of Religion*. New York: Doubleday, 55.

12. Political scientists Pippa Norris and Ronald Ingelhart offer a reason why modernity undermines core values. They argue that "the experiences of growing up in less secure societies will heighten the importance of religious values, while conversely experience of more secure conditions will lessen it." For them, individuals in dire situations tend to have strong religious faiths.

13. The Gallup Organization details the methodology of its World Poll at http://www.gallup.com/poll/105226/world-poll-methodology.aspx.

14. See http://www.gallup.com/poll/105226/world-poll-methodology.aspx.

15. The Gallup World Poll is a valuable and laudable achievement, but I must note some foreseeable weaknesses. First and foremost, cross-cultural survey data are rife with complications. How can we ever be sure that people from vastly different cultures understand questions similarly? An African tribesman on the savannah is going to understand the meaning of "fairness" or "time" or "satisfaction" differently than, say, a German banker. The process of translating questions into dozens of languages is a fathomless brainteaser, but I trust the Gallup Organization did as good a job as any. This makes the task of the statistician more challenging but potentially more inspired as she ponders the unsolvable riddles of cross-cultural surveys. In fact, the remainder of this chapter grapples with why the data look as they do.

16. I present cross-sectional data. This is unproblematic except for the fact that the issues under discussion are longitudinal. In other words, the effects of modernity are theorized to occur over decades if not centuries. This is a historical phenomenon, yet I begin with a

snapshot of one moment in time. Other studies of modernization have employed a cross-sectional approach. Although this is not ideal, comparing preindustrial, industrial, and postindustrial nations today allows us to guess at the various ramifications of transitioning through these different stages. One can only "guess" because modernization most definitely happened differently in preceding eras.

17. Gallup World Poll indexes of these concepts are strongly negatively correlated with GDP. Of course GDP does not capture of the concept of modernization completely. For instance, it is quite possible for nations with lower levels of GDP to have other aspects of modernity, such as good public education and a democratic political system. Conversely, some countries with high levels of GDP can be undemocratic and offer poor health care and public services.

18. A statistically significant correlation of −.434 to be precise, using a sample of 136 countries.

19. When encountering a new dataset I first familiarize myself by just running some basic stats to see if they are expect—really surprising results tend to suggest a data problem, not an alert-the-media moment. I first discovered that the poorer countries had *more* people without purpose. And this "fact" didn't surprise me in the least. Would it you?

20. Taylor, Diane. 2012. "Black Diamond: A Female Victim of Charles Taylor's Crimes Speaks Out." *The Guardian*. May 28.

21. This presents something of a problem for survey researchers. Questions that have no variation are branded "bad items," because they tell us nothing about differences between people. It is like having a survey item which asks, "Are you filling out a survey?" Actually, you might have some wise-ass answer, which would make that question valuable in terms of identifying wise-asses.

22. The existential urgency felt by Liberians is premised on their dire situation and also on the lack of time they have to ponder the meaninglessness of it all. As we shall see in the chapter *On Time*, time is luxury in the modern world, but one which many safe and well-off individuals avoid at all costs. Time on your hands can sometimes lead to hopeless thoughts, like what if everything is meaningless.

23. Norris and Ingelhart make the argument that people in the developing world lack existential security, in that they cannot ignore death in ways that postindustrial citizens can. Norris, Pippa, and

Ronald Ingelhart. 2004. *Sacred and Secular: Religion and Worldwide Politics*. New York: Cambridge University Press.

24. In Chapter 6, I discuss the joys and also the ramifications of living without existential urgency.

25. These are percentages supplied by the Association for Religion Data Archives. See theARDA.com.

26. A significant correlation of .639 for 127 countries. The religiosity of a nation and the purposefulness of its citizenry are not the same thing, conceptually or statistically. The strong positive correlation between the two indicates that religions certainly inspire purposefulness. Still the correlation is not perfect and regression analyses on purpose indicate that lower GDP is actually a better predictor of purpose than religiosity. This is the case at the country level of analysis. I shall show later that income or wealth is not a great predictor of purposefulness at the individual level; in other words, poor people are not more purposeful. Instead, it is something about the culture, community, and sacred canopy of a poorer nation that embeds an aggregate sense of purpose.

27. A significant correlation of –.557 for 133 countries.

28. Similar findings were reported in Oishi, Shigehiro, and Ed Diener. 2013. "Residents of Poor Nations Have a Greater Sense of Meaning in Life than Residents of Weathy Nations." *Psychological Science* 20(10): 1–9.

29. Dostoevsky, Fyodor. *The Brothers Karamazov*. Book X1, Chapter 9.

30. For instance, the brutal suppression of any and all intellectual discourse in North Korea is really an attempt to produce so much ignorance that informed debate is rendered impossible. Timur Kuran argues that certain oppressive social settings will lead individuals to consistently falsify their preferences. If this continues long enough, individuals will lose any and all sense of what their natural preferences are. While this is not technically "brainwashing," totalitarianism spreads ignorance so completely as to undermine free thought.

31. Epstein, Mikhail. 1995. *After the Future*. Amherst: University of Massachusetts Press.

32. Taylor, Charles. 2007. *A Secular Age*. London: The Belknap Press of Harvard University Press, 3.

33. See Norris, Pippa and Ronald Ingelhart. 2004. *Sacred and Secular: Religion and Worldwide Politics*. New York: Cambridge

University Press; and Baker, Joseph, and Buster Smith. 2015. *American Secularism.* New York: New York University Press.

34. Born in Germany in 1886, Tillich became one of the leading theologians of his era, holding positions at Union Theological Seminar in NY, Harvard Divinity School, and the University of Chicago, where he died in 1965. While not featured in Time's discussion of the "new" theology, Tillich's ideas were certainly influential in a larger intellectual movement to reanalyze what "God" means to Christians in the modern era.

35. Tillich, Paul. 1962. *Courage To Be,* New York: Yale University Press, 185.

36. Chris Bader and I find that Americans who believe in God overwhelming think that God is intimately involved in their daily lives. See Froese, Paul, and Christopher Bader. 2010. *America's Four Gods: What We Say about God and What That Says about Us.* Oxford: Oxford University Press.

37. Luhrmann, T.M. 2012. *When God Talks Back: Understanding the American Evangelical Relationship with God.* New York: Knopf, 312.

38. Ibid., 216.

39. Smith, Christian. 1998. *American Evangelicalism: Embattled and Thriving.* Chicago: University of Chicago Press, 106.

40. Rieff, Philip. 2006. *The Triumph of the Therapeutic: Uses of Faith after Freud.* Wilmington, DE: ISI Books, 46.

41. Ibid., 7.

42. Robert Nozick argues that what is real has an almost irrational lure. Nozick gives us this thought experiment: "Suppose there were an experience machine that would give you any experience you desired. Super-duper neuropsychologists could stimulate your brain so that you would think and feel you were writing a great novel, or making a friend, or reading an interesting book. All the time you would be floating in a tank, with electrodes attached to your brain. Should you plug into this machine for life, preprogramming your life's experiences?" You could experience happiness, fulfillment, insight, and love for your entire life. And you would never know you were just floating in a tank. The experience machine would answer all of life's questions, because you could program it to fool yourself into thinking you know the answers. Wouldn't that be better than the life you're living now? Not *really.* Or least Nozick theorizes that we would not choose to live out our days in the machine. Why? I want to write

great novels and be loved by millions and climb Mt. Everest. The machine is my only chance at that life. But that life is not *real*. Nozick asserts that over and above our fantasies and dreams of a perfect life, "what we desire is to live (an active verb) ourselves, in contact with reality. (And this, machines cannot do *for* us)." Within each of us is this profound urge—it says that being in contact with reality is important. This is what importance means. It is the self-evident value we place on what we feel and believe is *real*. As Nozick points out, the problem with virtual reality is that "there is no *actual* contact with any deeper reality, though the experience of it can be simulated. Many persons desire to leave themselves open to such contact and to a plumbing of deeper significance." Our ability to plumb the depths of reality creates the desire for a purpose in life which is not just enjoyable or convenient, but real. Nozick, Robert. 1974. *Anarchy, State, and Utopia*. New York: Basic Books, 64.

43. Illouz, Eva. 2008. *Saving the Modern Soul: Therapy, Emotions, and the Culture of Self-Help*. Berkeley: University of California Press, 5–6.

44. Ibid., 105.

45. Gallup World Poll has multiple religious measures, all of which indicate that the Netherlands is in the bottom tenth of most countries.

46. Sartre, Jean-Paul. 1956. *Being and Nothingness*. New York: Philosophical Library.

47. "The percentage reporting economic strain rises with increasing deprivation in every country with remarkable consistency." Whelan, Christopher T., Richard Layte, Bertrand Maître, and Brian Nolan 2001. "Income, Deprivation, and Economic Strain: An Analysis of the European Community Household." *European Sociological Review* 17(4): 357–372.

48. Kuran, Timur. 1995. *Private Truths, Public Lives: The Social Consequences of Preference Falsification*. Cambridge: Harvard University Press, 171.

49. Daniel Chirot explains the fickleness of modernity's rewards, "Modernization has weakened many old community ties and therefore created among some a sense of alienation and discomfort about the speed and nature of change. Modernity has spread unevenly, and there continues to be significant resistance to some of its aspects almost everywhere." Chirot, Daniel. 2011. *Contentious Identities: Ethnic, Religious, and Nationalist Conflicts in Today's World*. New York: Routledge, 62.

50. Jung and Rollo's critique of the psychological problems of mid-twentieth-century moderns suggest this trajectory. Marx and Durkheim provide reasons why industrialization and urbanization bring with them a new kind of isolation and alienation. And the idea that we are becoming "lost" is a ubiquitous theme in our popular culture, from sermons about the coming Rapture to science fiction tales of future dystopias.

51. Compassionate conservatism.

52. Liberal progressivism.

53. Chapter 7 looks at attempts to impose moral order from above.

54. In theory, the era-specific thesis is the closest to the truth, only because it tips its hat to a myriad of possibilities, eschewing the unidirectional assumptions of the moral regress and psychological progress ideas. For instance, the 1950s and 1960s are often depicted as an era of emptiness, usually attributed to something specific to this period, such as postwar trauma. But whenever an era-specific idea gets specified—as Sorokin does in his complex typology—or mythologized, as HBO's *Mad Men* has done with the 1960s, they too appear unduly reductionist and artificial.

55. Sorokin, Pitrim. 1957. *Social and Cultural Dynamics*. Oxford: Transaction Books, 337.

56. Jung, Carl. 1933. *Modern Man in Search of a Soul*. New York: Harcourt, 103.

57. Dreyfus, Hubert, and Sean Dorrance Kelly. 2011. *All Things Shining*. New York: Free Press, 26.

Chapter 4

1. Quote from Walt Whitman's "O Me! O Life!" read by Robin Williams in film *The Dead Poets' Society*.

2. This phrase—"What will your verse be?"—has become the marketing tagline for iPad Air. See https://www.apple.com/your-verse/.

3. Weber, Max. 1946. "The Social Psychology of the World Religions." In *From Max Weber: Essays in Sociology*. Translated by H. H. Gerth and C. Wright Mills. New York: Oxford University Press, 282.

4. Weber was fond of this line written by poet Friedrich Schiller; I think it is wonderfully evocative and sums up the grander idea that modernity brings with it secularization.

5. In 2008, China officially listed "Internet addiction" as a health epidemic affecting their teenage population; their curative is currently a bleak army camp-like psychiatric ward. See Shlam, Shosh, and Hilla Medalia. "Treating China's 'Web Junkies' at a Boot Camp." *New York Times*. January 20, 2014.

6. The full sentence is, "In modern societies, the foremost of [sacred objects] is the individual self, treated as if it were a little god." Collins, Randall. 2004. *Interaction Ritual Chains*. Princeton, NJ: Princeton University Press, 25.

7. The fact that only 25 percent of Americans feel that more money is required for better fulfillment in life indicates that most truly desire something out of life more than comfort and wealth.

8. Descartes, Rene. 2011. *Discourse on Method and Meditations on First Philosophy*. Translated by Donald Cress. New York: Hackett Publishing.

9. William James, following Descartes's lead, called this the *I*. Jonathan Brown explains that "the *I* refers to our awareness that we are thinking or our awareness that we are perceiving." In turn, the *me* "refers to people's ideas about who they are and what they are like." Consequently, it makes sense to say, "I see me." It expresses my awareness at having thoughts about a self.

10. Hood, Bruce. 2012. *The Self Illusion: How the Social Brain Creates Identity*. New York: Oxford University Press, xi.

11. Blackmore, Susan. 1999. *The Meme Machine*. Oxford: Oxford University Press, 228.

12. The best predictor of whether an American meditates is her level of education. Interestingly, income is negatively related to meditation. Source: Baylor Religion Survey, Wave 3. I am unclear about how Christian meditation differs from traditional Eastern forms of meditation. Some Christian meditators have told me that they understand it as a form of prayer—for this reason it differs from Eastern meditation by presuming the presence of God.

13. Gunaratana, Bhante. 2011. *Mindfulness in Plain English*. Boston: Wisdom Publishers, 33–34.

14. Breathing is of central importance in some forms of meditation. Gunaratana explains, "We use breath as our focus. It serves as that vital reference point from which the mind wanders and is drawn back. Distraction cannot be sees as distraction unless there is some

central focus to be distracted from . . . Breathing is a nonconceptual process, a thing that can be experienced directly without a need for thought." Gunaratana, Bhante. 2011. *Mindfulness in Plain English*. Boston: Wisdom Publishers, 65–66.

15. Gunaratana, Bhante. 2011. *Mindfulness in Plain English*. Boston: Wisdom Publishers, 25.

16. Hölzel, Britta K., Sara W. Lazar, Tim Gard, Zev Schuman-Olivier, David R. Vago, and Ulrich Ott. "How Does Mindfulness Meditation Work? Proposing Mechanisms of Action From a Conceptual and Neural Perspective." *Perspectives on Psychological Science* 6, no. 6 (November 2011): 537–559. Canter, Peter H. "The Therapeutic Effects of Meditation: The Conditions Treated Are Stress Related, and the Evidence Is Weak." *British Medical Journal* 326, no. 7398 (May 17, 2003): 1049–1050.

17. Here are some simple directions from Bhante Gunaratana: "Find yourself a quiet place, a secluded place, a place where you will be alone"; sit and focus on your breathing. "In spite of your concerted effort to keep the mind on your breathing, the mind will likely wander away." Gently direct it back to breathing, and "don't expect anything." He adds, "There is no hurry, so take your time." Gunaratana, Bhante. 2011. *Mindfulness in Plain English*. Boston: Wisdom Publishers. See book for detailed overview of the technique.

18. Hood, Bruce. 2012. *The Self Illusion: How the Social Brain Creates Identity*. New York: Oxford University Press, xi.

19. Damasio explains that "there is no single region in the human brain equipped to process, simultaneously, representations from all the sensory modalities active when we experience simultaneously, say, sound, movement, shape, and color in perfect temporal and spatial registration. We are beginning to glean where the construction of images for each separate modality is likely to take place, but nowhere can we find a single area toward which all of those separate products would be projected in exact registration." Damasio, Antonio. 1994. *Descartes' Error: Emotion, Reason, and the Human Brain*. New York: Penguin, 95.

20. Gunaratana, Bhante. 2011. *Mindfulness in Plain English*. Boston: Wisdom Publishers, 43.

21. Nasr, Seyyed Hossein. 2007. "Bearing Witness to the One God." *The Life of Meaning*. Edited by Bob Abernethy and William Bole. New York: Seven Stories Press, 292.

22. Stephen Prothero's *God Is Not One* very insightfully summarizes the fundamental ideological, cultural, and ritualistic differences between the world's most popular religions. The similarities are as fascinating as the differences. Prothero, Stephen. 2010. *God Is Not One: The Eight Rival Religions That Run the World and Why Their Differences Matter.* New York: Harper One.

23. For instance, the United Nations Universal Declaration of Human Rights begins with the assertion that "all human beings are born free and equal in dignity and rights." Individual sovereignty is one of very few widely shared global values and with it comes the idea that we *should* discover who we are and are equally justified in what we ultimately find. See http://www.un.org/en/documents/udhr/. Eleanor Roosevelt wrote about how the idea of self-sovereignty translates into philosophical relativism, describing a debate between representatives from China, Canada, and Lebanon. She writes,

   Dr. Chang was a pluralist and held forth in charming fashion on the proposition that there is more than one kind of ultimate reality. The Declaration, he said, should reflect more than simply Western ideas and Dr. Humphrey would have to be eclectic in his approach. His remark, though addressed to Dr. Humphrey, was really directed at Dr. Malik, from whom it drew a prompt retort as he expounded at some length the philosophy of Thomas Aquinas. Dr. Humphrey joined enthusiastically in the discussion, and I remember that at one point Dr. Chang suggested that the Secretariat might well spend a few months studying the fundamentals of Confucianism!

24. Leaman, O. 2008. *The Qur'an: An Encyclopedia.* London: Routledge, 36.

25. Psychologists tend to separate "private self-consciousness" from "public self-consciousness." The first refers to the examination of one's feelings and thoughts, and the second indicates our tendency to consider others' assessments of our selves. But a clear distinction between these two forms of self-consciousness is impossible, because how we self-assess is always tied to how we think others assess us. Abrams, Dominic, and Rupert Brown. 1989. "Self-Consciousness and Social Identity: Self-Regulation as a Group Member." *Social Psychology Quarterly* 52(4): 311–318.

26. Whitman is assumed to be gay or bisexual and there is evidence of him having male lovers. That said, Whitman never publicly announced his sexuality.

27. Whitman, Walt. 1855. "Song of Myself" from the collection *Leaves of Grass*.

28. See Cousins, S. D. 1989. "Culture and Self-perception in Japan and the United States." *Journal of Personality and Social Psychology* 54:124–131; Cheek, J. M. 1989. "Identity-orientations and Self-interpretation." In *Personality Psychology: Recent Trends and Emerging Directions*. Edited by D. Buss and N. Cantor. New York: Springer-Verlag, 275–285.

29. Jonathan Brown summarizes some general findings, including his own, on this topic: "Contrary to reports circulating in the popular press, research does not show that females have lower global self-esteem than men. Sex differences do emerge, however, with respect to how males and females evaluate certain of their attributes and abilities. For the most part, these differences mirror cultural stereotypes . . . women are more apt than men to develop a collectivist or interdependent self-concept, one that emphasizes their connection and relations to others." Brown, Jonathan. 1998. *The Self*. New York: Routledge, 208.

30. Mead, George Herbert. 1934. *Mind, Self, and Society*. Edited by Charles W. Morris. Chicago: University of Chicago Press, 174–185.

31. Mead famously used team sports to illustrate his point about how the self is only defined in relation to others.

32. Mead, George Herbert. 1934. *Mind, Self, and Society*. Edited by Charles W. Morris. Chicago: University of Chicago Press, 154.

33. Howard Becker explains how labeling lies at the center of construction of social deviance. "*Social groups create deviance by making rules whose infraction creates deviance*, and by applying those roles to particular people and labeling them as outsiders. From this point of view, deviance is *not* a quality of the act the person commits, but rather a consequence of the application by other of rules and sanctions to an 'offender.' The deviant is one to whom that label has been successfully applied; deviant behavior is behavior that people so label." Becker, Howard. 1963 (revised 1973). *Outsiders*. New York: Free Press, 9.

34. Tolstoy, Leo. 2012. *Childhood; Boyhood; Youth*. Translated by Judson Rosengrant. New York: Penguin Classics.

35. Neurologist Antoinio Damasio explains why mind-body dualism is a fiction. He writes, "Feelings are just as cognitive as any other perceptual image, and just as dependent on cerebral-cortex processing as any other image." Consequently, "feeling happy or sad also corresponds in part to the cognitive modes under which your thoughts are operating ... Which means that reducing depression to a statement about the availability of serotonin or norepinephrine ... is unacceptably rude." Damasio, Antonio. 1994. *Descartes' Error: Emotion, Reason, and the Human Brain*. New York: Penguin, 159. For Damasio and other neurologists, emotion and reason work in tandem, one never completely rid of the other. For instance, anxiety is not a synonym for a particular mix of brain chemicals; it also refers to an individual's perception of her reality.

36. Turner, Jonathan, and Jan E. Stets. 2005. *The Sociology of Emotions*. Cambridge: Cambridge University Press, 10.

37. Moll, Jorge, Ricardo de Oliveira-Souza, Roland Zahn, and Jordan Grafman. 2008. "The Cognitive Neuroscience of Moral Emotions." In *Moral Psychology, Vol. 3: The Neuroscience of Morality: Emotion, Brain Disorders, and Development*. Edited by Walter Sinnott-Armstrong. Cambridge: MIT Press, 12.

38. Here is a common list of moral emotions: guilt, shame, embarrassment, pride, indignation, contempt, pity, awe, gratitude, and righteousness. This list comes from Moll, Jorge; Ricardo de Oliveira-Souza, Roland Zahn, and Jordan Grafman. 2008. "The Cognitive Neuroscience of Moral Emotions." In *Moral Psychology, Vol. 3: The Neuroscience of Morality: Emotion, Brain Disorders, and Development*. Edited by Walter Sinnott-Armstrong. Cambridge: MIT Press, 13–16. Moral psychologists come up with varying lists of these "moral emotions," essentially picking favorite terms from the vast language we daily use to label emotions.

39. Jonathan Turner explains the evolutionary development of acting sad: "Episodes of sadness are highly associative because they mobilize primates to secure positive and reinforcing positive sanctions; and when such sanctions do indeed produce positive emotions like satisfaction-happiness, sadness becomes a marker to the individual and those in its environment that efforts need to be made to sanction positively those signaling sadness. In this way, sadness becomes a kind of trigger for the activation of more positive sanctioning

processes that ultimately produce the most solidarity." Turner, Jonathan. 2000. *On the Origin of Human Emotions: A Sociological Inquiry into the Evolution of Human Affect*. Stanford: Stanford University Press, 50.

40. This research was conducted in 1994, prior to the development of Viagra. See Wagner, T. H., D. L. Patrick, S. P. McKenna, and P. Froese. 1996. "Cross-cultural Development of a Quality of Life Measure for Men with Erection Difficulties." *Quality of Life Research* 5(4): 443–449.

41. Wagner, T. H., D. L. Patrick, S. P. McKenna, and P. Froese. 1996. "Cross-cultural Development of a Quality of Life Measure for Men with Erection Difficulties." *Quality of Life Research* 5(4): 443–449.

42. James, William. 1890. *Principles of Psychology*. New York: Henry Holt.

43. Scott Draper and I define *alienation* as "an imagined negative relationship between the self and macroreality." Froese, Paul, and Scott Draper. Forthcoming. "Alienation: The Social Construction of Macroreality and its Effects on Mental Health."

44. Seligman, M. E. P. 1975. *Helplessness: On Depression, Development, and Death*. San Francisco: W. H. Freeman.

45. Bandura A. 1986. *Social Foundations of Thought and Action: A Social Cognitive Theory*. Englewood Cliffs, NJ: Prentice-Hall.

46. Froese, Paul, and Scott Draper. Forthcoming. "Alienation: The Social Construction of Macroreality and its Effects on Mental Health."

47. Young, Michael. 1958. *The Rise of Meritocracy: 1870–2033*. New York: Transaction Publishers.

48. Jung, C. G. 1933. *Modern Man in Search of a Soul*. New York: Harcourt, 82.

49. These types are measured as mainly response styles. For instance, "Type A individuals respond to stress with hard driving, time-urgent, and hostile behavior. Type B individuals, in contrast, are easy-going, patient, soft-spoken, and more resilient." Nunes, Joao, and John Carr. 2012. "Predisposition." In *The Behavior Sciences and Health Care*. 3rd edition. New York: Hogrfe.

50. These are categories in the "Big Five" factors; they are *openness, conscientiousness, extraversion, agreeableness*, and *neuroticism*, sometimes referred to as OCEAN.

51. ESTJ = extraversion (E), sensing (S), thinking (T), judgment (J). INFP = introversion (I), intuition (N), feeling (F), perception (P).

52. Igo, Sarah. 2007. *Average Americans: Surveys, Citizens, and the Making of a Mass Public.* Cambridge: Harvard University Press, 289.

53. You can even go to http://www.thearda.com/whoisyourgod/ to fill out a survey which supposed tells your image of God. There are apparently four types. Who dreamt up that nonsense?

54. Fredrickson, Babara, and Marcial Losada. 2005. "Positive Affect and the Complex Dynamics of Human Flourishing." *American Psychologist.* 60(7): 678–686.

55. Fredrickson, Babara. 2009. *Positivity: Top-Notch Research Reveals the 3 to 1 Ratio That Will Change Your Life.* New York: Harmony.

56. Anthony, Andrew. 2014. "The British Amateur Who Debunked the Mathematics of Happiness." *The Observer.* January 18. http://www.theguardian.com/science/2014/jan/19/mathematics-of-happiness-d ebunked-nick-brown.

57. Shteyngart, Gary. 2010. *Super Sad True Love Story.* New York: Random House, 90–91.

58. Wieseltier, Leon. 2015. "Among the Disrupted." *The New York Times Book Review.* January 18, 1–15.

59. Weber, Max. 1958. *The Protestant Ethic and the Spirit of Capitalism.* New York: Scribner, 181.

60. Wittgenstein, Ludwig. 1918. *Tractatus Logico-Philosophicus.* Section 6.521.

61. The "real self" is a vision of "a persistent entity that lasts a lifetime, is separate from the brain and from the world around, has memories and beliefs, initiates actions, experiences the world around, and makes decisions." Blackmore, Susan. 1999. *The Meme Machine.* Oxford: Oxford University Press, 228.

62. The whole quote is this: "What I ask of the free thinker is that he should confront religion in the same mental state as the believer. He who does not bring to the study of religion a sort of religious sentiment cannot speak about it! He is like a blind man trying to talk about color." Durkheim, Emile. 1995 [1915]. *The Elementary Forms of Religious* Life. Translated by Karen Fields. New York: Free Press, 15.

63. Robbins, Anthony. *Awaken the Giant Within: How to Take Immediate Control of Your Mental, Emotional, Physical, and Financial Success.* New York: Free Press, 1.

64. Robbins, Anthony. *Awaken the Giant Within: How to Take Immediate Control of Your Mental, Emotional, Physical, and Financial Success.* New York: Free Press, 22.

65. Warren, Rick. 2002. *The Purpose Driven Life*. Grand Rapids, MI: Zondervan, 171.

66. Ibid., 10.

67. Smith, Christian. 1998. *American Evangelicalism: Embattled and Thriving*. Chicago: University of Chicago Press.

68. Warren, Rick. 2002. *The Purpose Driven Life*. Grand Rapids, MI: Zondervan, 69.

69. Baylor Religion Survey estimates from Waves 1, 2, and 3. See http://www.thearda.com for codebooks and data.

70. Claire Scobie. 2003. "Why Now Is Bliss." *Telegraph Magazine*. Retrieved on February 2, 2010.

71. Tolle, Eckhart. 2005. *A New Earth: Awakening to Your Life's Purpose*. New York: Plume, 208.

72. Ibid., 214.

73. Moral Foundations Theory searches for "universal moral taste receptors" which are *triggered* by social circumstances. It assumes that "cultural variation in morality can be explained in part by noting that cultures can shrink or expand the current triggers of any module." Haidt claims to have located six of these "moral foundations." They are 1) the care/harm foundation, 2) the fairness/cheating foundation, 3) the loyalty/betrayal foundation, 4) the authority/subversion foundation, 5) the sanctity/degradation foundation, and 6) the liberty/oppression foundation. Haidt, Jonathan. 2012. *The Righteous Mind: Why Good People Are Divided by Politics and Religion*. New York: Pantheon Books.

74. Jonathan Haidt argues that righteousness is a core moral emotion, one on which moral order is premised. In *The Righteous Mind*, Haidt argues, "I want to show you that an obsession with righteousness (leading inevitably to self-righteousness) is the normal human condition. It is a feature of our evolutionary design, not a bug or error that crept into minds that would otherwise be objective and rational. Our righteous minds made it possible for human beings—but no other animal—to produce large cooperative groups, tribes, and nations without the glue of kinship. But at the same time, our righteous minds guarantee that our cooperative groups will always be cursed by moralistic strife."

75. Haidt, Jonathan. 2012. *The Righteous Mind: Why Good People Are Divided by Politics and Religion*. New York: Pantheon Books, 190.

76. Chirot, Daniel, and Clark McCauley. 2006. *Why Not Kill Them All? The Logic and Prevention of Mass Political Murder*. Princeton, NJ: Princeton University Press, 27.

77. Turner, Jonathan. 2000. *On the Origin of Human Emotions: A Sociological Inquiry into the Evolution of Human Affect*. Stanford: Stanford University Press, 135.

78. This give and take is what outsiders often fail to understand about strict religions and absolutist ideologies. Why would someone accept the strictures of moral absolutism which so fully confine the self? Durkheim answers, "Society weighs down on its members with full authority. Does a mind seek to free itself from these norms of thoughts? . . . The necessity with which the categories [of normative thought] press themselves upon us is not merely the effect of habits whose yoke we could slip with little effort; nor is that necessity a habit or a physical or metaphysical need, since the categories change with place and time; it is a special sort of moral necessity" Durkheim, Emile. 1995. *The Elementary Forms of Religious Life*. Edited by Karen E. Fields. New York: Free Press, 17.

Chapter 5

1. Wittgenstein tells us why ontological, metaphysical, and theological discussions within the linguistic culture of scientific inquiry will always be fruitless. It is because participants in discussions of transcendental themes can never and will never specify the concepts they utilize to the degree that scientific discourse demands. Indeed, the very essence of a discussion of transcendental or metaphysical or absolute reality depends on the fact that it is a topic which can never be properly described. Even purveyors of exceptionally vivid religious descriptions of, say, the afterlife or the personality of God will still maintain the indescribable nature of their revealed Truth or God. Wittgenstein explains: "I see now that these nonsensical expressions were not nonsensical because I had not yet found the correct expressions, but that their nonsensicality was their very essence. For all I wanted to do with them was just *to go beyond* the world and that is to say beyond significant language." Ludwig Wittgenstein. 1994. "Ethics, Life and Faith." In *The Wittgenstein Reader*, edited by Anthony Kenny. Oxford: Blackwell Publishers, 296.

For Wittgenstein, discussions of "reality" or "God" or "Truth" or "absolute goodness" are nonsense, not because they are not true, but because there is no way to understand them in a concrete real-world way. We cannot point to any object or phenomenon and say *that* is "reality" or "God" or "absolute value." And if we can, then we have made the term relative to a situation and it therefore loses its transcendental or absolute quality.

If God is a person, or an experience, then science can evaluate God. If reality is a phenomenon or a perspective, then science can evaluate it. But it seems that words like "God" and "reality" and "goodness" seek to express something greater—in fact, so great as to be beyond language. As such, we cannot really talk about them scientifically. On the topic of faith, Wittgenstein tactfully responded that it is something that "I personally cannot help respecting deeply and I would not for my life ridicule." This is good advice. Scientists should not ridicule religious or transcendental language, not only because it is potentially offensive, but because religious and transcendental concepts paradoxically seek to express something which exists in a realm beyond language or, at least, the language that scientists use. See Froese, Paul. 2011. "Fact, Value, God, and Reality: How Wittgenstein's Ethics Clarifies the Fact-value Distinction and, in the Process, Perhaps Subverts a Scientific Holy War" (ARDA Guiding Paper Series). State College, PA: The Association of Religion Data Archives at The Pennsylvania State University, from http://www.thearda.com/rrh/papers/guidingpapers.asp.

2. Wittgenstein, 1994. "Ethics, Life and Faith."
3. Wittgenstein explains that statements of relative truth are easy to spot: "The word *good* in a relative sense simply means coming up to a certain predetermined standard. Thus when we say that this man is a good pianist we mean that he can play pieces of a certain degree of difficulty with a certain degree of dexterity." Wittgenstein, 1994, 290.
4. Hawking, Stephen, and Leonardo Mlodinow. *The Grand Design*. New York: Bantam Books, 46.
5. Wittgenstein explains: "What I wish to contend is that, although all judgments of relative value can be shown to be mere statements of fact, no statements of fact can ever be, or imply, a judgment of absolute value." Wittgenstein, 1994, 290.
6. James, William. 1961. *The Varieties of Religious Experience: A Study of Human Nature*. New York: Collier Books, 95.

7. Leon Festinger, a primary research of "cognitive dissonance," argues that we are hardwired to seek ideological coherency. See Festinger, Leon. 1957. *A Theory of Cognitive Dissonance*. Stanford: Stanford University Press.

8. A strong case can be made that the authors of Genesis understood their own text to be metaphorical or at least didn't make a big distinction between fact and good narrative.

9. Orwell, George. 2008. *All Art Is Propaganda*. Compiled by George Packer. New York: Houghton Mifflin Harcourt, 256.

10. Type of religion, political party affiliation, and level of education all significantly predict belief in "ultimate truth" using multinomial regression analyses. Gender, age, and income are also associated with Truth—women, people with lower incomes, and the young are more likely to believe in "ultimate truth." Source: Baylor Religion Survey, Wave 3.

11. Kuran, Timur. 1995. *Private Truths, Public Lies: The Social Consequences of Preference Falsification*. Cambridge, MA: Harvard University Press, 183.

12. Baylor Religion Survey, Wave 3. Seventy-one percent of survey respondents agreed with the statement, "I believe in ultimate truth in life."

13. Stark, Rodney, and William Sims Bainbridge. 1985. *The Future of Religion: Secularization, Revival, and Cult Formation*. Berkeley: University of California Press.

14. Christian Smith's study of American Evangelicals demonstrates the extent to which a religious group with growing political and economic power can instill feelings of "embattlement" with secular society. See Smith, Christian. 1998. *American Evangelicalism: Embattled and Thriving*. Chicago: University of Chicago Press.

15. Associate Justice of the US Supreme Court Potter Stewart famously said that hard-core pornography was hard to define but "I know it when I see it."

16. Sociologists tend to gauge religiosity by aggregating indicators of supernatural belief, the ritual behavior, and religious affiliation.

17. The Shadow knows.

18. A major dilemma with the concept of religious tension is the need to specify the cultural boundaries of one's analyses. For instance, a Buddhist will be in high tension in rural Mississippi but not in Tibet.

Admittedly, I switch between multiple levels of analysis with my examples; they are mainly an attempt to illustrate the ideas of the concept rather than present a more refined definition or more precise measure of tension. And I realize that an Evangelical Protestant is not in high tension in central Texas but is in relatively high tension with Americans overall. The studies which report that Evangelicals feel embattled support this perspective, namely, they indicate that Evangelicals feel in tension with secular society.

19. Stark and Bainbridge show that high tension Christian groups are more likely to believe that "Darwin's theory of evolution could not possibly be true"; "It is completely true that the Devil actually exists"; "Biblical miracles actually happened just as the Bible says they did"; "It is completely true that Jesus walked on water"; "Definitely, Jesus will return to the earth some day." See Stark, Rodney, and William Sims Bainbridge. 1985. *The Future of Religion: Secularization, Revival, and Cult Formation.* Berkeley: University of California Press, 55.

20. Pick up any religious pamphlet and you are likely to find some claim to Truth. For instance, Woo Myung created Maum Meditation in 1996, a practice which promises to "subtract" all of your false thoughts and images until you are left with only Truth. According to the Maum doctrine, we have the following choice: "The one who lives in the false world just dies and that's it. The one who is born in the True world. . . will live forever." Myung promises what all the great religious traditions do—access to the True world. Muam Organization. 2012. "Maum Meditation: Where Does Man Go When He Dies?" Published by www.maum.org.

21. The Anabaptist movement is framed around the idea of adult baptism—one can only come to Christ freely and with open eyes.

22. See *The Devil's Playground*, a documentary about rumspringa.

23. Smith, Christian. 1998. *American Evangelicalism: Embattled and Thriving.* Chicago: University of Chicago Press.

24. I met a number of Christians who were emotionally distraught over the issue of biblical literalism. Biblical literalists tend to think that anything less is a moral cop out. For them, faith requires unquestioned allegiance. But other Christians can see biblical literalism as the cop out. They believe biblical literalism is an abdication of one's critical thinking and an unwillingness to struggle with intellectually difficult topics. James Wellman describes how American Christians are divided

by differing perspectives of Truth: "A major critique of the evangelical community by liberals is that not only are the answers too simple but the messages (truth claims) are also created to be attractive and 'appealing' to people . . . in order to manipulate the masses. The same critique, of course, is what evangelicals use against liberals; the latter accommodates their message to people by soothing their conscience with a 'soft' gospel." Wellman, James. 2008. *Evangelical vs. Liberal: The Clash of Christian Cultures in the Pacific Northwest.* New York: Oxford University Press, 120.

25. Both the PEW and Gallup Organizations collect statistics on creationism belief. For latest numbers see http://www.gallup. com/poll/21814/Evolution-Creationism-Intelligent-Design.aspx. Some surveys put belief in creationism at over 33 percent. It is also important to note that around 30 percent of Americans believe that God created humans *through* the process of evolution. These believers easily reconcile their faith with current science.

26. From a 2012 GQ article "All Eyez on Him" by Michael Hainey. See http://www.gq.com/news-politics/politics/201212/marco-ru bio-interview-gq-december-2012.

27. Google it! And read the US Geological Survey website: http://pubs. usgs.gov/gip/geotime/age.html.

28. See http://thinkprogress.org/politics/2011/08/18/298998/ rick-perry-age-of-earth-evolution-creationsism/.

29. See http://www.slate.com/articles/news_and_politics/ explainer/2012/10/rep_paul_broun_says_the_earth_is_9_000_ years_old_how_do_creationists_calculate.html.

30. While the Bible never explicitly states that the earth is six thousand years old, biblical literalists claim to have calculated this fact from the Bible. Ken Ham is the CEO of Answers in Genesis, founder of a Creation Museum, and a popular speaker at biblical literalist events. He explains the logic: "Let's do a rough calculation to show how this works. The age of the earth can be estimated by taking the first five days of creation (from earth's creation to Adam), then following the genealogies from Adam to Abraham in Genesis 5 and 11, then adding in the time from Abraham to today. Adam was created on day 6, so there were five days before him. If we add up the dates from Adam to Abraham, we get about 2,000 years, using the Masoretic Hebrew text of Genesis 5 and 11. Whether Christian or secular, most scholars would agree that Abraham lived about 2,000 B.C. (4,000 years ago).

So a simple calculation is: 5 days + ~2,000 years +
~4,000 years = ~6,000 years. At this point, the first five days are
negligible. Quite a few people have done this calculation using the
Masoretic text (which is what most English translations are based
on) and with careful attention to the biblical details, they have
arrived at the same time frame of about 6,000 years." http://www.
answersingenesis.org/articles/2007/05/30/how-old-is-earth.

31. In *A Universe from Nothing* and other writings, physicist Lawrence
Krauss reasons that valid descriptions of how the universe formed
do not require a creator. In its Afterward, evolutionary biologist
Richard Dawkins warns that Krauss's "title means exactly what
it says. And what it says is devastating." Krauss, Lawrence. 2012.
*A Universe from Nothing: Why There Is Something Rather Than
Nothing*. New York: Free Press, 191. Dawkins hopes that science will
intellectually devastate the foundation of most religion—the belief
that everything was *created*.

   Stephen Hawking lightly agrees. In his most recent book *The
Grand Design*, Hawking and Mlodinow assert that questions about
the existence of the universe can be sufficiently answered "without
invoking any divine beings." The truth that theoretical physics does
not require supernatural beings has stoked public fears that scientists
have atheistic agendas. Hawking, Stephen, and Leonard Mlodinow.
2010. *The Grand Design*. New York: Bantam Books, 172.

32. Dawkins, Richard. 2011. *The Magic of Reality: How We Know What's
Really True*. New York: Free Press, 12.

33. Actually, Stalin probably didn't say this; it most likely was his
minister of anti-religious education. But it is more evocative to
simply quote Stalin. See Froese, Paul. 2008. *The Plot to Kill God*.
Berkeley: University of California Press.

34. Ludwig Fleck studied how "thought styles" which are formed within
collectives determine what can be considered a "fact." Consequently,
scientific explanations only shift understanding if and when they
adhere to a group's thought style. A scientific attach on the Truth
of a group can therefore bolster a group's belief that science is
non-factual. See Fleck, Ludwig. 1979. *Genesis and the Development of
a Scientific Fact*. Chicago: University of Chicago Press.

35. Sageman, Marc. 2004. *Understanding Terror Networks*.
Philadelphia: University of Pennsylvania Press, 135.

36. Conversely, Durkheim argued that self-destructive behavior can also be the result of too little social integration and moral regulation. People in these settings lack social ties and moral guidance. Their circumstances provide no sense of a righteous or even a good self, but rather distill an abandoned and isolated image of self. It is a self with a hostile social home. Durkheim's concepts of *egoistic* and *anomic* suicides reflect too little social integration and too little moral regulation respectively. Durkheim, Emile. 1951 [1897]. *Suicide: A Study in Sociology.* Glencoe, IL: Free Press.

37. For instance, President George W. Bush successfully got American public support for his planned invasion of Iraq by linking this military effort to fighting the "evil" in the world. He tapped into a narrative of good vs. evil, and for many Americans this vision of the war blanketed the intricacies of American foreign policy. See Froese, Paul, and F. Carson Mencken. 2009. "An American Holy War? The Connection between Religious Ideology and Neo-Conservative Iraq War Attitudes." *Social Science Quarterly* 90:1.

38. From President Barrack Obama's victory speech given on November 6, 2012.

39. www.realclearpolitics.com/articles/2007/03/ the_coming_backlash_against_th.html

40. Buckley, William F. 2008. *Let's Talk of Many Things: The Collected Speeches.* New York: Basic Books, 423.

41. Social theorists have long attempted to define the essence of what it means to be liberal or conservative. James Hunter, author of *Culture Wars*, explains that we are principally divided in how we understand moral structures. Conservatives, or "the Orthodox" as he calls them, believe in a transcendent moral authority. Progressives, his label for liberals, see themselves as arbiters of their personal morality. His schema maps directly onto belief in Truth (the Orthodox perspective) and denial of Truth (the Progressive perspective). Logically, Truth is the possession of the moral follower; he has clear rules. Moral doers, on the other hand, seek their personal truth.

　　The cognitive scientist George Lakoff offers a different yet compatible distinction between liberal and conservative moral traditions. He asserts that conservatives follow a "Strict Father" morality, while liberals perform a "Nurturant Parent" style of moral decision-making. The strict father defines the rules and hands out the punishments. The nurturant parent encourages and rewards good behavior. For Lakoff, these basic moral styles form the foundation of our disagreements about social welfare, the role of government, and the meaning of equal opportunity.

In sum, the conservative is a moral follower, who believes in Truth, thinks moral rules are absolute, and favors a system which defends these absolutes. In contrast, the liberal is a moral doer, who questions Truth, understands moral rules as relative, and favors a system in which individuals name their own values.

42. Based on findings of the Baylor Religion Survey (wave 3) belief in Truth is related to a whole host of political indicators. GOP party affiliation is strongly correlated with belief in Truth. Similarly, conservative identity is strongly correlated with belief in Truth. A believer in Truth is also more likely to have voted for McCain over Obama in the 2008 presidential election. Overall, Americans who vote Republican are more likely to believe in Truth regardless of their religious and political identities.

43. This makes sense. Strong attachment to a political party, like strong attachment to any group, suggests that the identities and beliefs of the group hold some special significance to the member. In turn, we would expect that a "strong" Democrat would be more likely to feel that their ideology is True than a "leaning Democrat." It could also be that individuals who believe in Truth are more likely to assert "strong" memberships regardless of their actual commitment. They have the cognitive style of understanding identities and affiliations in stark terms, as opposed to more fluid terms.

44. Mann, Thomas, and Norman Ornstein. 2012. "Let's Just Say It: The Republicans Are the Problem." *The Washington Post.* April 27, 2012.

45. Parents tend to very effectively socialize their children into similar political views; see Greenstein, F. I. 1965. *Children and Politics.* New Haven, CT: Yale University Press. Also, Kinder, Donald. 2006. "Politics and the Life Cycle." *Science* 312:30.

46. Bafumi and Shapiro (2009) show that partisan identity is much stronger than feelings towards the policies and ideologies offered by our different political parties. This indicates that we tend to value loyal membership over understanding the intricacies of policy differences. Bafumi, Joseph, and Robert Shapiro. 2009. "A New Partisan Voter." *The Journal of Politics* 71(1): 1–24. Also see Ura, Joseph, and Christopher Ellis. 2012. "Partisan Moods: Polarization

and the Dynamics of Mass Party Preferences." *The Journal of Politics* 74(1): 277–291.

47. Vishal Singh outlines clear distinctions in liberals and conservatives purchasing habits. See Singh, Vishal. 2014. "Ideology and Brand Consumption." *Psychological Science.*

48. Berry, Jeffrey, and Sarah Sobieraj. 2014. *The Outrage Industry: Political Opinion Media and the New Incivility.* New York: Oxford University Press, 7.

49. Zeki and Romaya find that "there is a unique pattern of activity in the brain in the context of hate. Though distinct from the pattern of activity that correlates with romantic love, this pattern nevertheless shares two areas with the latter, namely the putamen and the insula." Zeki, S., and J.P. Romaya. 2008. "Neural Correlates of Hate." *PLoS ONE* 3(10): e3556. doi:10.1371/journal.pone.0003556.

50. The Pew Research Centers and quantcast.com profile the demographic characteristics of Limbaugh listeners as well as viewers of Bill O'Reilly and Sean Hannity. They are similar. These political pundits appeal mainly to men (between 72 and 83 percent of Limbaugh listeners) and whites (92 percent). Quantcast.com estimates that the vast majority of Limbaugh listeners are between the ages of 35 and 65, and 33 percent have a college education. Sixty percent are without children, and most are in the middle class. Around 14 percent of the American public listens to Limbaugh sometimes, and around 29 percent of Americans watch O'Reilly "regularly or sometimes." While I do not have specific Truth statistics concerning Limbaugh listeners, the demographic characteristics of Limbaugh's listeners are good predictors of believing in Truth. Second and more interestingly, believing in Truth is a powerful predictor of whether an American listens to talk radio. Apparently, listeners to radio pundits have a firm sense that the Truth is out there. See http://www.people-press.org/2012/09/27/section-4-demographics-and-political-views-of-news-audiences/.

51. Faludi, Susan. 1999. *Stiffed: The Betrayal of the American Man.* New York: HarperCollins.

52. Moral enemies clarify moral order; our individual goodness becomes clear when presented with a wicked "other." We feel morally pure by comparison. The emotional power of this feeling is intoxicating and, as Daniel Chirot and Clark McCauley argue, can become the moral basis for extreme acts of political violence. This occurs when

political ideology objectifies our moral outrage as a grander Truth. When this occurs and is popular, it can become a more powerful motivator of political action than purely economic interests. Chirot and McCauley argue that one of the most influential rationales for political violence is the fear of "pollution" (ideological, ethnic, or religious). In this instance, outrage is interpreted as a legitimate and necessary response to the moral impurity of a whole class of people. For instance, Nazis believed that Jews were diseased; Catholics in sixteenth-century France believed Protestants were a religious cancer; and Stalinists and Maoists believed that capitalists were social malignances. Genocide and mass political violence are justified as a necessary operation to remove the disease, cancer, and malignances of society. The worst consequence of Truth occurs when emotional outrage is perceived as a moral crusade to rid the world of impurities. Chirot, Daniel, and Clark McCauley. 2006. *Why Not Kill Them All? The Logic and Prevention of Mass Political Murder.* Princeton, NJ: Princeton University Press

The American outrage industry wades in these dangerous waters. Radio and cable pundits are unconcerned with the facts of current events or policy outcomes. They voice the frustrations and humiliations of their listeners and wrap these feelings in a collective moral Truth. I expect that the outrage industry is not influential or hateful enough to inspire a modern American genocide. But if mass political violence ever did occur in the United States, it would surely be motivated by sentiments preached by the outrage industry.

53. Kuran, Timur. 1995. *Private Truths, Public Lies: The Social Consequences of Preference Falsification.* Cambridge, MA: Harvard University Press, 226.

54. Kuran, Timur. 1995. *Private Truths, Public Lies: The Social Consequences of Preference Falsification.* Cambridge, MA: Harvard University Press, 227.

55. *The New Yorker.* February 19, 2001.

56. Lietgeb, Hannes. 2005. "What Truth Depends On." *Journal of Philosophical Logic.* 34:155–192.

57. While this is not a universally shared opinion—just ask a Dittohead—I feel that insanely esoteric academic discourse serves an important historical purpose. Beyond solving problems within their individual disciplines, academics, as a whole, record human knowledge in all its countless and mind-boggling manifestations.

58. Having a PhD (any PhD) is one of the best predictors of whether someone will say that "ultimate truth does not exist."

59. Hitchens, Christopher. 1999. "It's Our Turn." *American Enterprise.* May/June.

60. *The Politics of Method in the Human Sciences: Positivism and Its Epistemological Others*, edited by George Steinmetz, presents a detailed history of the epistemology of the various social sciences. Steinmetz summarizes as follows:

> Anthropology has shown the strongest divergence from modern epistemological versions of positivism. History is a discipline that has been deeply influenced by two versions of positivism, one oriented toward the search for general laws and the other emphasizing what historians call a positivist approach to source material. But the discipline of history is also widely described as having moved into a state of epistemic and methodological pluralism in more recent years. Psychoanalysis contained both scientistic-positivist and radically antipositivist potentials from the outset . . . Diagnosing economics with respect to issues of epistemology turns out to be an extremely complex problem. Economics is described by the contributors to this volume variously dominated by epistemological positivism and empiricism, by a "depth realist" epistemology, or by an antiempiricist idealism . . . By contrast, most writers seem to agree that U.S. sociology was captured by scientistic positivism during the postwar decades, even if different explanations have been offered for this disciplinary transformation (4–5).

61. Nelson, Robert H. 2001. *Economics as Religion: From Samuelson to Chicago and Beyond.* University Park: Pennsylvania State University Press, 23.

62. Ecklund finds that "about 64 percent of scientists at elite research universities either are certain that they do not believe in God . . . or they do not know whether or not there is a God . . . In a radical show of difference, only about 6 percent of the general public consider themselves either atheist or agnostic." Ecklund, Elaine Howard. 2010. *Science vs. Religion: What Scientists Really Think.* New York: Oxford University Press, 16.

63. Ecklund, Elaine Howard. 2010. *Science vs. Religion: What Scientists Really Think.* New York: Oxford University Press, 6.

64. For instance, higher education is known to diminish the religious confidence of many believers. See Stroope, Samuel. 2011. "Education and Religion: Individual, Congregational, and Cross-Level Interaction Effects on Biblical Literalism." *Social Science Research* 40(6): 1478–1493.

    And secular ideologies are conversely strengthened in modern settings. Norris and Inglehart show that modernization has a secularizing effect world-wide. Norris, Pippa, and Ronald Inglehart. 2004. *Sacred and Secular: Religion and Politics Worldwide.* New York: Cambridge University Press. But while secular global purposes certainly come on strong in the modern era, they have yet to completely overwhelm religious ones.

65. Here is how the Hollywood version of this common story might be told. A sweet God-fearing farm boy goes off to college in the big city. His professors introduce to him ideas which were never discussed on the farm, in church, or in high school. He discovers that religion has been used to oppress workers, oppress women, and oppress minorities. In addition, the Truth of religion turns out to be just one small offering in a long list of philosophical systems developed over millennia. Sweet God-fearing farm boy returns home cynical, God-defying, and urbanized. This story is a contrivance but contains elements we might find in reality. And these instances led some conservative religious communities to fear higher learning.

66. Academics reading this chapter are reflexively tearing down my argument paragraph by paragraph.

67. Dawkins, Richard. 2011. *The Magic of Reality: How We Know What's Really True.* New York: Free Press, 22.

68. https://www.goodreads.com/author/quotes/12855. Neil_deGrasse_Tyson

69. Rorty, Richard. 1991. *Objectivity, Relativism, and Truth.* Cambridge: Cambridge University Press, 21.

70. Wittgenstein, Ludwig. 1918. *Tractatus Logico-Philosophicus.* Section 6.522

71. Wittgenstein also indicates in section 6.53:

    The correct method in philosophy would really be the following: to say nothing except what can be said, i.e. propositions of natural science—i.e. something that has nothing to do with philosophy— and then, whenever someone else wanted to say something metaphysical, to demonstrate to him that he had failed to give a meaning to certain signs in his propositions. Although it would not be satisfying to the other person—he would not have the feeling that we were teaching him philosophy—this method would be the only strictly correct one.

72. Durkheim, Emile. 1951. *Suicide: A Study in Sociology.* Translated by John A. Spaulding and George Simpson. New York: Free Press, 37.

73. Science and logic can certainly undermine faith in Truth. Claims of Truth which clearly counter facts that we know about the world will be extremely difficult to sustain even with social solidarity. Still, science and logic are not what make Truth seem real—the reality of Truth is wholly dependent on the confidence of our compatriots.

74. Arbitron data indicates that Rush Limbaugh's radio show attracts fourteen million listeners ever week.

75. Without a community of believers, a Truth holder is simply a lunatic. The lunatic sees a nonhuman reality which no one else does.

76. A common example of this dynamic occurs when a person refuses to visit the doctor for fear of the lab results. The patient feels healthy and does not want to risk the possibility of revealing an unwelcome truth. He is unwilling to question his faith everything is fine.

Chapter 6

1. They tend to be middle-aged men who are not very religious. Baylor Religion Survey, Wave 3.

2. The driving force in life's story is the quest to feel good about the self. Moral egoism frames the story and leads us to continually search for moral strategies and perspectives which will put ourselves in the best light possible. We latch onto popular narratives which justify our actions and circumstances.

3. Seneca. 1997. *On the Shortness of Life.* Translated by C. D. N. Costa. New York: Penguin Books, 27.

4. Becker, Ernest. 1973. *The Denial of Death.* New York: Free Press, xix.

5. Ibid.

6. Csikszentmihalyi, Mihaly. 1990. *Flow: The Psychology of Optimal Experience.* New York: Harper Perennial, 218.

7. Randall Collins explains how rituals "self-consciously link the community backwards to primordial time . . . This is most

characteristic of the Western religions, Judaism, Christianity, and Islam, which by their textual focus and commemoration of historical/mythic events are constantly reminding their members of their intergenerational community. In contrast, secular rituals tend to be oriented fairly closely to the near present." Collins, Randall. 2010. "The Micro-sociology of Religion: Religious Practices, Collective and Individual." ARDA Guiding Paper Series. State College: The Association of Religion Data Archives at The Pennsylvania State University, from http://www.thearda.com/rrh/papers/guidingpapers.asp.

8. Tolle, Eckhart. 2004. *The Power of Now: A Guide to Spiritual Enlightenment.* New York: New World Library, 24.

9. https://www.eckharttolle.com/article/The-Power-Of-Now-Spirituality-And-The-End-Of-Suffering

10. McCann, Colum. 2009. *Let the Great World Spin.* New York: Random House, 78.

11. Bergmann, Werner. 1992. "The Problem of Time in Sociology: An Overview of the Literature on the State of Theory and Research on the 'Sociology of Time,' 1900–82." *Time Society* 1(1): 81–134.

12. Ibid.

13. Werner Bergmann wrote an impressive overview of the sociology of time in his 1992 piece "The Problem of Time in Sociology" in *Time and Society.* He features Ottheim Remmstedt's four forms of time comprehension, which are 1) occasional time awareness (now/not now), 2) cyclical time awareness (before/after), 3) linear time with closed future (PPF), and 4) linear time with open future (continual movement/acceleration).

14. Maybe he does. Regardless, it would be a very fundamental form of social time, for instance, always heading toward the barn at sundown, because the pigs expect dinner when the world feels like this (dusky and colder) to them.

15. Durkheim, Emile. *The Elementary Forms of Religious Life.* New York: Free Press, 442.

16. A. J. Weigart makes the argument that modernity is only possible due to the increasing specificity and synchronicity of timetables. He writes, "The structure of society can be seen as the intricate joining of millions of individual daily rounds into a massive daily round of society itself." Weigart, A. J. *Sociology of Everyday Life.* New York: Longman, 205.

17. A number of researchers have described a transition from preindustrial to industrial norms of time as a function of time technologies and more complex coordinated activities. Specifically, work in a preindustrial society is defined by task, while work in an industrial society is defined by time. Thompson, E. P. 1967. "Time, Work Discipline, and Industrial Capitalism." *Past and Present* 38: 56–97.

18. Sorokin, Pitirim. 1964. *Sociocultural Causality, Space, Time.* New York: Russell and Russell Inc., 171.

19. Brisset, Dennis and Robert Snow. 1993. "Boredom: Where the Future Isn't." *Symbolic Interaction.* 16(3): 245.

20. It seems that premodern or preindustrial settings will also have cultural arrhythmia, at least according to the definition offered by Brissett and Snow.

21. Bauman, Zygmunt. 2000. *Liquid Modernity.* Cambridge: Polity Press.

22. Brigid Shulte muses on this prevalent topic in her latest book *Overwhelmed.* She notes time studies which indicate that individuals in wealthy modern societies are becoming more scheduled and multitasked. It is probably one of biggest complaints about the modern experience of life—everyone is overwhelmed by the rapidity of change and the ever-expanding plethora of focuses. Schulte, Brigid. 2014. *Overwhelmed: Work, Love, and Play When No One Has the Time.* New York: Sarah Crichton Books.

23. The specific congregation on which my observations and interviews rely was composed of mainly working-class minorities, many of whom had struggled with substance abuse and various domestic dysfunctions. In interviewing congregants after one service, I was struck by the traumatic life experiences individuals were willing to freely share with a complete stranger. The fact that congregants were writhing in religious catharsis a moment before explains their openness to releasing and addressing some of life's most devastating experiences.

24. Darren Sherkat explains that "religious goods are not simply 'experience' goods which must be consumed in order to be evaluated; rather, these goods must be experienced in communities which direct us how to evaluate them." Sherkat, Darren. 1997. "Embedding Religious Choices: Integrating Preferences and Social Constraints into Rational Choice Theories of Religious Behavior." In *Rational Choice Theory and Religion.* Edited by Lawrence A. Young. New York: Routledge, 65–85.

25. This is why logical or scientific arguments for atheism completely miss the point of ritual activity. Does Eli care that contemporary theoretical physics does not require a creator to explain the origins of the universe? No, he is in therapeutic bliss every week because he is speaking directly *to* the creator. Social harmony trumps theoretical physics every time.

26. Collins, Randall. 2004. *Interaction Ritual Chains.* Princeton, NJ: Princeton University Press, 48.

27. Swidler, Ann. 2001. *Talk of Love: How Culture Matters.* Chicago: University of Chicago Press, 113.

28. Tolstoy, Leo. 2008. *Anna Karenina.* New York: Oxford Paperbacks, 103.

29. Csikszentmihalyi, Mihaly. 2008. *Flow: The Psychology of Optimal Experience.* New York: Harper, 134.

30. Draper, Scott. 2013. *Effervescence and Solidarity in Religious Organizations.* Unpublished dissertation manuscript. 196.

31. There are two, if not many more, exceptions to this optimal schedule. First, some believers are forced to forego their ritual ceremonies. I have argued in *The Plot to Kill God* (2008) that the Soviet Union clearly limited and often eradicated most religious rituals. Jewish, Orthodox, Muslim, Catholic, and Protestant believers tended to keep religious faith, even under conditions of severe repression. This indicates that sacred symbols can have long lives even when separated from the energy source—rituals. Second, there are spiritual people who believe in a very rich and extensive supernatural realm and seemingly reject religious organizations. Here is an example of faith without traditional ritualistic elements.

32. Durkheim, Emile. 1995 [1912]. *The Elementary Forms of Religious Life.* Translated by Karen Fields. New York: Free Press, 425.

33. Believers equate the highs of ritual participation with the group and its conceptual framework. Scott Draper studied the effects of Jewish, Christian, Islamic, and Buddhist rituals and explains that "social solidarity is an experience of collective identity, morality, and truth that extends beyond the practice of the ritual. Solidarity is stored in the feelings and thoughts that arise when members of an organization encounter each other and/or their sacred symbols." Draper, Scott. 2013. *Effervescence and Solidarity in Religious Organizations.* Unpublished dissertation manuscript.

34. Swidler, Ann. 2001. *Talk of Love: How Culture Matters.* Chicago: University of Chicago Press, 114.

35. Ibid.

36. Ibid., 128–129.

37. In fact, this winking often occurs weekly. Randall Collins observes that "persons in stable couple relationships typically have sex about once a week, even at relatively advanced ages. This is the same order of time as the weekly scheduling of religious rituals, suggesting that both kinds of solidarity rituals operate the same way. Both imply that strong rituals keep strong group relationships only for about a week." Collins, Randall. 2004. *Interaction Ritual Chains.* Princeton, NJ: Princeton University Press, 237.

38. Csikszentmihalyi, Mihaly. 2008. *Flow: The Psychology of Optimal Experience.* New York: Harper, 152.

39. Lonnie Golden summarizes a general decline in workweek length over the past century for all modern industrial countries. Golden, Lonnie. 2009. "A Brief History of Long Work Time and the Contemporary Sources of Overwork." *Journal of Business Ethics* 84(2): 217–219. The Gallup World Poll furthermore indicates a strong positive correlation $r = .50$ ($n = 118$) between the per-capita GDP of a country and the number of hours of free time a citizen enjoys. The correlation between hours spent with family and per-capita GDP is also strong $r=.32$.

40. Ng, W. H., Kelly Sorenson, and Daniel Feldman. 2007. "Dimensions, Antecedents, and Consequences of Workaholism: A Conceptual Integration and Extension." *Journal of Organizational Behavior* 28(1): 111–136.

41. Some researchers even suggest that the happy workaholic can serve as a model manager. See Friedman, Stewart, and Sharon Lobel. 2003. "The Happy Workaholic: A Role Model for Employees." *Academy of Management Executive* 17(3): 87–98. Burke and Fiksenbaum indicate that some workaholics have a "harmonious passion" for work as opposed to workaholics who have an "addictive passion." Burke, Ronald, and Lisa Fiksenbaum. 2009. "Work Motivations, Work Outcomes, and Health: Passion Versus Addiction." *Journal of Business Ethics* 84(20): 257–263.

42. De Botton, Alain. 1997. *How Proust Can Change Your Life.* New York: Vintage Books, 48.

43. One of the many pieces of great advice given to me by my dissertation advisor, Daniel Chirot, was that an academic has to "take time to think." This is something that the current focus on publication undermines completely. In publishing more and more, we are giving ourselves no time to actually think.

44. Csikszentmihalyi, Mihaly. 1990. *Flow: The Psychology of Optimal Experience*. New York: Harper Perennial, 217.

45. Americans who are searching for purpose in life are the most unhappy. They feel lost regardless of their income, education, or religious activity. Baylor Religion Surveys, Wave 4.

46. With his novel *One Day in the Life of Ivan Denisovich*, Alexander Solzhenitsyn gave the world its first thorough account of the disturbing Soviet gulag. Since its publication in 1962, horrific tales of the Soviet genocide of intellectuals, religious believers, and nonconformists grow yearly as historians uncover previously hidden documents. Solzhenitsyn paints an intimate portrait of a singular experience—one day in a frozen hell. Here is a moment of it:

This was a game they played every day. Before quitting time, the workers would collect wood chips, sticks, bits of broken board, and carry them off tied up with a strip of rag or a bit of string. The first raid might come at the guardhouse. If the site manager or one of the overseers was waiting there, he would order them to drop the lot . . . But the workers had ideas of their own. If every man in a gang got home with just a stick or two, the hut would be that much warmer. Without this, there was only the five kilograms of coal dust issued to the hut orderlies for each stove, and you couldn't expect much warmth from that. So besides the wood they carried in their hands they broke or sawed sticks into short pieces and stuffed them under their jackets. That much they'd get past the site manager.

Day after day after day spent scrapping for a little warmth and a morsel of food. The meaning of this kind of life is simple and sad—one achieves a ghostly purpose at best. Still, transcendent moments occur, like when Solzhenitsyn describes the numinous quality of bread. His tiniest pleasures take on divine significance, prodding him to endure and persist. Solzhenitsyn's depiction of a day in the gulag makes our standard irritations and petty jealousies appear ridiculous. How can we legitimately complain about office politics and daily chores when no one is *preventing* us from keeping warm or eating? Still, the fact that things could always be much worse doesn't negate the fact that things could also be much better.

47. Lonnie Golden argues that basic economic theories of work time allocation cannot sufficiently explain the behavior of these workaholics. She explains:

> The recent run up of hours in the US cannot be attributed to changes in the demographic composition of the labor force, changes in the mix of occupations and industries or a simply reallocation of labor supply within workers' life cycles . . . Opening the "black box" of preferences would incorporate psychological, social and cultural sources of workers' constraints and preference adaptation, to arrive at a deeper understanding of the roots of trends in the time devoted toward work.

Golden, Lonnie. 2009. "A Brief History of Long Work Time and the Contemporary Sources of Overwork." *Journal of Business Ethics* 84(2): 220.

48. His workaholism is no professional passion. Burke and Fiksenbaum distinguish passionate from addictive forms of workaholism. Burke, Ronald, and Lisa Fiksenbaum. 2009. "Work Motivations, Work Outcomes, and Health: Passion Versus Addiction." *Journal of Business Ethics* 84(20): 257–263.

49. Gary might also be trying to avoid his life in general. Workaholism is correlated to various negative emotional and social problems. Burke, Ronald, and Lisa Fiksenbaum. 2009. "Work Motivations, Work Outcomes, and Health: Passion Versus Addiction." *Journal of Business Ethics* 84(20): 257–263. When I was working on a research project to study the family effects of erectile dysfunction, we found that men suffering from sexual problems tended to increase work time in order to avoid marital intimacy. Wagner, T. H., D. L. Patrick, S. P. McKenna, and P. Froese. 1996. "Cross-cultural Development of a Quality of Life Measure for Men with Erection Difficulties." *Quality of Life Research* 5(4): 443–449.

50. Quoted from Dreyfus, Hubert, and Sean Dorrance Kelly. 2011. *All Things Shining: Reading the Western Classics to Find Meaning in a Secular Age*. New York: Free Press, 31–32.

51. Marx, Karl. 1972. "The German Ideology: Part I." In *The Marx-Engels Reader*. Edited by Robert Tucker. New York: Norton, 110–164.

52. Workaholism is directly correlated to poor health, stress, anxiety, depression, marital estrangement, and mistrust of others. Still, some workaholics report higher job satisfaction and career success. See W. H. Ng, Kelly Sorenson, and Daniel Feldman. 2007. "Dimensions, Antecedents, and Consequences of Workaholism: A Conceptual Integration and Extension." *Journal of Organizational Behavior* 28(1): 111–136.

53. For instance, Michael Howard argues that militant nationalist movements are irresistible outlets for wealthy and bored societies. War becomes a twisted means to entertain a public who can revel in televised battles in the safety of their living rooms. See Howard, Michael. 2001. *The Invention of Peace: Reflections on War and International Order*. London: Taylor and Francis. Jorg Kustermans and Erik Ringmar explain: "Modern societies are . . . becoming more peaceful and their inhabitants are becoming more bored. As a means of overcoming our boredom, we are increasingly fascinated by violence, and war is glorified as a means of restoring our ability to act." Kustermans, Jorg, and Erik Ringmar. 2011. "Modernity, Boredom, and War: A Suggestive Essay." *Review of International Studies* 37:1775.

54. Balla, Bálint. 1978. *Soziologie der Knappheit*. Stuttgart: Kramer, 57.

55. See Figure 6.2.

56. Norris, Pippa, and Ronald Inglehart. 2004. *Sacred and Secular: Religion and Politics Worldwide*. Cambridge: Cambridge University Press, 14.

57. "The term 'stressor' is most commonly applied within the context of daily life events (i.e. changes in health, sleep habits, finances, or social interactions)." Carr, John E., and Peter P. Vitaliano. 2012. "Stress, Adaptation, and Stress Disorders." In *The Behavioral Sciences and Health Care*. Edited by Olle Jane Sahler and John E. Carr. Cambridge: Hogreffe, 60.

58. Ibid.

59. The Families and Work Institute report that the feeling of being overworked is on the rise; in 2009, 44 percent of working Americans felt overstressed by work. This is especially the case for workers across Asia. See Fry, Louis, and Melanie Cohen. 2009. "Spiritual

Leadership as a Paradism for Organizational Transformation and Recovery from Extended Work Hours Cultures." *Journal of Business Ethics* 84: 265–278.

60. Meek, C. B. 2004. "The Dark Side of Japanese Management in the 1990s: Karoshi and Ijime in the Japanese Workplace." *Journal of Managerial Psychology* 19(3): 312–331.

61. Ng, W.H., Kelly Sorenson, and Daniel Feldman. 2007. "Dimensions, Antecedents, and Consequences of Workaholism: A Conceptual Integration and Extension." *Journal of Organizational Behavior* 28(1): 111–136.

62. Fry and Cohen describe various causes of workaholism such as the need for money to buy increasingly extravagant goods (consumerism) and a fear of failing work expectations or appearing less than one's peers. Fry, Louis, and Melanie Cohen. 2009. "Spiritual Leadership as a Paradism for Organizational Transformation and Recovery from Extended Work Hours Cultures." *Journal of Business Ethics* 84:265–278.

63. How did Americans feel yesterday? Fifteen percent of Americans felt "really stressed and really bored" yesterday. Eleven percent were just really bored and a whopping 31 percent were really stressed. This means on an average day nearly 1 out of every 2 people you meet are "really stressed." Forty-three percent of the people you meet will be not bored or stressed—the time winners. Source: *Gallup World Poll*.

64. De Waal, Thomas. 2010. *The Caucasus: An Introduction.* New York: Oxford University Press, 95–96.

65. Frederikson, Martin Demant. 2013. *Young Men, Time, and Boredom in the Republic of Georgia.* New York: Temple University Press. Still, Georgians, Armenians, and Azerbaijanis remain relatively optimistic. Only around 10 percent of them think that their children will remain financially "the same" or "worse off." They continue to look pass their current doldrums with hope.

66. Rushdie, Salman. 2010. *Luka and the Fire of Life.* New York: Random House, 159.

67. Life's purpose creates a means to link together pleasing moments in consistent and frequent rhythms. The purpose of real love secures our moments of *true love.* The purpose of faith secures our moments of *collective effervescence.* The purpose of profession calling secures our moments of *flow.*

Chapter 7

1. Excerpt from a letter to close friend, quoted in Kelly, Aileen. 2013. "Getting Isaiah Berlin Wrong." *New York Review of Books* LX(11): 48.

2. Machiavelli, Niccolo. 1981 [1513]. *The Prince*. New York: Simon and Brown, 60.

3. Fischer, Louis. 2010. *Gandhi: This Life and Message for the World.* New York: Signet Classics, 7.

4. Hayek, Friedrich. 1982. *Law, Legislation, and Liberty.* Vol. 1. New York: Routledge.

5. Doestoevsky, Fyodor. 1960. *Notes from Underground*. New York: Dell Publishing, 28.

6. Ehrlich, Paul. 2000. *Human Natures: Genes, Cultures, and Human Prospect*. Washington, DC: Island Press, ix–x.

7. While Ehrlich remains committed to the idea that we will find an "evolutionary theory of culture that unites the social sciences," he has given up on describing human nature and now hunts for a myriad of "human natures." Ehrlich, Paul. 2000. *Human Natures: Genes, Cultures, and Human Prospect*. Washington, DC: Island Press, 231.

8. Doestoevsky, 1960, Notes from Underground, 36.

9. The Oxford Dictionary of Philosophy defines imagination as follows: "the faculty of reviving or especially creating images in the mind's eye . . . the ability to create and rehearse possible situations, to combine knowledge in unusual ways, or to invent thought experiments." *Oxford Dictionary of Philosophy*. 1994. Oxford: Oxford University Press.

10. Rank, Otto. 1932. *Art and Artist: Creative Urge and Personality Development*. New York: W. W. Norton and Company, 96.

11. Coleridge was one of the first to advocate that one's imagination could be purposely exercised to discover the transcendent. Coleridge scholar Jonathan Spencer Hill explains: "The relevance of neoplatonic pantheism to Coleridge's theory of the Imagination is made clear in his lecture on the slave-trade of June 1795: 'The noblest gift of Imagination is the power of discerning the *Cause* in the *Effect* [,] a power which when employed on the works of the Creator elevates and by the variety of its pleasures almost monopolizes the Soul. We see our God everywhere—the Universe in the most literal Sense is his written Language.' Imagination, then, is the mental faculty that

allows man to interpret the symbolic language in which God has written himself into the *natura naturata*." Hill, Jonathan Spencer. 1978. *Imagination in Coleridge*. London: McMillan Press.

12. Alexander, Victoria. 2006. *Sociology of the Arts*. Oxford: Blackwell Publishing, 143.

13. Bauman, Zygmunt. 2008. *The Art of Life*. Cambridge: Polity Press, 53.

14. Steven Mithen described research which suggests that other primates appear to have the imaginative ability of choice. Mithen, Steven. 2001. "The Evolution of Imagination: An Archaeological Perspective." *Substance* 30(1): 50.

15. Ibid.

16. Hechter, Michael. 1987. *Principles of Group Solidarity*. Berkeley: University of California Press, 41.

17. Hechter, Michael, and Christine Horne. 2009. *Theories of Social Order*. 2nd Edition. Stanford: Stanford Social Sciences, 1.

18. Dewey, John. 2005. *Art as Experience*. New York: Perigee, 43.

19. Bernays, Edward. 2005 [1928]. *Propaganda*. New York: IG Publishing, 61.

20. Propaganda is "the deliberate, systematic attempt to shape perceptions, manipulate cognitions, and direct behavior to achieve a response that furthers the desired intent of the propagandist." Jowett, Garth, and Victoria O'Donnell. 2006. *Propaganda and Persuasion*. London: Sage Publications, 7.

21. Bernays, Edward. 2005 [1928]. *Propaganda*. New York: IG Publishing, 57.

22. Ibid., 168.

23. Orwell, George. 2005 [1946]. *Why I Write*. New York: Penguin Books.

24. Bernays, Edward. 2005 [1928]. *Propaganda*. New York: IG Publishing, 62.

25. See Key, W. R. 1973. *Subliminal Seduction*. New York: Signet.

26. Jowett, Garth, and Victoria O'Donnell. 2006. *Propaganda and Persuasion*. London: Sage Publications, 149.

27. Ibid., 200.

28. Kuran, Timur. 1995. *Private Truths, Public Lies: The Social Consequences of Preferences Falsification*. Cambridge, MA: Harvard University Press, 212.

29. Pfaff, Steven. 2006. *Exit-Voice Dynamics and the Collapse of East Germany*. Durham, NC: Duke University Press, 138.

30. Kuran, Timur. 1995. *Private Truths, Public Lies: The Social Consequences of Preferences Falsification*. Cambridge, MA: Harvard University Press.

31. Jowett and O'Donnell explain that public perceptions of media messages are never "monolithic but rather subject to a wide range of possible interpretations." Jowett, Garth, and Victoria O'Donnell. 2006. *Propaganda and Persuasion*. London: Sage Publications, 149.

32. Ibid., 1.

33. Westen, Drew. 2007. *The Political Brain: The Role of Emotion in Deciding the Fate of the Nation*. New York: Public Affairs, 85.

34. Persuaders pray that we keep responding positively while they struggle with the fickleness of the modern voter. The popularity of any candidate is fragile, because a single setback can elicit a firestorm of negative emotions. Unlike the cultural values and preferences they exploit, politicians are expendable.

35. Because the world of public policy and social philosophy is so vast and complicated, citizens rely on whether they *like* a candidate, her narratives, and her key words. Stephen Vaisey investigates the logic behind our moral decision-making. Like Westen, he finds that we rely predominantly on emotions, explaining that "everyone does 'what feels right,' but the substantive content of those feelings varies a great deal." Doing what "feels right" is not an instinctual or even necessarily a selfish urge but rather an act which reflects one's moral socialization. Variation in the "substantive content of those feelings" maps onto the values and narratives of our community. Consequently, individuals may not be able to explain their moral or political ideology, but that does not indicate that they lack guiding principles. Rather, Vaisey explains, "*recognizing* a moral script that 'sounds right' is cognitively easier than articulating it from scratch." Individuals *feel* a logic to their attitudes and values, even when they cannot articulate it. Vaisey, Stephen. 2008. "Socrates, Skinner, and Aristotle: Three Ways of Thinking about Culture in Action." *Sociological Forum* 23(3): 603–613.

36. Jowett, Garth, and Victoria O'Donnell. 2006. *Propaganda and Persuasion*. London: Sage Publications, 200.

37. Ibid.

38. In addition, political success is fleeting in a culture that grows bored quickly.

39. Stark, Rodney. 2001. *One True God: Historical Consequences of Monotheism*. Princeton, NJ: Princeton University Press, 23.

40. Ibid.

41. In *The Plot to Kill God*, I argue that "the idea of the supernatural and, more specifically, the idea of God is a fundamental cultural element common to all modern societies, so common as to make it a core belief from which a multitude of radically divergent worldviews spring." Froese, Paul. 2008. *The Plot to Kill God*. Berkeley: University of California Press, 2.

42. Prothero, Stephen. 2010. *God Is Not One: The Eight Rival Religions that Run the World and Why Their Differences Matter*. New York: HarperOne, 3.

43. Ibid.

44. Stark, Rodney. 2001. *One True God: Historical Consequences of Monotheism*. Princeton, NJ: Princeton University Press, 32.

45. See Froese, Paul, and Christopher Bader. 2010. *America's Four Gods: What We Say about God and What That Says about Us*. Oxford: Oxford University Press.

46. See Froese, Paul, and Christopher Bader. 2010. *America's Four Gods: What We Say about God and What That Says about Us*. Oxford: Oxford University Press.

47. Luhrmann, T. M. 2012. *When God Talks Back: Understanding the American Evangelical Relationship with God*. New York: Knopf, 216.

48. Norris, Pippa, and Ronald Inglehart. 2004. *Sacred and Secular: Religion and Politics Worldwide*. Cambridge: Cambridge University Press, 57.

49. Ibid.

50. Prothero, Stephen. 2010. *God Is Not One: The Eight Rival Religions that Run the World and Why Their Differences Matter*. New York: HarperOne, 166.

51. Yang, Fengang. 2006. "The Red, Black, and Grey Religious Markets of China." *The Sociological Quarterly*. 47(1): 93–122.

52. http://www.brainyquote.com/quotes/quotes/f/franciscol555159.html

53. McGinn, Colin. 2013. "Neuromania." *New York Review of Books* LX(12): 50.

54. Harris, Sam. 2010. *The Moral Compass: How Science Can Determine Human Values*. New York: Free Press, 2.

55. Ibid., 104.

56. Sciences can become religions. We often think that religions melt away with scientific progress. Science definitely eats up large amounts of intellectual space, taking physics, chemistry, economics, sociology, and psychology from religion as societies modernized. But science can also inspire cultist behavior which bleeds into a kind of mystical faith. The Soviets did it with the science of Marxism, going so far as to create rituals and sacred texts around what they believed to be "a science" (see *Plot to Kill God*).

57. Changeux, Jean-Pierre. 2013. *The Good, the True, and the Beautiful: A Neuronal Approach*. New York: Yale University Press.

58. McGinn, Colin. 2013. "Neuromania." *New York Review of Books* LX (12): 50.

59. Ibid.

60. Wittgenstein, Ludwig. 1994. "Ethics, Life and Faith." In *The Wittgenstein Reader*. Edited by Anthony Kenny. Oxford: Blackwell Publishers, 296.

61. Rorty, Richard. 1979. *Philosophy and the Mirror of Nature*. Princeton, NJ: Princeton University Press, 43–44.

62. Wuthnow, Robert. 1987. *Meaning and the Moral Order: Explorations in Cultural Analysis*. Berkeley: University of California Press, 201.

63. Sennett and Habermas fear that the ethos of individuality leads us away from our public obligations. John F. Kennedy famously counseled, "Ask not what your country can do for you, but what you can do for your country," in a push against the self-centered excesses of individuality. But today's tactics of political persuasion assert little if anything about the obligations of public service, seeking instead to accommodate and charm our individual fancies. In striving to satisfy this self-absorption, many throw themselves into work. For their tireless efforts, some of these workaholics are rewarded with wealth and esteem. In addition, they solve the problem of meaning by not thinking past their next career move or lavish purchase. Still, many lackadaisically accept a concept bequeathed by centuries of religious history—God. For these tacit believers, the idea of God, and the vague sense of moral order it implies, provides necessary ballast in those sporadic times of existential angst.

Others throw themselves wholeheartedly into religion. For these more serious believers, God is the source of all meaning. They passionately and incessantly imagine God and, if lucky, even hear his voice. But this enchanted relationship is at odds with a world bent on disenchantment. Modernity does not kill God but it can muffle his voice. In wealthy and technologically advanced countries, God is becoming more distant. Modern believers still sense God's presence, but often only dimly through the imposing paradigms of science and rationality. Yet the modern ethos of individuality creates an expansive space for God within the self.

64. Wittgenstein, Ludwig. 1998. *Culture and Value.* Edited by Georg Henrik von Wright, rev. ed. London: Wiley-Blackwell, 14.
65. Rorty, Richard. 1979. *Philosophy and the Mirror of Nature.* Princeton, NJ: Princeton University Press, 370.
66. Ibid.
67. Chabon, Michael. 2013. "The Film Worlds of Wes Anderson." *The New York Review of Books* 60(4): 23.

Chapter 8

1. Self, Will. 1991. *The Quantity Theory of Insanity and Other Stories.* London: Vintage International, 134.
2. The wise reader turns to the back first, where the sound bites of nonfiction reside.
3. I address the topic of life's purpose from multiple perspectives. In this way, I hope to demonstrate *through* mixed methods that the topic itself is endlessly fragmented. Specifically, I looked at: *Discussions:* from over 200 interviews and focus groups conducted for various research projects, chance meetings I had with strangers, and participant observations of life all around me. *Surveys:* the Gallup World Poll, an international dataset with questions about purpose from over 140 countries, and The Baylor Religion Survey (waves 1, 2, 3, and 4), a representative survey of Americans which contains hundreds of questions relating to religion, politics, morality, and purpose. *Prior Research:* I drew from hundreds of research papers and books by historians, economists, political scientists, cognitive scientists, anthropologists, and sociologists. As best I could, I sought to weave together disparate findings on the topic of purpose into an organic whole. *Literature and Philosophy:* So much of life's meaning cannot be captured by observable evidence. Feelings and imaginative processes are unseen; great writers provide us a window into their mental worlds with concise and beautiful language that the rest of

us lack. As you have seen, I relied most heavily on Russian writers simply because they resonate with me. *Popular Culture:* I followed popular discourse pertaining to life's purpose. While this could very well have been the entire focus of a book on purpose, I found that purveyors of purpose mainly reflect rather than create popular conceptions of self or life. I attempted to draw from all of these empirical sources within every chapter. In sum, this hodge-podge of methods was conducted *on purpose.*

4. Dunbar, Paul Laurence. 1993. *The Collected Poetry of Paul Laurence Dunbar.* Edited by Joanne M. Braxton. Charlottesville: University of Virginia Press, 102.

Index

existential meaning, and modernity, 68–69
existential urgency, and sense of
    purpose, 50–54

failure, 31, 81–83
faith. *See also* religion
    interdependence of love and, 107–8
    production of, 96–97
    as purpose, 23–24
    rational dilemma of, 99–101
    reality of, 91
    security's impact on, 193n12
    and self-discovery, 74
    social support and, 16–17
    and time victimization, 140–41
    Truth and, 123
    Wittgenstein on, 208n1
    as work, 64–65
family, as source of purpose, 61
Fathers and Sons (Turgenev), 42–43
feeling, 13–14, 15
Festinger, Leon, 209n7
"50,000 Elvis Fans Can't Be Wrong"
    (Warhol), 123
film, 41
financial worth, 82–83
Fleck, Ludwig, 212n34
"flourishing ratio," 87–88
flow, 135, 137–38, 141–43
flowers, 2–3
Frankl, Victor, 4–5, 182n13
Frederiksen, Martin Demant, 148
Fredrickson, Barbara, 87–88
Freud, Sigmund, 190n32
Friday Night Lights, 7

Gandhi, Mahatma, 151
generalized other, 78
genocide, 216n52
Georgia, 147–49, 227n65
Gilbert, Daniel, 21
globalization, 69, 146, 170–71
God. *See also* atheism
    and Alcoholics Anonymous, 124
    belief in, 162–67, 217n62, 232–33n63
    as common idea, 231n41
    as instrument to mitigate
        despair, 36–37
    and spiritual self-discovery, 58–60
    as transcendent source of existence and
        morality, 190n35
    views on, 57–58
    and Warren's articulation of
        self-enchantment, 93–94

Wittgenstein on discussions of, 208n1
God Particle, 39
gods, 34
Golden, Lonnie, 223n39, 225n47
good
    definitions of, 38
    finding inner, 24–25
good times, 133–35
Grayling, A. C., 188n29
gulag, 224–25n46
Gunaratana, Bhante, 72, 199–200nn14, 17

Haidt, Jonathan, 97, 206nn73, 74
Hale, Nathan, 8
Ham, Ken, 211–12n30
Hannah and Her Sisters, 11
Hannity, Sean, 215n50
happiness
    as by-product of moral egoism, 22–25
    and knowing purpose, 181n12, 186n2
    as purpose, 21–22
    wealth and, 27–29
"happy workaholic," 138–39, 142–43
Harris, Sam, 167–68, 169, 189n29, 191n44
Harrison, George, 96
hate, 215n49
Hawking, Stephen, 101, 182n12,
    189n29, 212n31
Haybron, Daniel, 45
Hayek, Friedrich, 152
Hechter, Michael, 156
helplessness, learned, 83–84
Herzog, Werner, 189–90n30
Higgs boson particle, 39
history, epistemology of, 217n60
Hitchens, Christopher, 119
Homo economicus, 26–27
Hood, Bruce, 72, 86
hope, Obama's vision of, 112
Horne, Christine, 156
Howard, Michael, 226n53
human nature
    imagination and, 153–57
    notions of, 151–53
    and propaganda versus persuasion, 161
Human Stain, The (Roth), 117–18
Hume, David, 72–73
Hunter, James, 115, 213n41

I, the, 199n9
Igo, Sarah, 86–87
I Know Why the Caged Bird Sings
    (Dunbar), 177–78
Illouz, Eva, 60, 61

on fruitlessness of ontological, metaphysical, and theological discussions, 207–8n1
on problem of life, 90
on purpose of life, 21
on scientific answers to philosophical questions, 169–70, 218–19n71
on statements of relative truth, 208nn3, 5
on transcendent concepts, 99
on uses for word "truth," 101

work, purpose in, 3. *See also* overwork; workaholism
workaholism, 138–39, 142–44, 145–46, 223n41, 225nn47, 49, 226n52. *See also* overwork
worth, 82–84
Wuthnow, Robert, 171

Young, Michael, 84–85

Zeki, S., 215n49